Woman's worth

Woman's worth

Sexual economics and the world of women

Lisa Leghorn *and*
Katherine Parker

Routledge & Kegan Paul
Boston, London and Henley

First published in 1981
by Routledge & Kegan Paul Ltd
9 Park Street, Boston, Mass. 02108, USA,
39 Store Street, London WC1E 7DD and
Broadway House, Newtown Road,
Henley-on-Thames, Oxon RG9 1EN
Set in 10/12pt Century by
Elephant Productions, London
and printed in the United States of America

British Library Cataloguing in Publication Data

Leghorn, Lisa

Woman's worth
1. Women – Economic conditions
I. Title   II. Parker, Katherine
305'.3   HQ1381

ISBN 0-7100-0836-8
ISBN 0-7100-0855-4 Pbk

Str. 19,95/12.00 /8/5/82

To the women who have been developing these ideas for centuries, and the millions of women who are continuing that work in their own ways every day

Contents

Tables

Preface and acknowledgments

During the last-week push to finish this book, while we were reworking parts of the last section and finalizing the other chapters, we were aided non-stop, twenty-four hours a day by shifts of friends editing, typing, massaging and bringing gourmet delights. It became crystal clear that this book is a product not just of a vast community of women locally, but of the fight for freedom of women the world over. Our putting the ideas to paper was only a portion of the total energy that made it possible.

First of all, many of the ideas were already 'out there' – we heard them voiced by women in supermarkets, discussed by feminists, and we read them in the letters and novels of women the world over.

Our work on this book really began in embryonic fashion several years ago, when Kathy worked with women discussing wages for housework in Montreal and Boston in 1975, and Lisa worked with Betsy Warrior on the *Houseworker's Handbook*, which was first published in 1974. Since that time we have been collecting materials and developing our analysis through our work with a variety of people and projects, without whom this book could not have been what it is, and probably would not have happened at all.

Thanks must first go to Charlotte Perkins Gilman, author of *Women and Economics* (1898), and Betsy Warrior, author of 'Slavery or a Labor of Love?' (1969, reprinted in *Houseworker's Handbook*) for their crucial work in forging an explicitly women-centered economics. It is with such work that we are hoping to continue in this book.

In 1976 Angela Miles introduced us to each other, and we later worked together with dozens of women on the 'Women

Support Women' march and rally that took place in Boston on 26 August 1976. That same summer Lisa worked with Mary Roodkowsky on the booklet, *Who Really Starves? Women and World Hunger*, and in the process collected valuable reference materials and further developed much of her analysis. Molly Lovelock, with whom we had worked on the march, was offering a course for the 1976-7 Goddard-Cambridge Graduate Program in Social Change on Women and the Economy, in which we subsequently enrolled along with Alemnesh Bulti who had also worked on the march. Though the course only formally consisted of the four of us – Kathy, Lisa, Alemnesh and Molly, other women participated in some of the readings and discussions, including Karen Lindsey and Helen Gray, and it was during these discussions that many of our ideas began to take form. In the course of our research we met with several women who were from, or had lived in other countries. Susan Bourque, Ann Froines, Zarina Patel, Rochelle Ruthchild, Judy Sutphen and Kay Warren gave extremely valuable presentations as a part of an International Speakers series that we sponsored at the school as a part of our research.

The first draft of the book was written as our MA thesis for Goddard-Cambridge, and Rochelle Ruthchild, as our adviser on the thesis, was a tremendous source of support and valuable feedback. From that time until the present, Karen and Molly have worked tirelessly with us on the book, providing everything from pages and pages of invaluable criticism and copyediting, to typing, rides and quiches. At several crucial points when we were about to give up entirely on the project, it was their support, suggestions and encouragement that persuaded us to continue. It is safe to say that this book never would have happened without them and in a very real sense it is as much theirs as ours.

Our deep gratitude also extends to the readers of various drafts for their patience, determination and invaluable critiques: Renée Norma Franco, Richard Leghorn, Karen Lindsey, Molly Lovelock, Billy Pope, Adrienne Rich, Kris Rosenthal, Barbara Smith, Laura Sperazi, and Kay Warren. Michelle Cliff, Patricia Eakins, Adrienne Rich and Dale Spender have been tremendous aids in dealing with the publishing world. And Renée Norma Franco, Rachel Hyde, Kathie O'Brien and Claire Potter offered much emotional support along with expert typing.

Then when it came to the crunch, our final week's work to meet a publishing deadline, it was the twenty-four-hour shifts of friends who sustained us. Their love, help and support so freely given was both a mirror of the total energy of women that has gone into making this book possible, and a foreshadowing of our own matriarchal visions: Eileen Eby, Renée Norma Franco, Susan Galvin, Yvonne Kendall, Karen Lindsey, Kathie O'Brien, Chip Parker, Billy Pope, and Laura Sperazi.

Many thanks also to Eileen Doolittle, who came up with our title as we were beginning to despair. And last, but by no means least, our thanks go to our friendship networks for the love, encouragement and many forms of help that kept us going: all of the above and also including Weka-Yawo Aladji, John Arden, Kathy Barry, Gabrielle Bernard, Connie Breece, Nancy Carter, Bill Dougherty, Dorienne Doyle, Ida Gbadago, Ann Kaufman, Freada Klein, Ken Leghorn, John Lombardi, Jimmy McHugh, Tina Montes de Oca, Judith Moore, Judy Norris, Calvin Ramsey, Melinda Rand, Jean Rioux, Lisa Rofel, Martha Shea, Katherine Triantafillou, Anna Whiteside, Kathy's friends in Customer Engineering at IBM in Boston and many others. Whether or not they've agreed with everything the book has said, they've given unstintingly of their time and support.

We are grateful to St Martin's Press for permission to quote Ntozake Shange's poem 'With No Immediate Cause', from *nappy edges* (1978); and to *The Second Wave* for permission to quote Adrienne Rich's poem 'The Phenomenology of Anger', from vol. 2, no. 2, 1972.

We want to thank Philippa Brewster of Routledge & Kegan Paul for her patience and encouragement.

Finally, we want to thank each other for the process of growing through our own disagreements, providing ongoing mutual support through many very hard times, and for the hard work and commitment that made the completion of the book possible while keeping a very important friendship intact.

Introduction

In a small Ewé[1] village near the Ghana-Togo border in the
summer of 1975, the queen mother's husband publicly
accused her of using a jinx on his second wife to prevent
her from having children. Dealing with the accusation was
considered a matter far too serious to go before a family
tribunal, and was brought instead before the entire village.
As is the custom with village tribunals, both husband and
wife expressed their points of view before the assembled
group, which was composed of almost all village members, of
all ages and both sexes. The matter was discussed thoroughly
by the group and then by the chiefs and elders (all male).
The unanimous decision was reached that the husband was
acting out of place in speaking in such a way and implying
such a thing of the queen mother, who warranted more
respect than that. He was obliged to apologize to her and her
family, as well as to the chief and elders, and to pay for the
judgment proceedings.

   This incident brings to light questions we might ask
concerning the role of women in the kind of society which
accords ultimate power and authority to men, but which
recognizes that in order for women to be productive and
healthy, there must be institutions that are supportive
of them and their needs. Sometimes the institutions thus
created serve to protect women from the abuse of power
by men. They also serve as a voice for women and their
needs, as a mechanism for women to express their concerns,
or as a means for women's wishes to be recognized and
acted upon. Depending on the society concerned and one's
own perspective, these institutions can be seen as viable
mechanisms for representing, expressing and carrying through

1

women's concerns, or they can be seen as safety-valves, providing the illusion of self-determination and channelling women's energies into institutions and processes which depend ultimately on men for approval and actually thwart attempts by women to gain real power.

To examine the difference between power and supportive institutions in any culture, one must look at everything from the division of work and money within the family and the society at large (thus gaining an understanding of who really makes the decisions controlling the use of money and resources) to the nature of the relationships between women and women, women and men, and men and men, and to the ways in which conflicts arising among them are resolved. For example, in the confrontation in the Ewé village, what authority does the queen mother hold relative to the chief and elders? What is the nature of her relationship to the other women in the village, and to what extent does her presence provide them with a tool for recognition of their own concerns? What is her relationship with her husband's second wife, and why haven't they resolved the matter between themselves? How does the role of women as priestesses and healers affect their status and interrelationships in their society, and what authority does it give them vis-à-vis the political authority of the chief and elders?

Finally, it is necessary to understand how the many aspects of Ewé women's lives fit together, and affect the women's sense of themselves and their direction, both individually and as a group. How does this fabric of women's lives express and reflect the economics of their society? In what ways are all these relationships economic relationships? If a queen mother uses her authority to call a strike of all women trading in the market in behalf of five women selling cornmeal cakes, who are losing money because the men who grind cornmeal have raised their prices, to what extent is hers an economic power that is sanctioned by the entire society? Could she use this authority to effect more fundamental changes in women's lives – has it been tried, and with what results? To what extent have Ewé women's networks been used to help them survive, to maintain existing power, or to create change?

Beginning from women's perspectives

> The labor of women in the house, certainly, enables men
> to produce more wealth than they otherwise could; and in
> this way women are economic factors in society. But so
> are horses. The labor of horses enables men to produce
> more wealth than they otherwise could. The horse is an
> economic factor in society. But the horse is not
> economically independent, nor is the woman.
>
> Charlotte Perkins Gilman,
> *Women and Economics*, 1898[2]

In virtually all existing cultures, women's work, though
usually invisible to the male eye, sustains the economy and
subsidizes the profits, leisure time and higher standard of
living enjoyed by individual men, private corporations, and
male-dominated governments. In spite of this, women live
almost universally without the corresponding economic,
political and social control over their lives that such a crucial
role should mean. How does this happen?

In every patriarchal culture (by 'patriarchal' we mean a
male-dominated culture in which traditional male values are
institutionalized in the family, the economy, and social and
religious life), the institutions and ideologies which govern
the society also serve to define women's place and to keep
women in that place. In nearly all cultures, women's work is
not thought of as work, but as an act of love for their families
or as a domestic duty (even if it involves huge amounts of
subsistence agriculture). It is not treated as serious labor by
society, perhaps because it is not men who do it. Women's
work in the home has been a common denominator in
women's lives throughout the world. The institution has
become so internalized in male-centered thought that almost
everyone believes that it is not productive in the 'traditional'
(male) sense of the word.

Traditionally social scientist and economists have looked
at women's lives through male eyes, and have only seen those
aspects of women's lives which overlap men's. They therefore
tend to understand and to categorize women's experiences

only in male terms. These analyses totally disregard the major components of women's lives which men never share, and which differ dramatically from men's experiences.

Therefore, when we look at women's place in the economy, we cannot begin from traditional male concepts of what is valuable and productive, and what are commodities. We must begin from women's perspectives. We must question and reevaluate all the institutions and concepts with which men have defined, measured and understood the economy, and develop a woman-centered perspective for attempting to understand women's lives cross-culturally.[3]

If we look more closely at our lives without preconceptions, in the way anthropologists try to do when studying cultures unfamiliar to them, we see that we have many day-to-day customs that have economic functions or that affect us economically. Many forces we think of as social, political, religious, or emotional serve economic functions as well. In order to include women's experiences in our analysis, we must develop an economics of social and emotional life. We have to look at the institutions that have economic implications on women's lives: the family, the educational system, the dominant ideology as it concerns women and their options and the forms of violence against women that sustain that ideology, the male-defined economy, and the political organization of the culture. From the shared experience of women must come an attempt at exploring just what that experience has meant in economic terms. For women to have equal power, they must have equal control over the organization of survival. To do this, it is necessary first to understand women's place within it.

This book explores new ways of looking at women's lives in order to create a woman-centered perspective of their place in patriarchal economies, an understanding of the basis of female culture, and a vision of what a female-value-based economy might look like. Such a perspective must be grounded in the everyday experiences of women throughout the world. It will be necessary to create a woman-centered viewpoint of what is valuable and useful, new definitions of work and productivity, and woman-centered theories to attempt to understand women's collective experience.

Although we will be exploring change strategies that have been used by women throughout the world, we do not have an outline of how we think further change might happen in different cultures or what the end results should be. Ultimately, while women across cultures can learn from each other's successes and failures, the most effective tactics can only be developed by each group of women in response to the conditions of the time and place in which they are living.

Unfortunately, most of the information available to us in the USA about other countries has been written by members of our own culture, whose cultural biases almost inevitably affect the accuracy of the data. The most common bias found in much of the social science literature analyzing non-western cultures is the male bias, which is often unconsciously shared by women as well. Men's experiences and values are used as a standard of measure for discussing society in general, and this results in glaring oversights or misinterpretations of the meaning of a given cultural institution, within the context of that particular society. Consequently, we have not used some of the most distorted available data.

Such distortion has happened, for instance, in most material written on gathering and hunting societies (the way of life for 99.5 per cent of human existence up to the present). It has been assumed that men, by virtue of their hunting, played the major role in those economies and thus held greater prerogative in the society in general. Hence, many male anthropologists have neither been aware of, nor gathered data on, women's sources of power or women's networks, and consequently no data is available that would enable us to attempt to interpret these cultures differently. This view has been so institutionalized in evolutionary thinking and theories that it is commonly believed that across cultures, male hunting has predominantly contributed to technological development, early social groupings, and leadership, as well as language development. In fact, in hunting and gathering cultures, it is women's gathering (often as much as 80 per cent of total food) that has sustained people nutritionally, because meat brought from hunting has come irregularly and infrequently.[4]

However, some data is available which, though interpreted

from a male bias, is in itself accurate. A typical example is the characterization by a male economist of a polyandrous marriage system (one woman with several husbands) used by the Nayar in India as a system where several men held a wife in common.[5] The information itself is accurate, but the language completely alters the reality of the power relationships. In such cases we use the literature, hoping that there are not too many distortions, and draw our own conclusions.

In the course of familiarizing ourselves with the range of relevant literature, we realized that it was not adequate – that we would be forced to seek out new sources of data for the work we were doing. Most of the cultures we have chosen to describe are cultures in which women have published accounts of their experiences, or from which we have known women who could give us an initial picture of what women's lives are like there – pictures which we supplemented with more traditionally-gathered data. We also use studies done by western women in other cultures in those cases where we feel they have a minimum of cultural and male bias in their research. Women as a group *have* developed an understanding of their place in the economy. And they have tried to communicate it, though their efforts have been neither rewarded nor recognized by the patriarchal cultures they live in. Women have written – so we have explored novels, journals, poems, and unpublished papers. Women have passed on information verbally – so we have spoken with women from different cultures, and women who have visited, lived in or studied in such cultures.[6]

Our analysis should make it clear that whether a society is western or third world, capitalist or socialist, does not by itself determine what women's position within the society will be. (By the term 'socialist' we mean a political and economic system advocating collective rather than private control of the means of production, distribution of goods, and decision-making. By 'third world' we mean non-western countries which have been colonies and now stand in varying relationships of neo-colonialism, independence and interdependence with the countries who colonized them, or people from those countries and their descendants. Although 'first world' is also used, to denote a political priority placed on these countries, our use of 'third world' is in no way meant to indicate they are less important than others – simply that it is the more common usage.) When looked at from women's perspective, a woman in a highly developed socialist economy might have similar social authority and economic power to a woman in a non-technological society. This might differ radically from the experience of a woman living in another socialist society, but which she might share with a woman in a capitalist society. Women's oppression is so deeply institutionalized world-wide that it is firmly entrenched in all social, political and religious systems. To get to the roots of this oppression necessitates that we hold no culture or tradition immune from the questioning of its relationship to women.

Throughout this book there is a predominance of examples taken from third world and socialist cultures. This in no way represents a belief that these cultures are more oppressive to women. Rather, we feel that since the USA and European nations control most of the world-wide information networks, many people throughout the world know more about white western culture than Europeans and Americans know about other cultures. We want to include enough examples to de-mystify many of the stereotypes, point to the problems in this model of 'development', and speak to the experience of American and European women. However, western culture and people are a minority on the planet and should not domi-nate any such discussion.

In introducing a cross-cultural perspective such as ours, there is no way we could begin to discuss all variations in every village, region or cultural area. We often choose to discuss only one particular segment of a society, i.e. women from one particular region, class, age, racial or occupational background. We have the space to present only a few examples, which does not mean that other examples are less important, just that we cannot cover them all. The value of our observa-tions lies not in believing they hold true in every instance, but rather in developing a mechanism for approaching new information. They help us to understand certain societal constructs and trends, how they affect women, and the vital importance of new questions applied to each instance.

What we have written here represents simply an attempt to lay out a perspective. Much more work needs to be done, but we hope that this will encourage women to question assumptions — which they have considered facts — and to look with fresh eyes at their everyday lives and shared female experience.

1 *Sexual economics explored*

Remember the Golden Rule:
He who has the gold, makes the rules

Economics: the power to intimidate

'Economics' is a powerful term. It has the power to intimidate, to alienate, and to imply to large numbers of people, especially women, a huge body of knowledge which we can never comprehend. This vast 'scientific force', we know, somehow intimately affects many aspects of our lives. But we usually feel powerless to stop the machine, to question or understand the vague and abstract mechanisms by which the value of our work is determined, and what our work, in turn, ostensibly entitles us to.

There are many reasons why economics as a system seems so divorced from our everyday lives. The most important is probably that most women have little or no say in those decisions governing what work is to be done, who should do that work, and what they should receive in return. In most societies, greater value is put on men's activities, and women, in many cases, are told that what they spend their days doing isn't even work, and that it produces nothing of 'economic' value. Since they are 'producing' nothing, they deserve little financial remuneration in return. With so much less money than men, women have less power, and often find themselves economically dependent on men and their economic systems. Male theory and perspectives have usually been blind to women's existence and point of view, so it's not surprising that many women find those theories boring and highly irrelevant. In addition, the nature of economic systems are mystified by those in power, so that most people (female and male) believe they can't understand how it works even if they try. And most people have neither the time nor the inclination to try to understand something that seems totally out of their hands.

But economics is, in fact, built on the daily ins and outs of our lives. Each choice we make – the work that we will do in the home or outside, what we will buy with what we earn, whether we will marry and/or have children, what we will do with our spare time – each of these choices affects the economy in some way. And the choices available to us are, in turn, determined by the kind of economic system we live in. The economy is a combination of structures and institutions based on a value system that we usually don't think about. This system of priorities is sustained by those in power. In most countries they are not the same people who do the work that keeps the economy going. The system that gives a certain group of people power determines what work will be done, what work is considered 'productive' and is well-paid, what work is not considered work and thus is unpaid, who will benefit from society's resources, whose needs will be met, and what new needs will be created. (Resources include all those things needed for human survival, from natural resources such as land, the raw materials coming from land, to the material means by which natural resources are converted for human use, such as money, factories, and human labor.)

The economy institutionalizes and sustains the value system of the society of which it is a part. Each society makes certain assumptions about human nature and creates an economy based on those assumptions. The basis of some societies is a belief that people are essentially harmonious and cooperative and work best when they feel they are working towards a common goal. Other societies are based on a belief that people are more hostile and individualistic, and that the best motivating factor is competition. Some people assume that everyone isn't capable, or willing, to be a part of the economic decisions that a society as a whole makes. (This philosophy is usually promulgated most forcefully by those people who are in a position of authority making those decisions about other people's lives.) Other people assume that people can't and won't work effectively unless they are an integral part of all the decision-making processes that affect them, and some economies attempt to carry this out. Some economies are structured in accordance with the assumption that fast economic growth, high profits, and high production rates will accommodate all the relevant needs of the society. The values implicit in other economies place no importance on growth in and of itself, but on the quality of human life and interactions. In these cultures it is accepted that a great deal of communication and planning is needed to insure an awareness of all the needs of all the individuals of the society, and to make sure that all those needs are met. The rate of growth and production are important only in so far as they insure that those needs are met.

The underlying values of a social system in turn affect the future choices people will make, and what factors will motivate them. In a society where people are rewarded (financially, socially or emotionally) for putting the interests of the common good before their individual interests, and are punished for pursuing private interests which might harm the group as a whole, it becomes a matter of economic, social and emotional survival for people to continue to think and act in terms of the common good. Conversely, if one lives in a society where economic 'success' is often possible only at the expense of other people's success, individuals find themselves making selfish choices daily. In a society where great emphasis is placed on producing high quality goods, custom-made to personal preference and sold with a great deal of personal accountability and responsibility, individuals attempting to sell poorly-made factory goods in an impersonal environment would probably go out of business, or be forced to change their workstyle. Individuals learn to change their values relating to their worklives, or are unable to survive doing that work. Once an economy is developed and structured along a certain value system, people's behavior, whether conforming to or questioning the status quo, is a response to, and is evaluated in terms of, these underlying values.

Perhaps the most important question that any economy must deal with is that of what mechanisms it will use to meet human needs. Does a society produce enough to feed, clothe and shelter all its people, or does it produce large profits for some through a lower standard of living for the majority? Does it respect people's differences, or capitalize on them and exploit them? Is women's capacity to bear children highly valued and supported by an entire culture taking responsibility for childcare, and do women have any control over their reproductivity, or is it exploited, leaving mothers alone to fend for themselves? Are the physically and emotionally different people scorned and ostracised, or provided with an active role in society? Does a society value the creation of surplus, and if so does it reinvest that surplus in meeting the needs of its members, or in making possible a higher growth rate to produce more surplus? Who benefits ultimately from this surplus?

A look at some of the diverse methods societies use to distribute their 'surplus' illustrates the variety of answers that societies have come up with. Two very different groups, the Pilaga of South America and certain low-income urban black families in the USA, have both created survival structures that recognize that surplus comes seldom and in small quantities.[1] In both societies people who have more goods than they immediately need share with others who have less at the moment, recognizing that soon enough they themselves will be doing without and will have to depend on others. Such a mechanism not only insures the survival of a group; it is also a means of 'storing' surplus, acting at the same time as a kind of social cement, holding people together as they perceive their common interests.

Among the Kawelka people in the highlands of Papua New Guinea, a custom called 'moka' serves the same function. Through the moka ceremony, a man gives away large numbers of pigs and sometimes other goods to other men within his community and in other communities, and these gifts are later returned with interest. Done to acquire prestige the moka ceremony in fact serves to strengthen bonds between communities and distribute surplus.[2] (While this surplus will eventually be shared by all members of a household, it is the man who receives the prestige of presiding over the moka, and his wife or wives do the work of tending the pigs and the sweet potato gardens from which the pigs are fed, making both the surplus and the moka possible.)

The space program in the United States, which periodically sends spaceshots to the moon, to Mars, or wherever, represents a very different use of surplus. The justifying ideology is that knowledge is obtained and that therefore the money is not thrown away. However, huge volumes of money are poured into a program with no cash returns or material benefits. In the moka ceremony surplus is given away after all individuals within the group have received enough to eat and wear, while the space program in the United States takes place while 20 per cent of the population is malnourished.[3]

Economics is simply a system of distribution of the work, resources, and wealth of a society. It is the sum total of all decisions regarding what work is to be done, who will do that work, and who will benefit from it, and the allocation of capital, resources and wealth. Our part in this system continually shapes our daily lives, and what we do becomes part of the economy and forms it at the same time.

Why the hand that rocks doesn't rule

A man may work from sun to sun,
A woman's work is never done
                    American Proverb

Specialization of labor takes place in all societies to varying degrees, and it is usually those with more status and income (men) who do the highly specialized (and therefore more limited) work. (By 'specialized' we mean work that is narrow in its focus, permitting concentration and a sense of accomplishment.) The work that is least specialized, no matter how tedious, difficult and all-encompassing, usually carries the least economic and social value, and is performed by the people of the lowest status in society (women). Their service and maintenance work permits those with more power to do their more specialized work. Without all the basic life-sustenance work necessary for survival taken care of, those with more power would not have the time and resources at their disposal to do their work.

The most basic and widespread division of work is that between men and women. Women the world over perform a wide variety of services for their families (from childcare and home maintenance to subsistence agriculture), which often enables those in a more powerful position – men – to pursue other interests such as religion, government and art. This has a further effect on women's position. Since women do the least specialized, low-status work, they do not have the same access to the crucial resources that would enable them to wield more power within their families and their communities. Because women are identified with their work in and around the home, they are told that they are incapable of more. They are denied access to other work, paid less, given less property, and permitted little or no control over the resources of their families and society. In other words, the position of women in the family is used to prevent them from holding equal power in society. Ironically those persons who do the work that sustains personal and future life have the least power and prestige.

Women are one-third of the world's formal labor force, and do four-fifths of all 'informal' work, but receive only 10 per cent of the world's income and own less than 1 per cent of the world's property.[4] A 1957 study of thirteen states in India found that roughly two-thirds of the women received wages that were 60 to 80 per cent of those paid to men.[5] In many western industrialized countries women's formal participation is lower and they earn 40 to 70 per cent of what men earn.[6]

Many men won't do the work to which society gives such low value (such as service work, which engages one-half the female work force in some countries[7]). Much of the work that women do (in the home as well as childcare and 'volunteer' work) isn't paid for at all. What money married women (even women married to wealthy men) do have access to is usually given to them and can be taken away if they stop playing their expected role. With less money, women have far less access to the goods which are produced by the society of which they are a part, and their unpaid work severely limits their leisure time, a social benefit falling almost entirely to men.

Women's continued low-cost production of services is so crucial to patriarchal economies that most cultures go to great lengths to insure that women will continue to see this work as their natural realm and as an expression of their love for their families. Thus women undergo tremendous socialization in heterosexuality to insure that they see men as primary in their emotional, sexual, and material lives, and that their unpaid work in the home is mystified as love. Therefore the extent to which lesbianism is rejected by a given culture reflects the degree to which that culture has a vested interest in maintaining a rigid division of labor and power by sex within the family and outside the home. In this sense, the freedom of sexual preference, especially for lesbians, is a barometer of women's options, or the repression and exploitation women experience.[8]

There are also many other forms of social stratification that affect women since they belong to all other social groupings. The next most widespread basis for division of work and power is by age. It is quite common, in cultures where there is no social stratification other than by sex, to also find a strict division by age, the youngest in any familial or social grouping having less power and enjoying the least specialized work. Thus, in some societies women who have no other access to decision-making roles grow into roles reserved exclusively for older members of the community. Ironically, with the increasing social stratification and industrialization that comes with westernization, many older people now have less power and respect than younger people (who are perceived as more marketable). Consequently older women in many cultures are losing one of the only sources of authority they ever enjoyed and now have an even lower status than younger women.

When women's work is ignored or undervalued, there is often strong class stratification, which almost always involves racial and religious oppression as well. A model of women doing menial, subservient work for men who have more power, resources, leisure time, and a higher standard of living, has been replicated in most cultures on a class and racial basis. (This model is also replicated when third-world nations service western countries which receive all the benefits of the poorly-paid labor and the resources that the third-world countries have produced.)

In the United States, in 1953, 11 per cent of the people owned 60 per cent of the private assets, and 2.1 per cent of the common-stock shareholders owned 58 per cent of the common stock.[9] These few wealthy people, mostly white and male, made many of the decisions affecting the lives of other people. Although the United States is among the most highly class-stratified societies, with great extremes in poverty and wealth, the same class system operates in many other societies as well.

Women from lower economic backgrounds, and racial, ethnic and religious identities that are discriminated against, have even less access to crucial resources than do other women. In the United States, for example, full-time 'minority' male workers earn 74 per cent of the salary of white men. 'Minority' women earn 94 per cent of the average for women, and 54 per cent of what white men earn.[10] (We prefer not to use 'minority' because on the planet it is white people who are the minority. When we use 'third world' to mean people of color, we do not mean that all people of color share a common culture, but a common experience of living in white-dominated society.) In fact, the sex/race hierarchy in the USA can be seen clearly by looking at the figures in Table 1.

Table 1   Median wage or salary income in 1974, by race and sex[11]

Race	All workers		Year-round full-time workers	
	Women	Men	Women	Men
Total	4,850	10,404	6,967	12,072
'Minority'	4,751	7,617	6,611	9,082
White	4,863	10,745	7,025	12,343

This income hierarchy is reinforced by the same underlying

hierarchy concerning the value attributed to different kinds of work that we discussed earlier. High status-related, well-paid work tends to be available only to white males whose class backgrounds permit them to attend schools where they can gain the appropriate credentials and friends. Consequently, these privileged white males have access to much greater wealth and a higher standard of living, and may earn twenty times as much as poor black females.

Sometimes the white-collar (or academic) work that women do is considered to hold higher status than that attributed to blue-collar jobs. In these instances, their status or their greater self-esteem and the respect they receive from others is used as a substitute for money, obscuring the true economic relationship.

The assumptions underlying the relative value of work are tremendously important in understanding how wealth is distributed. The division and organization of work in USA society is such that simply the fact of being female, black, or working class determines what training, work, pay scale and standard of living is available. And we can be sure that this standard is consistently lower than for those people who have the 'privileges' this society gives to some male, white, and middle-class people.[12]

These divisions of labor and benefits raise many questions about the meaning of the word 'class'. In highly complex western cultures, it is clear that class means a lot more than one's relationship to production. The large numbers of workers in the service, clerical and bureaucratic sectors raise questions as to what is considered 'production', even within the limits of paid work. There are many arguments as to whether one's class position is defined by the type of work one does, the income one makes, one's family background, and/or one's social and educational aspirations.

One model proposed by John Lombardi suggests looking at USA society as a system of three spheres – occupation (or income), wealth (or property) and ascription (status deriving from friends and family, and residence). People's status consists of the combination of their status in all three hierarchies, and the highest status necessitates high ranking in all three spheres. (Women's status, we might add, comes from a combination of those same spheres, and in addition their relationships to the spheres of the men they in effect belong to.) Various conversion mechanisms exist through which one's status can change by transforming an advantage in one sphere to an advantage into another. For example, one can convert a high income into a higher status in social circles (ascription) by attending prestigious schools. Marriage, friendship networks, education, and changing residence are some other common conversion mechanisms.[13]

For women, the class status of the men they belong to gives varying access to these patriarchal resources. Women can sometimes convert advantages gained through their relationships to men into resources that they control independently. However, women never have equal power because their biological 'ascription' is not convertible.

I am pounding for John: women in patriarchal economies

Na ba sitela bo Njoni,	I am pounding for John,
Ba sa liku sama bo Njoni,	He is sitting idle,
Ni simba-tuna bo Njoni	With his big stomach

Lozi pounding (of grains and meal) song[14]

By using women's experience as a standard of measure for economies cross-culturally we can interpret the nature of an economy as a whole, and the extent to which all people – children, the physically different, people of diverse ethnic and racial backgrounds – either benefit from, or are oppressed by, the system they live in. This is partly because women belong to all classes, races, and religions, to every majority and minority group. By including the experience of all women, we will understand the relationship of all these shared identities to the economy. More fundamentally, women as a group have historically been so exploited and undermined, and this oppression has been so highly institutionalized, that for women to have power necessitates a culture radically different from those where women are exploited, with values, family, social and economic structures that are more egalitarian and less hierarchical and oppressive in general. Women's exploitation is an integral and taken-for-

ing the various forms that women's powerlessness takes. Only by asking new questions about women's relationships to the societies in which they live can we understand the extent to which those cultures are male-centered and male-dominated. When we look at social institutions through women's lives and from women's experience, male-made distinctions between different types of societies, and their social, economic, political and religious institutions break down. The distinctions made by men to define their lives and their relationship to the economics in which they live help to define and understand female experience only when it overlaps with male experience.

Although women's lack of power in many social institutions can be traced to their lack of economic power and independence, the reverse also holds true: their lack of economic independence is often rooted in social norms and political obstacles that afford women few opportunities. When it comes to women's lives, distinctions between 'social' and 'economic' become blurred and often barely distinguishable, since so much of women's economically productive work has been mystified as 'personal'.

In evaluating women's position in society, it is important to take all these 'social' factors into account along with economic factors. It is also important to keep in mind that social institutions may affect women's standing within the family and outside the home in different ways. For example, in the USA racial and class discrimination gives some black women extremely low status in the society at large, while providing certain employment opportunities that enable them to bring in the majority of the family income, and thus raise their status within the family. On the other hand, some women married to wealthy men have high social status, but very low status within the household. Throughout this book we will be evaluating both spheres, for a good position in either can be used by women to increase their status in the other arena. Women's status in society and their personal power is the lowest when they have low status in both spheres, and highest when they enjoy relative power in both.

To order our thinking it helps to develop categories for defining women's experience of power and powerlessness within the family and society at large. But at the same time it should be remembered that such definitions are only important in so far as they help us to understand this experience. If they are adhered to rigidly, it can prevent the flexibility necessary to understand the complexity of women's lives. In creating our own classifications for women's experiences in different cultures, we have developed the following criteria to gauge women's status: (a) valuation of women's fertility and physical integrity, (b) women's access to and control over crucial resources, including property, paid and collective labor, training and education, and (c) women's networks.

Fertility and physical integrity
The role of fertility in these classifications is especially important because in every culture around the world the division of labor by sex has in some way been linked to women's reproductive work. In cultures where children, and thus child rearing, are highly valued, women (or at least mothers) have often enjoyed more prestige than women in those cultures which ignore or disdain women's reproductive capacities. Where reproductive work is valued by the society as a whole, women have also usually benefited from greater institutional support for this work (in the form of shared childcare responsibilities, pregnancy and maternity leaves and benefits, etc.), than they have in cultures where they are left with the total responsibility for child-birth and child rearing. The differing treatment of women's fertility also greatly influences the organization of the family, which in turn has a profound effect on women's access to and control over work done elsewhere. Further, the extent to which women have had control over their reproductive functions has had a tremendous influence on the control they exercise over their lives generally. Keeping women 'barefoot and pregnant' has been a standard method of repression cross-culturally. When women have no control over the number and spacing of children to whom they give birth, they are left to the mercy of their reproductive functions and to manipulation by the male economy. Perpetual pregnancies also limit the extent to which women are capable of participating in the labor force outside the home and of developing access to vital cultural resources.

Conversely, women's status outside the home, by virtue of their access to economic resources and wage labor, affects the extent to which the society values women's reproductive role. When women are more economically independent, they serve another useful purpose in men's eyes in addition to child-bearing – they bring in extra income. When men's wages must support women because their services in the home are not paid, women are seen as a burden and their existence justified largely through their production of children, especially male children.

Social attitudes towards women's reproductive capacities actually form one part of a broader gauge of women's status. By women's 'fertility and physical integrity' we mean the sum total of all societal values and institutions affecting woman's sexuality and physical well-being. This broad range includes the socialization, legal and economic institutions and social punishments that covertly and overtly induce women to heterosexuality to insure their further unpaid labor; the sexual taboos, restraints and customs that demean or harm women, ranging from ignorance about their bodies leading to perpetual pregnancies, to forbidden sources of female sexual fulfillment including masturbation, relations with other women or choice in male partners, to female circumcision; the dominant healing profession's treatment of women; and interpersonal forms of violence against women, from rape to battering and sexual harassment.

All these social forces are deeply rooted in attitudes towards women that reflect women's power in society at large. And they all serve economic functions, usually insuring women's continued production of children and household labor at no cost to society, and men's control over women and thus over their products. Cross-culturally, the higher a woman's status is, the less subject she is to violence and repressive sexual customs, and the more tolerance she will experience as a single, childless, and/or lesbian woman.

Resources
The extent to which women have access to, and a measure of control over, crucial societal resources also determines their general power in their culture. In a culture which is

highly dependent on a given service, commodity, or natural resource to sustain its economy, and women produce, mine, own, or control the distribution of that resource, women clearly have a great deal of bargaining power. Similarly, women's access to resources needed within the family greatly heightens their status within the family. If women have no access to the resources that sustain the economy they live in, they are entirely dependent on men for the goods and services that keep them alive (while men have access to virtually *all* that women produce).

Women's access to resources is affected by their class, racial, ethnic or religious identity. A woman belonging to an upper-caste or class family may in some situations have access to some resources through her affiliation with the men in her family, not enjoyed by men of other classes. Yet this access is a privilege bestowed by the male relatives and easily and frequently revoked. For *within* each social group, women's position is inferior to men's, and the women who belong to the most empoverished social groups are sub-servient to all other persons.[16] In the United States, for example, third-world women of all classes have the least access to resources.

Perhaps the most crucial resource for women cross-culturally is that of land, and other forms of property, especially their homes. Since so many women throughout the world partially or completely support themselves and their families through their agricultural work, a major determinant of their status is the ownership of the land they work. In cultures where women, along with men, form part of the agricultural work force for wealthy landowners, they are powerless to the degree that they are non-unionized and unable to exert control over the conditions or products of their work. Women in these cultures usually have even less power than men since their wages are lower, and they are often treated as a temporary work force, last hired and first fired. If men own the land their family works, women's status may be the same as in landless families if the products of women's work are expropriated by their husbands. In fact, they may have less money and independence than when working for landowners where at least they receive a wage, however paltry. In some other societies women have rights to the land they farm and so have incomes and status independent of their husbands.

An example of how women's power, status and access to resources such as property rights vary according to divisions by class, race, caste and religion, is a study by Ann Stoler of Kali Loro, a village in rural Java in Indonesia.[17] Stoler points out that in practice, women from all classes have almost equal rights over rice land as men (although according to Islamic and Javanese customary law, known as *adat*, sons inherit twice as much as daughters). The economic power that access to this property accords women varies greatly according to the amount of property (and hence the economic status) held by the family as a whole. Women from families who own little or no land must do wage labor in the fields of the large landowning families, whereas women from families with much more land are often in a position to oversee the distribution of work and rewards that the poorer women do. With westernization the disparity in women's incomes is increasing. In the early 1970s, imported rice hullers eliminated 133 million workdays and $50 million in potential income for the poorer women.[18] Women from large landowning families now have less harvest management work and are able to use their capital to invest in lucrative trading. Their profits bring them an important source of social power outside the home and within. The poorer women's relatively high contribution to their families' total income which provides them with an important source of power and respect *within* the home is declining as they lose their jobs, and their social status is lower due to their families' class status.

In more highly industrialized societies, ownership of other forms of property or capital make a tremendous difference in women's power if laws and male relatives do not prevent them from controlling their assets.

Clearly, cash is also an extremely important resource for women in most societies. The extent to which women's work is supported or respected is always an important standard of measure for women's status, especially when their labor is remunerated with a wage. It has been said that women's presence in the paid labor force reflects the level of a country's development.[19] In all economies where some form of money or barter is used, it is used to exchange goods and services *between* households. Women's money is never acquired in the form of a wage for doing work in their homes for members of their own family. They only receive room and board and possibly petty cash for this work. On this most fundamental level, men in every culture have organized a distribution of work and its benefits to the nearly total exclusion of women's work in the home. Therefore, the extent to which women participate in the external economy and labor force is the extent to which they have their own money and access to the goods and services this money can buy. (Even in the situation of inherited wealth women perform services for the men they acquire wealth from – these services just aren't recognized as work by male economists.)

Women's participation in paid labor, rate of pay, and access to more specialized, high status jobs are also greatly affected by their access to training and education. The kinds of jobs open to women, the levels of responsibility and decision-making impact are affected by a woman's education, whether it be on a grammar school or graduate level. Education is a major mechanism used to convert social and economic status, especially by women, who through social sanction are commonly denied access to male spheres of work.

Yet if women don't have some degree of social power and access to resources to begin with, they are not even able to make independent choices regarding salaried employment. In Morocco, for example, a woman may not work outside the home without her husband's approval.[20]

Low status in other areas, such as the acceptance of male domination by women within the family, can reduce the effect of any independent income women might have. According to Yolanda Moses, on the West Indian island of Montserrat[21]

The status of employed women has less to do with economic contributions per se than with the presence or absence of a male in the household and the degree to which women have internalized and perpetuate ideologies of male dominance.

She describes how employed middle-class women continue to be responsible for all home maintenance and childcare work and do not compete in traditionally male arenas outside the home. Therefore they do not threaten the traditional male/female power relation. She points out that even though the women in working-class families usually provide at least half the family income,

> the boys are made to feel like pampered strangers in the household, catered to by mothers and sisters . . . when the males grow up they will expect a similar kind of treatment from their wives or girlfriends, who will be trained to give it to them.

Thus even though women's access to and control over the resources important for physical and social survival in their culture are a determinant of women's status within that society, this is not the only important factor. The acceptance by women of dominant male ideology and their inability to meet to share experiences, and to support efforts to change also drastically affects women's status.

Networks

> She was a middle-aged Hispanic woman, who was taken by a neighbor to the emergency room of the hospital . . . Her husband has threatened to kill her if she left or sought help.
> She had no other choice but to run out of her home to the safety of a neighbor . . . She was born and raised in a rural community in Northern New Mexico . . . All of her support systems are there, . . . friends, neighbors, church, and most important to her – 'La Familia' (extended family). Now she finds herself in a situation whereby she is forced to look for . . . help from people she doesn't know, support in an area unfamiliar to her, as well as a language and/or ways other than what she knows. Where does the help really lie? Is she changed to fit into this new

world or, instead, is she helped to be herself and change the conditions of the world around her?[22]

A mechanism that women have used to make changes in their lives in all cultures, as well as to help them survive in hostile environments, has been that of networks. Networks can vary from extended family to matrilocal (when husband and wife live with the woman's family), arrangements in which women support each other emotionally and materially, to neighborhood based childcare cooperation, to powerful national systems of goods distribution by market women.

One of the crucial functions of networks lies in providing women with a context in which they can share feelings and problems. The validation they receive from each other is a tremendous influence on the degree to which they accept and internalize male values and thinking. The more support women get for their own perspectives, the closer they come to questioning male perspectives and priorities, a crucial first step in the process of change. The development of women's networks has been tremendously important in laying the groundwork for making changes in women's lives in any culture. For example, women in the Congo in Africa traditionally formed groups called 'Musiki' or 'Kiterno', through which they helped each other in life crises such as births, deaths, and wakes, and in their daily work. These groups were later replaced by the URFC, the Revolutionary Union of Congolese Women, through which women became involved in issues of national development. Because the groundwork of women's networks was already laid, it was far easier to organize women around an issue than it would otherwise have been.[23]

In pre-revolutionary China, peasant women frequently came together in informal groups to talk as they sewed on their front doorsteps or washed clothes along streambanks. They developed support networks that were used to apply neighborly pressure to family members who they felt were wronging a woman in the work group. By threatening a man with the loss of 'face' by discussing his undesirable behavior towards his wife where men would hear and then discuss it as well, these networks were able to wield influence in the community. During the revolution, the women used similar problem-solving techniques. The skills and networks that they had developed before the revolution were translated into effective Women's Associations and 'Speak Bitterness' sessions.[24]

The degree of development of women's networks is not only an important indication of women's position in itself. It serves as a conversion mechanism for women's status because women acting together are more powerful than each individual member of a group. The creation or dissolution of networks can radically improve or destroy women's authority. Consequently, the nature of women's networks in each culture we discuss plays a major role in our evaluation of women's position.

Minimal, token and negotiating power
Using the criteria and perspectives discussed above, we have developed an alternative women-centered way of looking at and understanding the economic organization of cultures throughout the world. We will be exploring several examples of cultures which fall into the following categories:

1 Societies where women have *minimal power*: minimal access to crucial resources, low valuation of their capacity to reproduce and little freedom in it, high incidence of violence against women, and infrequent occasion to share experiences, support and resources.

2 Societies where women have *token power*: varying access to resources, including paid work, though little substantial power to affect those institutions in which they participate; varying perspectives on reproductivity, usually involving mixed messages which change as men's needs change (including the male-dominated government's need for more workers); and some freedom to create networks, though these networks may be undermined when they become effective bases for change.

3 Societies in which women have *negotiating power*: greater access to resources often different from men's resources, enough economic independence and leverage to give them a social bargaining tool; high valuation and support for their reproductive work; and highly developed networks for support and change.

All three of these categories exist within a basic patriarchal context. Even in societies where women hold negotiating power and have (or have had) a higher status than in any other cultures we know of, men still subtly or overtly hold the greater prerogative in all areas and women still service men in the home free of charge. Within each category women's experiences are very different. The power of women in cultures around the world exists along a continuum. We have grouped cultures together into these three categories along the continuum, based on the criteria we discussed.

The kind of culture that women live in always determines the specific strategies they will use in gaining control over their lives (or in simply trying to survive). Male processes of change, whether through 'development' or revolution, often completely ignore or bypass women, if they don't actually exploit them more deeply. Depending on whether women have minimal, token or negotiating power, changes in their lives come through creating, developing or increasing the potential for networking, access to resources and paid work, or developing and strengthening alternative institutions through women-centered networks. In each and every culture, however, women's networking is essential to the building of an independent power base that would allow them to take back the expropriated money, time and control over their lives, step by step.

In order to understand better the strategies that are needed for change, we will also examine ways in which women are prevented from having access to the time and wealth they create, and what mechanisms women can use to gain power. Understanding women's part in the economy is important if that understanding can be used to make much needed changes. Women can learn which institutions and changes have helped women in other cultures, and which have only further entrenched the male status quo in more sophisticated ways. Learning from the experiences of other women is the best way to develop that tool of understanding which women can wield in their struggles to change their lives.

Women across cultures

It is exceedingly difficult, when talking about women's experiences cross-culturally, to understand the impact that customs have on the life of a woman living in a specific culture, unless one has an understanding of how those traditions fit into the entire social and cultural context. For example, although heterosexuality is a common social institution, the ways that it structures and controls women's sexual relationships varies a great deal across cultures. Laws enforcing monogamous marriage might serve a progressive function for some women living in a polygynous society while serving to inhibit the freedom of women living in a culture where legal monogamy has been the norm but where *social* monogamy is enforced only for women. (Polygyny means multiple wives, whereas 'polygamy', despite its common, though patriarchally-biased usage, in fact means multiple spouses.)

Because of the tremendous diversity in the relationship of these institutions to women, it is critical to develop an understanding of how such institutions function *within* their cultural contexts. For this reason, we include some more in-depth descriptions and analyses of women's lives in several cultures, spanning the spectrum from minimal to negotiating power. This lays the basic framework for later discussion of the commonalities in women's experiences.

The cultures we have chosen to explore are included for a number of reasons. To start, we wanted to be sure to cover examples from four major male-defined categories of economies: non-technological (hunting and gathering) low-energy consumption societies, sometimes with non-plow agriculture, which are not territorial or class-stratified (we do not use the term 'primitive' because it comes from a white/ western cultural bias, using the degree of technological development as a standard of measure for the society's development, and therefore has an extremely derogatory connotation); third world; capitalist, meaning other countries with private ownership of property and resources and not including state capitalist societies (by state capitalist societies we mean countries such as the USSR where large volumes of capital are concentrated in and controlled by an élite running a centralized state, rather than by private corporations); and socialist (including state capitalist and communist countries, who have arrived at some degree of socialism through revolutionary change). Within each of these male-defined economies, women's experience varies from minimal power to negotiating power. The countries we will describe where women hold minimal power are Ethiopia, Peru, Algeria, and Japan. The countries we will discuss where women hold token power are the USA, Cuba, the USSR and Sweden. We have used China, Ewé and Iroquois cultures as examples of societies where women have held negotiating power. We describe in less detail those societies on which there is more written material available.

Before we discuss these countries in detail, however, we are going to address the issue of development and its effects on women cross-culturally. Many of the themes in the history of development efforts are similar across cultures, and discussion here of what they have meant for women will help to clarify some of the changes that are taking place in each of the countries we discuss later.

2 *Shouldering the high cost of development*

Twenty years ago . . . the living seemed in constant
motion. The men and their women plied the paths
between the villages and the minuscule fields, hauling
grain or grapes or fodder, olives and wood, . . . Now, in
the 70's, there are fewer people and fewer donkeys to click
the rhythm of their perpetual march. Some of the men no
longer go out to the fields but are content to roost on the
low stone walls in front of the church or opposite the
market . . . Those who still go to the fields are older. They
are the ones who stayed at home. To them the factories of
Milan and Germany were more frightening than the stingy
land of Lucania. The women had had no such choice, nor
even the luxury of fear. As they have for centuries, young
and old alike, they leave for the fields in the false light of
dawn and return at dusk, plodding slowly, heavily,
stopping occasionally to shift their loads.[1]

Ann Cornelisen,
Women of the Shadows:
The Wives and Mothers of
Southern Italy

'Development' has traditionally been assumed to entail
'progress' – for women as well as men, but in fact often has
the opposite effect. Since the lives of so many women around
the world and in the countries we will be discussing are
affected by the development process, we are including here
a brief examination of the changes it brings to the society at
large and later to women in particular. (Since we are questioning what 'development' really means for most 'developing'

and 'underdeveloped' countries, we put it in quotes here. As many 'developed' countries can easily be considered 'over-developed', it is important not to make them the standard of measure. We want to call attention to the fact that development does not always mean improvement. Although we will not continue to use quotation marks, it is important to remain critical of the terms.)

Development has been used to imply economic development, as opposed to social or moral development, and in this context has meant increasing technology, greater division of labor and the accumulation of wealth.

One traditional economist unwittingly pointed out one of the basic problems with accepting the premise that rapid growth, in and of itself, will be of the greatest economic benefit to a society:[2]

> It is a generally accepted economic rule that a wide disparity in income will result in a large savings, and if these savings are invested wisely the economy will grow rapidly. A more even distribution of income, on the other hand, will tend to increase consumption and reduce savings and thus the rate of economic growth. The political idea of a modern democracy – greater equality of income – may thus be in conflict with the economic necessity of increasing the rate of savings in order to speed the nation's economic development.

The honesty of this statement is surprising after all the myths that have been perpetrated, which assert that 'true democracy' goes hand in hand with 'free capitalism'.

What a 'growth' model for development means in most developing countries is accumulation of wealth for a few at the expense of the health and economic viability of the many; an increasingly complex division of labor which results in extreme class stratification and debasing poverty for the overwhelming majority; technological advances which only the ruling class élite have access to; technological aid to men for their work and no or little aid to women; massive migration by men to urban areas to find work where they are greeted by extensive unemployment; a greater burden on women who must continue their own work, plus take over the men's work, and try to earn some cash on the side.[3]

There is a wide variety of western-modelled development programs, ranging from national economic planning programs to increase production, to teams of foreign agricultural 'experts' teaching methods to increase production for purposes of exporting. Almost all of these programs have been motivated by, and structured to benefit, western governments and corporations, not the majority of people in developing countries. In a speech on development in the West Indies, Robert Cuthbert questioned the notion of modernization:[4]

> there is a large and growing body of opinion that sees 'development talk' as a deliberate attempt to cover up the real issues. 'Development,' it is felt, is merely a call for modernization. Modernization increases the dependency of the region on external metropolitan centres.

All western countries, in fact, went through their most rapid industrialization at the same time that their colonies afforded them vast natural and human resources to exploit. The western nations actually developed and industrialized at the expense of third-world countries and poor and working-class people in their own countries. Third-world countries are in fact 'underdeveloped' to the extent that the nations exploiting them have become developed.

Fatima Mernissi, a Moroccan, has pointed out what a western-modelled development has meant in many Arab cultures:[5]

> The dilemma is that modernization, progress, came to mean aping the West. To ape the West is to deny one's identity, to bury one's glittering past, to give in to the conqueror. To modernize is to recognize the West's supremacy.

There have been, however, alternative models of development. Instead of linking an ideal of economic growth to the presence of foreign capital and industry, the former Indian government and China, for example, concentrate on domestic industry. Their policies were designed to utilize small amounts of capital, local rather than foreign expertise and labor-intensive methods to manufacture products for domestic consumption.[6] In the early stages of the revolution, China went even further, with a model for development which placed a priority on shared resources rather than economic growth. Technology took a second place to the maximum utilization of labor, and industry was de-centralized. In the process, the standards of health, education and employment for most of China were significantly raised.

Because we will go into China's development process in greater detail later, and because there are so few alternatives at present to western-modelled development, this 'Development' section will be devoted to an analysis of western-modelled development only.

Domination in the name of progress

The reasons that economic development is even an issue for most third-world countries are rooted in their colonial history. This history is consistently obscured in news reports and analyses originating in the west, most of which directly or indirectly imply that countries in need of development are culturally backward, uncivilized, immature and incapable of ruling themselves without help from the outside. Such arguments are also used by multi-national corporations in justifying their presence in third-world countries where they appropriate raw materials, pay meager wages, send the profits back to the home country, and sell finished products back to the third-world countries at exorbitant prices. Such corporations say that they're providing people with jobs, and ask what the underdeveloped countries would do without them.

One of the ironies of development has been that the colonizing countries entered by force nations which were culturally and technologically more sophisticated but not militarily. Throughout Asia and Africa, highly developed systems of medicine and of psychic healing once existed which were later suppressed by colonizers. Universities and libraries were burned, as in Alexandria in 700 BC, where one library destroyed by the Romans took six months to burn down, it was so large.[7] People have been imprisoned or fined for inventing new tools. For example, in south-east Togo the Germans imprisoned a man who invented a paddle-boat in the late nineteenth century.[8] Other work has been appropriated and claimed as the work of the colonizing power. Two-thirds of the Greek scientists and philosophers we know of today studied in ancient Egypt, where they learned mathematics, astronomy and medicine. Pythagoras spent twenty years studying in ancient Egypt, and Aristotle's books were based on information taken from the royal libraries of Egypt.[9]

Although the primary motivations behind colonialism were economic, the process itself had devastating social, cultural and religious repercussions. This process, described here by Josephine Trinidad as it occurred in Curaçao and the rest of the Caribbean, is representative of the same process of acculturation that occurred the world over:[10]

> After 1863 when slavery was abolished in Curacao, the economic situation did not change, simply because the 'liberated' slaves had to work for the same masters in exchange for very low wages. These blacks were adapting European family systems which were completely strange to them; they had to contract matrimonies and educate their children along the European train of thought.
> The Catholic Church in Curaçao did a lot to 'educate' those people. And the churches brought a series of values and norms that spelt 'perfect family' – values which our ancestors had to comply with if they wanted to be accepted (tolerated) in the community.

As colonized nations around the world were split up and appropriated by different European powers, western institutional models were imposed which led to urbanization and industrialization. The extended family units also broke down, as did other social and religious institutions that had served to hold pre-colonial cultures together.

Much of the economic exploitation that took place during the process of colonialism was justified in the name of

Christianity, with the claim that the purpose of colonialism and slavery was the education and enlightenment of non-Christians. One Jamaican minister points to similar contradictions in the role of the church today:[11]

> Have we not launched out on social services in rural
> communities with the aim of relieving the oppressed only
> to strengthen the oppressors by courting their favor?
> All Caribbean denominations share responsibility here
> for all have had an excessive emphasis on the after-life that
> promises liberation from poverty. But how about
> liberation in this life?

Part of the negative role the church has played has been in introducing male domination in spirituality to many cultures which formerly worshipped female deities and communicated through priestesses. Commenting on this same sexual bias today, John Hood points out the role of women in the Caribbean church, which reads like Christian churches the world over:[12]

> The institutional Church, committed to the salvation of
> all persons, has somehow allowed itself to become sexually
> discriminatory, in massive favor of women membership
> but of men for leadership.
> The communal picture of the Church is therefore one of
> men, pulpit-high, talking to women, at pew level.

In the wake of the West

Although much material and cultural destruction took place during the process of colonization, many changes affecting colonized countries have taken place after colonization ended, during a period of continuing imperialism or 'neo-colonialism' (this occurs when economic ties remain after political ties have ostensibly dissolved, and the imperial powers continue to use their former colonies as a source of revenue). Since independence, for example, all of France's former colonies have been used as markets for products which glutted French markets and are sometimes so poorly made that they do not sell in France.

The transformation of many social, cultural, and religious institutions was so profound under colonialism that eventual political independence could not reverse the process. One of the reasons that such changes did not take place at the time of independence was that the newly established governments and economies were modelled after those of the colonizers, with their interests in mind. As colonial powers officially withdrew from their former colonies, they left puppet governments in charge. The new regimes, composed of people favored by the former colonizers, often simply continued the economic and social policies of their predecessors. In so doing, they insured continued profits and benefits to the former powers, as well as to themselves.

Multi-national corporations, originating in and benefiting primarily Europe and the United States, enter former colonies and offer jobs, pay low wages, few or no taxes and do not share their profits with the host countries. They export minerals, cash crops and high profits to the nations they come from. Although multi-national corporations have invested over $70 billion in third-world countries, this investment has resulted in less than four million jobs, while approximately 680 million people are unemployed.[13] Contrary to the popular rationalization that multi-nationals' presence creates jobs, they often render existing jobs obsolete. With the use of foreign-built equipment, many jobs are often lost. In Indonesia, capital-intensive factory-made goods such as bricks, soap and shoes undersell traditional industries that employed more people. One study in Tukdana, in West Java, found that each of 5 Japanese-built power tillers eliminated more than 2,000 days of work each year, rechannelling $2,650 away from the laborers, to the owner, dealer and manufacturer.[14] While the wages in Indonesia are among the lowest in the world, (with more than 50 million of the 140 million people subsisting on less than 25 cents a day) multi-national corporations obtained a 56 per cent return on their investments in 1977 alone, and the landowning minority is becoming extremely wealthy, with government tariffs continuing to support imported capital and mechanization rather than labor-intensive policies and programs.[15]

The process of imperialism creates 'needs' where they didn't formerly exist, which are 'met' by multi-national corporations who are eager to make new sales in countries not already glutted with their products. In much of Africa and South America, baby bottle formulas are sold by sales-people, dressed in nurse's uniforms, who tell village women that their babies will be healthier and stronger if they are fed the imported formulas. In some cases women are given enough free or low-cost samples to last until their breast milk dries up, at which point they are obliged to buy the high-cost formula. In 1973, formulas cost about $140 annually. This sum represents 100 per cent or more of the average family's annual income in Peru, Indonesia or Nigeria, and many women are forced to dilute the formula to make it stretch farther while breast milk is free, comes naturally 'mixed,' in sterile 'containers,' and with antibodies to help prevent infection and disease.[16] Many babies are malnourished as a result and drink from containers and water that are unsterile, both of which greatly increase the death-rate among infants. In Chile, for example, the infant mortality rate has increased threefold since the baby formula was imported.[17]

Developing countries around the world, devastated by colonialism and imperialism, are then given 'aid', with strings attached, that keeps them dependent on the sources of this 'aid' – the western countries. France, for example, gets back 80 per cent of the 'aid' that it gives to Togo, one of its former colonies, in the form of salaries that go to French people, French textbooks, French technicians, etc.[18] The World Bank (the International Bank for Reconstruction and Development) itself admitted that loan regulations often stipulate that the funds must be spent outside the host countries, for machinery and technology that creates high unemployment but insures profits for the buyers and sellers of the equipment.[19] Ironically, even aid in the form of material goods sent into many third-world nations during crises benefits mostly the élite (through pilfering at each step of the distribution process) while relatively little goes to those who need it most. Economic policies favorable to the élite result in atrocities such as the starvation during the drought in sub-Saharan Africa in the 1970s when export of cotton and peanuts from some nations receiving aid actually increased.[20]

Host nations, unable to accumulate surplus, become more and more economically dependent on the nations giving them 'aid.' This further insures the industrialized nations higher profits, which are used to buy third and fourth homes for corporate owners, to raise the standard of living and benefits of a select group of workers in the developed countries (thus insuring their national allegiance and hostility towards third-world countries demanding control over and profits from their resources); and allow one-third of the world's population to consume over 80 per cent of global resources each year.[21] If these foreign governments and their corporations were not a presence, the products of third-world countries would belong to those countries, and poverty and development would not be the issues they are currently.

Robert Cuthbert, in *The Role of Women in Caribbean Development*, discusses how western modernization perpetuates problems within developing nations:[22]

> Modernization also tends to emphasize changes within one sector of society. Groups privileged in terms of income, education, colour, cultural background and religion have been progressively integrated into an international market structure. The tastes, values, and dynamism of this group originate in the metropolitan centres and work to the advantage of these centres.

This process is inevitable in all countries where industrialization takes place along a western model. Along this model, the number of households in industrial urban areas increases, while the percentage of the population engaged in agriculture decreases. In third-world countries, policies have increasingly emphasized export-oriented agriculture, and heavy industrial and urban growth, concentrating the capital and profits in the hands of a few, instead of decentralizing the production, control and benefits among the entire population. Thus development along a western, capitalist model has also meant increasing class-stratification and resulting poverty.

Left behind to slave

Men are moving ahead. Men and women are growing
apart. Men look down on us – I don't know why.
                    Village woman to Peace Corps Director[23]

Colonialism and development have, directly and indirectly,
affected women's status in complex ways. In most pre-
colonialist cultures, women were second-class citizens, a role
reinforced by institutions that varied from subtle assumptions about women's and men's proper roles to devastating
isolation, exploitation and violence.

Because women's role was secondary in virtually all
cultures before colonialism (whether those assumptions and
values were overt or subtle) the existing norms and institutions made it possible for western-based forms of sexual
oppression to be superimposed. This often resulted in an
increasing disintegration of women's status, compounding
women's oppression. In cultures where women held negotiating power traditionally, their status declined with the new
norms, and laws introduced by the colonial powers of countries
where women often had less power. When countries where
women held token power were colonized by other cultures
where women held token power, women's traditional forms
of oppression were institutionalized in new ways, superimposed upon the old. When token power societies colonized
cultures where women held minimal power, certain benefits
accrued to some women, though their new and more liberal
forms of oppression became further entrenched in more
subtle ways.

Even in cultures in which women held greater power and
prestige than in many cultures today, there were still underlying assumptions of women's inferiority that provided the
basis for a later acceptance of degrading imported attitudes
and behavior towards women.

In traditional Ashanti society in Ghana, for example, the
term in the Twi language for elders going into consultation
is 'consulting the old woman,' the image of the older woman
symbolizing wisdom. Although in this society a woman's age
gives her higher status, and the queen mother has the im-

portant role of carrying the genealogical information necessary for choosing the next king, there are underlying sexist assumptions in these traditions. They are revealed in the following statement made by J.B. Danquah, a prominant Ghanaian thinker, in an article he wrote for a Ghanaian paper in the late sixties:[24]

> woman is the goddess behind the scenes who is consulted in case of the need for a high decision, but she is never to expose herself to the slings and arrows of outrageous politics. Women should be more concerned with the permanent – inheritance and tradition.

This statement reads something like the common western male assumption that women are the vessels of conservatism and only show concern with stability, lack foresightedness and fear change.

Annie Jiagge, Ghana's first woman lawyer, has pointed out how these assumptions affect women today:[25]

> Many serious problems bedevil the advancement of women. First on the list perhaps is prejudice against women based on traditional attitudes and customary practices that relegate them to an inferior position in society. Lack of adequate education and professional and technical training is another. . . . Heavy domestic commitments make pursuit of knowledge difficult . . . . Due to tradition, affairs of State, unfortunately, have been reserved to men in Ghana. It is true that Queen mothers have always had a big say in certain aspects of state matters but generally it has been the domain of men, and they are now so well entrenched that the tendency is to carry over this tradition into modern forms of government.

The centralization of colonial and neo-colonial government meant that the male power that was often diffused in traditional societies has become more absolute since it is so removed from women's spheres.

Another example of colonial sexism compounding traditional oppression is the erosion of women's status through the heavy taxation the European powers instituted almost immediately upon occupying the colonized countries.[26]

In many nations the impact of the sudden need for cash was more devastating than the steep taxes themselves. Only two mechanisms for acquiring cash existed – producing the new export crops and working for wages – both of which were made available only to men. Men were forced to leave their villages and farms to work in mines, plantations or factories, at extremely low wages. Women were often left doing their own as well as the men's work, while most of the men's wages went to taxes and to support themselves at the higher standard of living in urban areas.[27] As men who remained on the farms were taught how to cash crop, most technological aid and education went only to them, and women were left maintaining the subsistence agricultural economy that sustained themselves and their children. In Africa women still do 70 per cent of the agricultural work while almost all the agricultural aid has gone to men.[28] With little or no education, women have not even been able to take advantage of those programs that might otherwise have admitted them.

Similar policies have continued into the present, and enormously affect the ways in which development changes women's lives, often for the worse. Ester Boserup, a leading economist concerned with the issue of women and development, has summed up the difficulties facing women in developing countries:[29]

Although both men and women may become victims of development, it is more difficult for women to adapt to new conditions, because (1) Family obligations make them less mobile than men, (2) Their occupational choice is more narrowly limited by custom, (3) They usually have less education and training, and (4) Even without these handicaps they often face sex discrimination in recruitment. Moreover, in Third World countries, a much larger percentage of the female than of the male labor force is engaged in traditional occupations, which are precisely those gradually replaced by modern enterprises in economic development.

Since education, including agricultural and industrial training, and clerical jobs, have been made available primarily to men, the only waged work left for women has been the most menial, difficult and lowest paid work, and prostitution. Women's work in the home or compound, as well as their work in the fields, is usually not recognized as work, so they seldom are given technological aid in the form of water pumps or wells, running water, electricity, household tools and appliances, etc. Ester Boserup has also pointed out that since many countries cannot afford the wide-scale capital investment needed to institute technological improvements in agriculture, they will continue to call on women to perform the more menial and back-breaking agricultural work.[30] The extensive poverty and hunger that exists the world over is rooted in this division of labor and resources which leaves women and their subsistence agriculture as the sole support of several generations.

Another problem affecting women's agricultural work in some cultures is that as land ownership shifts from the collective 'land-use rights' of traditional village life, in which women shared in the distribution of land, to the European concept of private ownership, it is usually only the men who have the necessary cash to pay for it (by virtue of their cash-cropping income). In addition, some men traditionally 'owned' the land, while women 'owned' the crops as in the Cameroons in West Africa. As land becomes increasingly scarce, men begin to rent and sell 'their' land, leaving women with no recourse but to pay for land or stop their agricultural work.[31]

It is also increasingly difficult for women to support themselves and their children in subsistence agriculture due to inflation and other effects of development. Consequently, many women also have to take on other remunerative activity to supplement their families' income – for instance, weaving clothing and baskets in South America. So these economic shifts have brought women increasingly more work with little or no technological aid, and less wealth and a lower standard of living than men in the same cultures.

Apart from almost universally placing a greater work burden on women, development has had other negative impacts on women's lives in different cultures.[32] In some African cultures where women traditionally had supportive institutions and some control over their lives, their condition has deteriorated in direct proportion to western influence. For example, in much of West Africa, South-east Asia and parts of Latin America, trading has been a major source of employment and income for many women because it does not require specialized training, it affords flexibility in schedule and permits their children to stay with them. In traditional Ga society in West Africa, women controlled the trade in fish – buying from fishermen along the coast, smoking fish to preserve it, and transporting it to the northern areas of Ghana to sell. However, when the N'Krumah regime established a system of cold storage for fish and moved the harbor from Accra to Tema in Ghana, it made obtaining fish a great deal more difficult for the Ga women, most of whom lived in or near Accra. The few women who could afford to go to Tema to obtain the fish found themselves competing with larger businesses owned by men who refrigerated the fish. Today, only women from wealthy families can continue the fish trade, because only they have the necessary capital to pursue it. Young women who would have grown up apprenticed to their mothers instead go to school where they learn very different skills, for which there is currently no market. They leave school only to confront massive unemployment and sex discrimination, and are often obliged to turn to prostitution, the only consistent employment the west has offered them.[33]

In other countries as well, colonial and neo-colonial regimes have attempted to limit market women's power. In Kenya, just before independence, only 20 per cent of hawkers' licenses were given to women, and consequently many women were prosecuted for illegal hawking. In the Cameroons, similar attempts were made in efforts to get more women back to the fields, but they met with such resistance from women that they were abandoned.[34]

In Morocco, where women had little authority or independence before colonialism, they have even less now. Women who previously lived in extended family networks where they could at least get advice and support from older

women, are now often isolated in nuclear families in unfamiliar urban settings. This is well articulated by an Indian
housewife:[35]

> In the joint family, a woman got rest during pregnancy
> and menstruation. And children grew up almost without
> one's realizing it. Older people would help take care of
> the kids. Now, all the work has descended on the head of
> one woman. Yet, husbands have the same old expecta-
> tions . . . . She has to slave at home and toil outside too.
> Her husband will still consider it a disgrace to enter the
> kitchen. The child may be crying while she is cooking;
> why should the husband bother?

The presence of other women in the compound, in the
neighborhood and in the extended family in rural India, as
well as in many countries around the world, afforded women
far more mobility and shared responsibility than they now
have. Now, with large-scale migration to urban areas in many
countries, there is little, if any, childcare available in cities
and that which is available is prohibitively expensive. So the
care of children is becoming an increasingly burdensome
task to each woman.

Moroccan women did weaving as a source of income, but
the lack of commercial outlets and difficulties in obtaining
raw wool prevent the continuation of this work in urban
settings, where they moved with their husbands in their
search for employment. Consequently the women became
more economically dependent on their husbands. Among
poorer families recently arrived in urban areas only 7 per cent
of women working outside the home are married. Men who
are unemployed spend hours with other men drinking or
playing cards, refusing to help women with their domestic
work or childcare for fear of seeming 'feminine' (a fear that
is backed up with scorn or deprecating jokes when a man
does outstep his role). Without the help of older female
family members in matters of health care, pregnancy and
birth, urban women now can turn only to the Public Health
Service. Its extreme bureaucracy and impersonality requires
that the women spend hours and even days of waiting for

inadequate services while watching several children.[36]

Development has negatively affected women in some cultures by totally ignoring traditional social and economic structures in which women had played a major role. In Mexico, for example, modern laundries which were installed as part of a World Bank-funded tourism program employed only men, even though women had previously done the laundry for the tourist industry.[37] In Kenya women had traditionally done most of the work and received most of the benefits from production of chrysanthemums. When development programs intervened, there emerged economic superstructures which paid the men in the families for the work that women were doing. With no more incentive for women to work, production dropped to almost nothing.[38] European models of sex discrimination and division of labor had been imposed on a far more egalitarian structure without any thought to the women's possible reaction or resistance. It was not only European influence, but other male-dominated influences as well which affected women's status harmfully. For example, Taiwanese agricultural instructors failed in their efforts to introduce new rice paddy methods in Senegal, West Africa, because they did not teach the women, who were doing all the work, and addressed only the men, who largely ignored them.[39]

Even in cultures where women were exchanged like commodities, such as in the Tiv in Nigeria, their status declined with colonialism. The pre-colonial Tiv economy was based on a system of three spheres – subsistence goods, valuables including cattle and slaves, and rights to non-slaves, especially women. Goods (including women) within each sphere held equivalent value and could be exchanged but could not be exchanged with goods from another sphere. Men could only obtain the right to marry a woman in another family by exchanging the right to marry a woman in their own family. When Europeans introduced money, it began to be used interchangeably for goods within all the spheres. Consequently, there was a 'devaluation' of women, as the bride price was reduced to money, which could be exchanged for objects.[40]

In addition to the economic policies which often place a

greater work load on women, change institutions that had formerly been supportive of women, and ignore traditional social and economic structures in which women had played a major role, western-modelled industrialization has brought with it values and new methods of social organization that have negatively affected women.

As agricultural work in developing countries is increasingly relegated to cash-cropping and replaced by industrial work, families leave rural areas where they were able to support themselves through agriculture and cottage industries in which women played a large role. Industrialization, however, is less labor intensive and so creates high unemployment. Consequently, women must work at the only tasks available, primarily 'informal' labor (trading, domestic work and other erratic part-time work), usually service work of some sort. Although early in the development of industry, there is often a huge need for cheap labor and women can find jobs (and even predominate in such industries as textiles), with the development of greater technology, it is the women workers who are usually displaced. In Brazil, for example, women comprised 45.3 per cent of the labor force in 1900, and only 21 per cent in 1970, in spite of a tremendous growth in industry.[41]

Women have also been affected by a more subtle process of acculturation which includes an implicit acceptance of western materialism and industrialism and forces women to work even harder to be part of industrializing society. Rural families the world over are being affected by this process as described here by Tomiko Shimado concerning Japan:[42]

Since our industrialization has made its great progress, starting about 1956, men in rural areas began to work in paid employment in factories. The living standard of rural areas is improving by using gas, washing machines, refrigerators and T.V. But to buy these things the rural family needs money which they can not gain by farm work alone.

Also parents wish their children to go on to high school or even college. This also costs much. Many industries are now building their factories near agricultural areas so farm people can find jobs. Also the Central and Local Governments are making efforts to build roads and develop other public works so the head of the farming family can find his work.

Because of all this, women in rural areas are compelled to do both farm work and home work. They have to work harder than ever in the fields often with old grandfather or grandmother. Home work may be easier by gadgets but they still have to cook, sweep, take care of children.

Many overwork and are taken ill . . . . Young sons and daughters do not want to stay on the farms. There is a keen shortage of brides willing to come to farm families. They prefer to go to factories which put up clean, modern dormitories for them in order to attract girls to work, for even the big industries are short of workers. After this relatively free and lucrative life, they are not anxious to return to farms where hard work and family discipline wait.

There are also many changes in cultural attitudes towards, and expectations of, both mothers and children. A frequent consequence of rapid development along a western, class-stratified model, is that children are raised with a set of social values and expectations based on traditional economic requirements, while the changing social and economic mores often make it impossible for them to live up to those expectations. This poses a major problem for mothers raising their children with the assumption that they are preparing the family for a secure economic future, while the conditions for that future are rapidly deteriorating. On the island of Montserrat in the West Indies, for example, most women spoil and pamper their sons with the hope of ensuring their continued emotional and economic loyalty to their mothers in their old age.[43]

Ideally, mothers believe their sons will have a good 'position' [job] in life and that they will dote on an aged mother who may have no man of her own to depend on. Sisters do it because they say they need to have a man around to help them. But, due to the lack of economic alternatives these working class men will have to face in life, they are not being socialized by their mothers to survive. Girls are actually better equipped to survive, although it is still ideally believed and valued that men should be economically superior at providing and at decision-making.

Clearly, women's work around the world has remained invisible to the male eye, a major reason why development has so negatively affected women. Much of women's work is never even recorded in statistical analyses of work, or census reports, rendering them extremely inaccurate when concerning women's role in their economies.

Hanna Papanek, a sociologist, points out some of the reasons why male definitions of work and productivity make their statistical analyses and census reports so hopelessly off base:[44]

> Available methods of analysis . . . draw a sharp distinction between work that results in a product that can be sold and work that does not. This entails a parallel distinction in terms of reward systems. 'Market' activities receive wages, 'nonmarket' activities do not. This has also led to economic analyses that differentiate between the 'modern' sector, entirely market oriented, and the 'traditional' sector, partly involved in subsistence. The preoccupation with wage labor in economic analysis and development planning, while relevant to industrial societies, may be much less so for largely agricultural nations. New analyses which meet their needs are particularly relevant for women.

Women's subsistence agricultural work, for example, is not even considered to be productive, nor is it entered in the agricultural statistics in census reports or economic studies, as is men's cash cropping.

Usually crafts and trading are not recorded in census reports either, nor is work done for a family business (for which women receive not a wage, but room and board), nor is irregular part-time work done outside the home. In Mexico, for example, the census report records only women's 'primary activity', which is assumed to be domestic work and which is not classified as an economic activity. Consequently, 79.9 per cent of Mexican women are classified as 'economically inactive', and their frequent involvement in many different forms of work is thus obscured. If the 'economically inactive' women are added to the 'active', then 94.7 per cent of women over 12 are working, as opposed to 89.7 per cent of the men. However, only 17.5 per cent of the women receive a wage for their work, as compared to 90.3 per cent of the men.[45]

Much of the work that women do around the world has been considered a part of the 'informal labor sector' by male economists, as opposed to the 'formal labor sector', which is included in national measurements of production and is predominantly 'men's' work. Ironically, most social scientists and policy makers have overlooked the fact that the informal labor sector exists largely because women are restricted from the formal occupational structure.[46] This informal labor includes both jobs performed by women only (within and outside the home) such as paid and unpaid domestic work, prostitution and volunteer work, and jobs that men also share, such as work in a family business, irregular part-time work, trading and street vending. Consequently, it can be said that the definition of informal labor, which includes low-status, low-income and less specialized work, closely resembles women's work around the world. Of course, measuring women's work is not important in itself, but the fact that it is not even counted shows how little it is valued by society.

When informal work is recognized, marginal, temporary service work has often been held up as an 'opportunity' for women. Shirley-Ann Hussen, in discussing options available to West Indian women, points to the fallacy of this argument:[47]

Take the case of the domestic workers. A development institution should be involved in more than placing these women in domestic jobs as this makes no dent in the society. It merely rearranges the same order. Domestic labour will have to be done away with in any serious attempt at social and economic reorganization. A more useful exercise for a development institution would be district nurseries and food services, run by the present domestic workers.

Something for some at what cost?

In spite of these examples, women's status has not universally declined with western influence. The European norms imposed on third-world countries, coming from societies in which women held token power, had a negative impact on cultures in which women held negotiating or token power. However, in cultures where women held minimal power, they stood to gain from certain aspects of development.

French colonization brought women new freedom from seclusion in Algeria, and in countries such as Japan and Cuba access to employment outside the home has enabled women of all classes to share experiences and perceptions, a crucial first step in the empowerment process. Infibulation, a form of female genital mutilation whereby the clitoris and vaginal lips are removed and the outer lips sewn together (leaving only a tiny hole for blood and urine to pass through), has been widely practiced for centuries throughout North Africa and other Moslem countries. Women were formerly infibulated in unsterile conditions, often on dirt floors with razor blades or broken glass, frequently resulting in sterilization or death. Although the mutilation continues women are increasingly being infibulated in sanitary hospitals.

Because the colonialist countries were all highly class-stratified, they brought with them their economic hierarchies, and often the benefits accruing to women were only enjoyed by upper-class and in some cases, middle-class women. In Latin America, development has increased some middle- and upper-class women's educational and employment options,[48] and more and more upper-class women in Ethiopia are able to obtain education. Access to education has also changed the lives of upper middle-class women in Japan, Peru and

Algeria, though neo-colonialist regimes in these countries have kept most poorer women illiterate.

Women traders from wealthier families have also benefited from development more than women from low-income families. In some West African cultures such as in Ghana and the Yoruba society in Nigeria as many as 70 per cent of women trade, though there is tremendous variation in the volume sold and income produced.[49] Some women trade thousands of pounds sterling worth of goods, and others walk 15 to 20 miles to sell one or two litres of milk.[50] Trading is the predominant reason for much of the female travel and migration in many countries of coastal West Africa. In the past 25 years women have become even more likely than men to move to urban areas, seeking education or training, employment and/or marriage.[51] Women from wealthy families with access to a lot of capital for initial investments are now able to accumulate large profits from trading, and they have a major effect on the economies of their countries. Wealthy women traders often enjoy a high social status, and income from sales of *all* traders is sometimes greater than their husband's incomes, affording them a higher status within their families than if they did not have this income.

In some countries where development has benefited women married to wealthy men, it has hurt women from poorer families, as increasing class division severely limited and sometimes erased what access to economic resources women previously had. Ann Stoler's description of a Javanese village, discussed earlier, demonstrates how, for many rural women, the decline in status came not so much with increasing sex-role differentiation, as with their deteriorating class position and corresponding loss of access to land and jobs.[52] More often than not the benefits for women of westernization are mixed, and positive developments have been combined with other forms of imported, western-style oppression that maintain women's powerlessness and isolation.

In Egypt, for example, as families migrate to Cairo, women's lives become far more isolated than they were in the villages, where they played large roles in social and religious festivals.

In the city, men have access to other men through male institutions such as the coffee shop, while women are isolated in their immediate neighborhood.[53] In Turkey a similar phenomenon often takes place, though it contains mixed blessings. Though isolated, the newly urban women also have more access to the kinds of employment, education and training that were unavailable in the villages. It is questionable, however, whether women without moderate to high incomes really have access to such institutions. Most women in industry do the lowest paid, least skilled work. One study in Istanbul and Izmit showed that only 2 per cent of the wives of male industrial workers work outside the home.[54] With childcare unavailable and the lack of female relatives to help, urban women are less able to work outside the home.

Other changes have also brought bad results mixed with good. Throughout Africa, the digging of village wells has saved women enormous amounts of time which they formerly spent trekking long distances to obtain water. But it has often simultaneously destroyed their only chance to get together and share information and experiences. Technological advances such as household appliances do not free women from domestic drudgery in any society. Many of the household appliances that decrease women's time in the home are expensive and therefore available to few women. When traditional women's work is transferred to businesses outside the home, it is usually poorly paid women who do them under tedious and gruelling conditions. Relatively few women can afford such services because of the high prices which line the pockets of the men who own the laundries, cafeterias and daycare centers where women work. Only in some socialist societies (such as China and Cuba), where a few home maintenance chores are being collectivized as the society as a whole begins to take responsibility for them, are the advantages of large-scale production a real alternative for women. Yet even here it is still women who do collectively the work which individual women did formerly.

For those women who can afford the household appliances industrialization makes available, the influence of western consumer society creates more work for them to do.[55] There are new social requirements and standards of cleanliness, childcare and consumption which require more work than has been saved through technology. Rhona Baptiste described this process as it affected the Caribbean woman:[56]

> To further complicate the plight of the Caribbean woman, a western capitalist society continues to tempt her with the materialism of the 'good' middle class life which holds her capitve in a certain unquestioning conformity of 'decency' while allowing her to become the object of sensual advertising and the subject of greedy consumerism.

There are other superficial changes as well, that seem to work to women's benefit but only alter the form that marriage takes, not the economic base or distribution of authority within the family. In upper-class India, for example, marriages are often still arranged, sometimes through classified advertisements in newspapers. Although the dowry system is now illegal, and some advertisements indicate 'no dowry' or 'simple marriage', many fathers of future husbands insist on it. Likewise, a person's caste, ethnicity and skin color are often mentioned as criteria for marriage candidates. Eligible young women are advertised according to their looks, culinary and mothering skills, and, increasingly, for their ability to bring in a second income.[57] This is yet another example of westernization which changes traditions but does not change the basic power relation between men and women within the family.

Development for whom?

It is important to keep woman-centered criteria in mind while evaluating the effects of development. Many people who are critical of western-modelled development romanticize pre-colonial cultures. During many countries' struggles for independence especially, there was a great resurgence in pride and respect for values and traditions that had existed before colonialism. After independence, these cultures reclaimed many of their traditional customs, many of which were extremely oppressive to women in cultures where women had held minimal power. As a consequence, women found themselves losing gains that had been made during the colonial era. Although women were extremely active in the Algerian revolution, for example, they experienced great repression afterwards, though the new male-dominated culture was reputed to be far more progressive than that of the French regime.

Today in Iran, with the end of the Shah's regime, many women are losing gains that had been made at a high cost since the rule of Reza Shah Pahlavi. Feminism in Iran had its roots in the early nineteenth century, in a revolt against the veil and polygyny. Feminists persisted through the 1920s during the reign of Reza Shah Pahlavi, even though the founders of *Messenger of Happiness*, a women's magazine and organization, were jailed, and the Shah's brutal method of 'lifting of the veil' was by having police tear them off women in the streets.[58] They were also active against the recent Shah, the son of Pahlavi, and fought in support of Prime Minister Mohammed Mossadegh's attempts to nationalize the oil industry. Although the Shah banned feminist publications and meetings, and his secret police force, SAVAK, was responsible for the torture, rape, and death of many female political prisoners, he did introduce some reforms including equal pay, legalized abortion, a family protection law and the right to vote. These were an attempt to absorb and diffuse intense feminist pressure and a response to his twin sister, Princess Ashraf, who worked actively for reforms for educated women. Yet the equal pay law was not enforced, few adequate abortion facilities were available, the right to vote was meaningless under his one-party system, and Islamic law was kept basically intact. (Men still have the rights to polygyny and child custody and can kill their wives if they are suspected of adultery).

Even though women were active participants in overthrowing the Shah and welcoming the Ayatollah to power, within five weeks they were denouncing his stands on women: women had been barred from the armed services and the Ayatollah announced his disapproval of the family protection act, abortion, and women 'who are naked', saying that a Muslim woman should cover her hair, arms, legs and hide her *zinnaat* (enticing parts) – in other words, don the veil once again.

The long fought-for liberation from the Shah's repression recalled some of the old forms of women's repression in the name of Islam and liberation from western influence. As in many countries, the male-defined 'revolutionary' edict to maintain or reclaim traditions is done at women's expense. It is usually the women who maintain the traditions (through unpaid subservience in the family) while men are educated, trained and enjoy some of the benefits of technology.

As we have seen from the previous examples, development, whether planned or unplanned, usually takes place in a totally male context, with male needs, desires and priorities in mind, to the total exclusion of women's priorities. When social change takes place, whether within governmental contexts, or through rebellion from outside forces seeking to change the institutional structure, it is usually controlled by men. When social change has positive effects on women it is usually by accident, or because of the changing needs of the male economy. In countries where there are labor short-ages due to war, rapid industrialization or social revolution, women are swiftly directed to meet the newest ideal of womanhood and jump into the job slots made available to them. Then when the labor market is flooded, they are herded back into the home and encouraged to be the dedi-cated wife and mother, a role which flimsily disguises their widespread unemployment.

The problem then, is *not* that women need to be 'inte-grated' into the development process, a concept recently articulated by the United Nations and International Aid agencies in the wake of the UN Decade for Women. Women have always played a huge role in their economies, within their families and in social change, and actually shoulder the immense social and economic costs of development. In fact, in most industrialized and third-world nations, develop-ment has only been possible due to women's 'invisible' labor.

Male-controlled political interests and the presence of foreign political and economic powers have still, directly through policy choice and indirectly through cultural shifts, actively prevented women from participating in planning that could change their lives. Male interests have ignored women's needs, then accused them of being 'backward,' and finally turned around and expressed the questionable desire to 'integrate' women into a development process over which they have no control. As Achola Pala, a Kenyan sociologist, has aptly pointed out, 'Member states that pursue a program of development that negates equity can only be paying lip service to the issue when they agree to establish a woman's bureau or commission.'[59] Their lip service is only an attempt to assimilate women's real desires for change into the existing power structure. A woman from rural Kenya described the problem in a conversation with Ms Pala:[60]

> During the anticolonial campaigns we were told that
> development would mean better living conditions.
> Several years have gone by, and all we see are people
> coming from the capital to write about us. For me the hoe
> and the water pot which served my grandmother still
> remain my livelihood. When I work on the land and fetch
> water from the river, I know I can eat. But this
> development which you talk about has yet to be seen
> in this village.

Clearly the only answer to development which will truly work in the interests of all is a development process which is not imposed from the outside by foreign powers with vested interests, but is created by all persons who will be affected. For development to be useful and sensitive in any society, those people (women) who have sustained the development process must play a leadership role in defining the terms of that development. If men continue to control the development process, women may simply refuse to be a part of it. A new model for change necessitates women holding control over their own lives and power within their communities.

3 As a woman, I have no country: the diversity of male power

As a woman, I have no country.
As a woman, I want no country.
As a woman, my country is the whole world.
Virginia Woolf

Very few of the countries we use to illustrate minimal, token and negotiating power societies fit solidly into their category. Categories are inherently rigid. So it is important to use them more as a mechanism for freeing our thinking from old concepts and definitions, rather than as something that must be strictly adhered to.

There is a broad range of experiences within each category and the distinctions between cultures in adjacent categories may be very fine. Women's status may be higher than other societies in the same group, according to a couple of the criteria we are using for comparison, while it is lower in other areas. The greatest factor in each categorization has usually been that of women's networks, because it is the existence, building or dissolution of these networks that determines women's status and potential for change in all areas of their lives. We include less information on some of the countries where material is more easily available.

Most cultures around the world are undergoing rapid transformation. We attempt to deal with the present realities of women's lives rather than idealized versions or anthropological reconstructions of ancient societies. Women in most countries are caught in the awkward moment between tradition and rapid development. When we discuss each country, we will try to delineate the forces that are affecting women's status negatively or positively.

Heaven under his feet: minimal power societies[1]

A woman's heaven is under her husband's feet.
Bengali expression

In societies where women hold *minimal power*, they have almost no control over their lives and no influence on the institutions which affect them. One of the premises of these societies is that the highest benefits to those in power are gained by overt exploitation. Women receive few rewards for their participation in the economy, and their status is so low that pretentions of equality are not needed. Women's participation in work (often unpaid) is frequently maintained by force.

The status of women's labor force participation and fertility, and their access to resources, is almost uniformly low in all the societies in this category. Women have no collective strength, and do not meet together without men except under strictly confined circumstances (though this may be changing in some of the countries we speak of, as women begin to organize). Women's physical and emotional well-being has little value for the men in power in these societies, and they are subjected to tremendous institutional and interpersonal violence. Their labor power is cheap, since they are rarely rewarded for their work except in so far as it is necessary to keep them alive. In some minimal power societies, women's lives are not valued unless they are performing an important social or economic function.

The low quality of life and the extremely limited resources of women in these societies mean that issues such as nutrition, medical care and housing are central to changes in women's lives, whether in a non-industrialized third-world country such as Ethiopia, or an industrialized country such as Japan. In each of the societies we describe here – Ethiopia, Peru, Algeria and Japan – women have almost no power in their own lives. They contribute heavily to their economies without much in return. The standard of living of women in these societies is exceptionally low in relation to that of men.

Ethiopia

Ethiopia is characteristic of countries where women have minimal power. (For the purposes of this discussion, we are excluding Eritrea which is separating from Ethiopia.) The powerful Ethiopian Christian church emphasized female subordination in conjunction with similar Moslem teachings. Traditional customs, particularly as regards marriage, keep women in the lowest economic position, and in some cases, as with land reform, modernization has worsened their lives.

Women are alone responsible for unpaid work far beyond childcare and household work. A typical peasant woman rises at 5 a.m. to do household chores before her day's work in the fields while watching the children. All that she produces in the fields is expropriated by her husband and/or landlord. Later she returns home to cook dinner (always eating last herself), wash her husband's feet, put him and the children to bed, and do more household chores, including food preparation for the next day and care of livestock.[2]

Women have few means of participating in the paid labor force. The little paid work available includes gathering and selling wood, carrying water, cooking and cleaning for wealthy families, working in low-level factory jobs, and prostitution. In urban areas, prostitution is often the only option for women of all classes.

Women's ability to raise children is valued only as an asset that totally belongs to and is controlled by men. Marriage is the mechanism for this control. Girls are typically married at age 15 or 16 and have no voice in the decision. A bride price is negotiated by the father or other male relatives. In the majority Oromo culture, if a wife dies, her husband may take one of her marriageable sisters as a new wife. A man lacking a bride price may give his sister to the brother of his prospective bride. A bride may also be obtained by kidnapping and raping a marriageable girl, forcing her parents to agree to the marriage. The fear of kidnapping means that girls and women are unable to travel alone. The widespread practice of infibulation and clitoridectomy (a form of female genital mutilation involving the removal of the clitoris) further illustrates the lack of control women

have over their bodies and the association of female reproduction with male needs. Once married, wife-beating is a
frequent mechanism for husbands to exert and maintain
control over their wives.

The isolation of women and their control by men makes
networking very difficult for Ethiopian women. In polygynous marriages co-wives are often kept in a state of competition for their husband's attention and financial support,
encouraging hostility among them.[3]

Except in a few rare cases, no women own land in Ethiopia.
With land reform in recent years husbands could only register
for land with one wife. Where polygyny is practiced the
husbands had to divorce their other wives who were left on
their own with no land or other means of support.[4]

Not surprisingly, the oppression of women in Ethiopia
goes hand in hand with the oppression of different cultural
groups and class stratification. The ruling Amhara, for instance, have deprived the Oromo and other people of official
use of their own languages by instituting Amharic in the
schools and government. This is a particular burden on
women who are unable to go to school and learn the dominant language. (According to official 1972 statistics, 73 per
cent of the adult female population, compared to 38 per cent
of the men, had *never* been to school.)[5]

Peru

Although the military government of Peru in the late 1960s
and early 1970s is reformist in orientation, it is no less
patriarchal than in the past. Women's status varies to some
extent between classes but always within severe limits.

In the mountainous regions of Peru, women are subject to
very strict male control. They are expected to have many
children to provide security for themselves and their husbands
when they grow older. While there is some support from the
community for single mothers, they usually find it very
difficult to make a living. Women are supposed to have many
children, but must do all the work that goes along with
reproduction. Babies are carried along while women do

housework and work in the fields. Women's ultimate responsibility for the management of the family and their crops is
illustrated by the drinking habits of the community. The
men drink together for long hours, socializing with their
friends, and spend many hours the next day recovering.
Few working hours remain before they go drinking again.
Women rarely drink except at celebrations, and then do not
get drunk. They always have responsibilities.[6]

Beatings are an acknowledged occurrence, even among
'happy' couples. Women are beaten or strongly reprimanded
for any infraction of the male rules, such as 'henpecking'.[7]

Women do some spinning and weaving to take to market,
in addition to household maintenance and work in the
fields.[8] In the fields, women's and men's tasks are separated.
The tasks defined as male are those considered crucial in any
area. For example, women who harvest potatoes to take
to market must have a man to tie the sacks to the burros
because 'only the men can make the knot' that will secure
the sacks during the long ride down the mountainside.[9]
Women share much of the burden of the agricultural work,
while men receive the credit for that work.[10]

Women's access to resources is limited. A woman cannot
use community lands for staple crops unless there are no men
in her family that could take her place. Even a relatively
rich woman who owns her own land as a widow is not a full
comunero (one of the landowners who control shared community resources). She is responsible for all the communal
work that a male *comunero* shares with his wife, but is not
eligible to be a village official.[11]

In the commercial towns closer to the coast, women may
have more varied work opportunities. Many women work
in stores and their husbands' businesses, and in some towns
a high percentage of retail establishments are run by women
alone. But it is often difficult for them, because men control
the economy and norms of behavior. The district officials
that distribute rationed goods (largely according to local
political considerations which exclude women), such as food
staples, are all male. Male truckers transport all the goods
from the coastal cities. The woman must deal with drunken-
ness and sexual harassment, from men whom they cannot

afford to alienate, without support from the police.[12]

Women's status in the coastal cities has changed somewhat as more women join the labor force, but they still have few opportunities to be financially independent.

In Peru women have many more opportunities to communicate with each other and share work than do women in Ethiopia. They have not totally internalized the low regard that men have for them. In the villages women may talk together in the fields, and share work in their homes while their husbands are together. In the towns women gather together in the afternoons and talk while they crochet or sew in the absence of men. In the city this happens less often. But though women can talk with each other, their actions are severely limited by men. A group of town women who were discussing organizing to build a water-pump to make their work easier dropped their idea when they realized the ridicule they would face from the men.[13] These business women felt that even this one task was beyond their resources.

The separate spheres of women and men in most work and social areas allow women to communicate within their local regions and create a women's space. The 'separate but equal' myth falls short, however, when it comes to the control women have over their sphere. Men's needs must always be met first and may interrupt any of the women's activities. Though women work very hard, they have few rewards, and no power in the institutions affecting them or in relation to the men surrounding them. Their lack of resources and the battering and ridicule they are subject to, have kept them from making changes that they might imagine or talk about.

Algeria

Women left behind the traditional veil and seclusion in the home to contribute actively in the guerilla efforts during the seven-year Algerian revolution of independence (1955-62) against the French. For a brief while, the status of women began to shift from minimal to token power.

But when independence was achieved, Algerian men used the traditional Moslem laws to bring women back under their control, claiming that the French had 'robbed' them of 'their' women.[14] French reforms had brought women new freedoms with campaigns against the veil and to send girls to school, but had also molded them into European sexual objects, causing women to lose one of their traditional sources of respect.

Women have been almost entirely resegregated into the sphere of private life. The feminist Fadela M'Rabet says that the suicide rate for young girls who refuse arranged marriages and seclusion has risen dramatically.[15] Women who attempted to continue their political work, or spoke out against polygyny were ridiculed.[16]

The status of Algerian women within the home is dependent mainly on their ability to bear children, especially sons, who give them some authority in old age. Even the lucky event of child-birth (lucky for the pleasure it gives the husband, and the security it may give the woman) is of course a burden for the woman, especially if she has had five to ten children. Women are generally seen as an economic burden because their work within the home brings in no income, and they are subject to beatings and threats that they will be replaced by another wife. No changes were made in the marriage laws that allowed men to murder wives that were suspected of infidelity.

Today, a very few women are secretaries and professionals in the cities, and as industry grows a minority of women are employed in segregated textile and clothing factories.[17] Because of the limited job opportunities and the fact that women do not own or control property, they must be attached to men to survive.

Women may communicate with each other alone since they are segregated socially, but they rarely leave their homes without permission. There is now an organization of women, the National Union of Algerian Women, that argues that divorce by male repudiation, 'djebr,' the right of a father to determine his children's marriages, and women's lack of legal protection should not exist.[18] But there was no independent organization of women during the revolution and immediately afterwards that might have had more influence in the formation of post-revolutionary Algeria. Women's present total economic dependence and their suppression in the name of 'revolutionary Islamic humanism' make reforms impossible to obtain without male approval or a huge reactivation of all women.

Japan

Traditional economic definitions usually separate Japan from the other countries we've discussed in this section because of its position as a wealthy industrialized capitalist economy. But there is a huge gap between the standard of living of men and that of women.

At the end of the Second World War the American occupation administration issued several directives which gave Japanese women equality under the constitution. On the surface it seemed that these laws 'liberated' Japanese women but, at the same time, thousands of women were laid off in a deliberate measure to give all available jobs to men. Women were forced to work as 'war consolers.' At one time, 13,000 women were assigned as public prostitutes to the occupation army by the Japanese government.[19]

The industrialization of the country has taken away most of the family businesses and agriculture, where women had some influence, though some women do have power in management of household property, such as managing tenants.[20]

The production of children to strengthen Japan is considered women's most important function. Participation in the paid labor force must be staggered around their childbearing years, or they suffer from the severe social stigma of appearing to neglect their children. Birth control exists, but social pressure is put on women to have children. Most childcare centers are unregulated and have very high ratios of children to attendants. Their inadequate care has resulted in the deaths of several children and mothers were blamed for not caring for them themselves.[21]

Women have traditionally been excluded from the seniority system through which Japanese workers are promoted and receive raises and benefits. Women are only considered occasional help, with no job security even after twenty years with many firms, working an average of 54 hours a week.[22]

In 1969 'Woman Power' policies were instituted, supposedly to expand career opportunities for women. In reality it divided women into a small minority who work within the male sphere, and the rest are still denied the vested rights of a full-time employee. A 1974 study of Japan's largest trading company found that 40 per cent of their workers were women, usually graduates of junior colleges (graduates of four-year schools were not hired), who were employed for the average continuous time of three or four years. Only women living at home with their parents were hired, and their mothers had to attend the job interviews.[23] Other companies are not much better.

Industrialization, while destroying other networks, has helped women to form some grass-roots 'democratic' women's organizations as a part of the peace movement and within unions, but many have been taken over by male political groups.[24] The assumption that the American occupation forces laid out a 'democratic' family system had kept many women from challenging their treatment as house, office and factory workers without rights. Recently, expanding upon women's previous networks, an independent women's movement has begun mobilizing around issues of childcare, consumer affairs and work, and are moving Japan towards token power.

After work all married women are expected to return home to have dinner ready when their husbands return from drinking with their buddies. Women thus do not have the opportunity to socialize with female co-workers, and urbanization destroyed the few supports traditionally given by the extended family. Suicide rates are especially high among young women workers. 70 per cent of marriages are still arranged, though women's consent is obtained. Women are idealized in their feminine roles as wives, mothers and sexual objects. (Japanese women consume 50 per cent of all Christian Dior's beauty products in their service of men.)[25] Women's status is that of a servant, with few exceptions. They receive little reward for their work and are expected not to complain about it.

The illusions of token power

Women have token power in those societies where they appear at times to have influence within the general society, and have some spheres of activity that are not strictly regulated by the male power structure. They usually do not have a solid basis of equality in any area that allows them to maintain helpful reforms and to prevent male encroachment upon, and ultimate control over, every area of their lives. In these societies women may meet together and even have independent organizations. A few alternatives to the heterosexual, child-producing family lifestyle are tolerated in some cultures, such as the United States and Sweden, as long as they do not interfere with the male business at hand. In many of these societies women are increasingly taking part in the labor force outside the home, but this is always subject to change with the needs of the male economic structures, as the experience of women in the Soviet Union and Cuba illustrates. No religious, political, social or cultural institutions that are powerful in the mainstream society represent women's needs as a major priority, though some may claim that they do. Pressure (in the form of ideals and norms), economic deterrents, and the fear of violence, regulate women's reproductive functions, working hours, pay and access to resources. Women's contribution to society is given lip service, and some women who are exceptionally visible benefit economically, so that women often feel a part of the social process and seem to have more power than they actually do.[26] Women's token power is based on the male assumption that women should receive some benefits from their work, and have some protection from abuse to maintain social stability and a high quality of production in the home and in the labor force.

USA

In the USA the image of the ideal American woman varies from the housewife caring for her husband and children full-time, to the woman who works outside the home and manages the family too. While government policy and the dominant culture give women token power, there is tremendous variation in women's power within the society, from the minimal power of a Puerto Rican welfare mother in New York City, to the token power of a black professional woman in Los Angeles.

There is generally a very low regard for women's reproductive powers in the USA, in spite of Mother's Day and other token gestures of respect for women. Most women have almost no maternity benefits available to them.Wife-beating often begins or accelerates when a woman is pregnant.[27] Violence in the form of battering and rape is a prevalent problem in the home, and on the streets.

Women make up more than 40 per cent of the labor force (this has decreased from 64 per cent at the end of the Second World War), and are only paid 59 per cent of what men earn on average.

Legislation aimed at improving these proportions gives the impression of an attempt to change more than is the case.[28] And as limited as it is, there is a tremendous backlash against it from personal male resentment to court cases.

Women are in a position of economic dependence on men. One recent study by the social services system of the effects of proposed family allowances showed a sharp increase in family break-ups when mothers were given money.[29]

Alternative institutions and businesses created by the women's movement of the late sixties and seventies give a few women more freedom than those working directly for male-dominated corporations. These alternatives allow women to develop skills and their own ideas among a feminist community and are among the few jobs where open lesbians are supported or even tolerated. But alternative jobs are few and are allowed to exist only as long as the economy is in good working order, and the participants do not become effective in changing the norm to any appreciable extent.

From the dominant system's point of view, these institutions make people happy who would otherwise rebel, and save the system money by providing necessary services. The liberal policies of token power countries allow exceptions for some, to maintain the illusion of progress while not changing the underlying power relations. On the other hand, alternative institutions form a very important part of women's networks (especially the most highly developed ones) and allow discussion outside of male institutions, even though they are always subject to the laws and economics of a hostile system.

A few women in the USA control some services and exchange of goods through private ownership, but their businesses form a tiny part of the economy. Women make up only 2 per cent of corporate boards of directors and 1 per cent of top management.[30] Women have few positions of leadership in business or government, though the few are deliberately made to seem more numerous by the visibility accorded them. In total, there have been 11 women in the United States Senate compared with 1,715 men, 87 women in the House of Representatives compared to 9,591 men, and no women among the 101 people that have been appointed to the Supreme Court.[31] Women's control of wealth and resources has changed little since they got the vote in the 1920s.

Women have always formed some networks on a grassroots level, from Parent Teacher Associations, auxiliary groups, to sewing bees, church groups and coffee klatches as an exception to their basic isolation in the home. Feminist refuges for battered women find themselves part of a longstanding 'underground railroad' of women trying to help other women escape from violent situations. As the feminist movement grows, these networks are increasing in size and versatility. Few organizations have existed for women to come together in the workplace, particularly since their work in the home and lack of job security limits their activity. But recently, a few unions have been formed for secretaries, waitresses, prostitutes and other segregated fields.

Cuba

Cuba is a country undergoing rapid transformation. In twenty years, the status of women has risen from minimal to token power, but whether women obtain negotiating power or equality will depend largely on the development and sincere enforcement of current policies towards women. In Cuba, after the revolution, women were strongly encouraged to take on jobs outside the home, in fields or factories, to aid in the national development process. Ideology reinforcing women's role changed drastically, coming to define desirable womanhood as participation in the revolutionary struggle through employment. Many women did so; however, it became apparent that women were not as 'productive' as men, that they frequently missed work and eventually left their jobs. In 1969 there was a 76 per cent drop-out rate among women workers.[32] When their situation was examined more thoroughly, it was 'discovered' that they were working a second shift — doing all the childcare, cooking and home maintenance work that they previously had all day to do. Institutional supports from laundry services to childcare have slowly been developed, but in 1973 only 16 per cent of children with working mothers could be accommodated by existing facilities.[33] Expanded family networks (mostly other women) took on much of this work, in addition to 'guerilla day care' organized by and among rural women. The burden of the 'second shift' still fell squarely on women's shoulders, thus contributing to continuing attrition on the job.

In 1966 Fidel Castro had stated that 'women in a social revolution should be doubly revolutionary,'[34] sometimes interpreted to mean that women should perform without complaint a full-time job outside the home, and a second job at home when they returned.

In 1974, the Family Code was enacted, which called for equal participation and responsibility in the home. It was a practical attempt by the male-centered government to draw women into fuller participation in the national development effort. Nevertheless, it institutionalized a national commitment towards addressing women's slavery in the home, and provoked much hot debate and resistance from men. The Family Code was also a response to pressure from women, and as one woman said, 'Young women around here drew up this law before the Government ever thought about it . . . and young men just have to go along with it these days!'[35]

In 1974 a maternity law was passed, which Margaret Randall called 'probably the most far-reaching maternity law in the world.'[36] The law requires pregnant women to take an 18-week paid leave of absence, and permits a mother to take a one-year unpaid leave, with her former job guaranteed.

The gross enrollment ratio (the number of students divided by the number of people in the relevant age group) for women in Cuba is only slightly less than for men in primary school, 123 per cent in 1974, representing the large number of older women currently going to school. The Cuban government has placed a great priority on literacy. But the underlying assumption that men have more use for higher education than women is reflected in the 12 per cent male gross enrollment ratio in universities, as opposed to 6.5 per cent for women.[37]

In spite of the progressive changes and support by the government for women, much remains to be done. According to one (male) doctor, there is a fair amount of resistance by women to birth control, reflecting a widespread assumption that women's first duties are as mothers and wives.[38] The most popular form of birth control is abortion, followed by the IUD, and, less frequently, the pill.[39] There are no vasectomies. Both female sterilization and abortion must be approved by hospital personnel, though both are free and legal.

Most workers in the childcare centers are women, and when this fact is questioned, it is supported with the old adage that female love and care is of primary importance to a child. In spite of the Family Code, most men perceive their role in the home to be 'helping' their wives. Though homosexuality has not been illegal since 1964, it is still considered a social pathology. Homosexual men and women must be careful to hide their personal lives; no gay custody matters have been heard in the courts.[40]

These stereotyped sex-role attitudes reflect deep-rooted assumptions of the 'naturalness' and importance of differences between the sexes. Given that most of the changes in women's lives have come about through government intervention, and the government has recognized and articulated a crucial need for women to participate in national development, the critical question remains whether women's gains will be compromised if the needs of the male-dominated culture change.

The national women's organizations reflect the ideals and priorities of the government and do not provide mechanisms for women to voice and express disagreements. The Communist Party established the Federation of Cuban Women (FMC) in 1960 to 'organize and mobilize women's active participation in society.'[41] In 1969 the Confederation of Cuban workers established a Feminine Front in each work-place to make sure that women received the necessary social services. The Feminine Front representative is selected by both men and women at each work-place, and the Front is clear to state, 'We are a feminine, not a feminist, organization.'[42]

When women do articulate disagreements, it is often among themselves outside of these organizations, or at frequent block group meetings, where local and national policy issues are discussed. Such disagreements are currently tolerated and even encouraged, possibly to allow women to let off steam in a context not threatening to the power structure. What will happen to women if such objections are discouraged or punished? These questions, and the development and strength of independent women's networks, will determine whether the Cuban government consolidates power in the hands of men, or redistributes it more equitably.

USSR

The status of women in the USSR can also be considered 'token'. Since the revolution in 1917 many reforms which support women's work in the labor force have been enacted, and women receive approximately equal pay for equal work. Yet the needs of the over-all economy still determine the focus of women's lives on almost every level. Relatively few positive changes have occurred in the status of women in the last few decades. And as the post-Second World War demographic imbalance has evened out, the government has sought to lower the percentage of women in certain professions such as medicine.

Independent feminist activity is discouraged, as is any independent political activity. In 1929 the Working Women's Section (*Zhenotdel*) of the Central Committee of the Communist Party was abolished, ostensibly because 'an independent women's movement was no longer necessary.'[43] Most recently, the authors of the first feminist anthology to appear in that country (in Samizdat) have been threatened with imprisonment if their collection of essays is published abroad.[44]

Women's fertility has been used as a tool for economic efficiency at different periods. Following the Revolution new family codes and marriage laws were enacted and there were some experiments with living situations. But many oppressive traditional attitudes were later reinstated, causing the status of women to fluctuate according to the need for greater production of birth-rate. For example, government encouragement of marriage and motherhood to increase population growth at the end of the Second World War resulted in 'hero mothers' receiving stars from the State for producing large numbers of children.[45] Abortion was forbidden and homosexuality was a criminal offense.[46]

The harshest measures have gradually been revoked since the 1950s and more supportive services now exist for women than in most countries. Services which support large families continued, taking some of the burden of past policies off women, though women still are responsible for childcare and maintenance at home. Leaves are now available for parents, mothers are allowed a one-year maternity leave with the option of returning to the same job, and childcare is widely available although facilities are not adequate in every region. A full one-tenth of all births are to single women. Abortion is available on demand, and surveys show that women who desire abortions usually get them, even if their husbands disagree. Birth control devices are sporadically available, and knowing the 'rhythm method' is a sign of being well-informed.[47]

In formal labor force participation, the USSR (and the Eastern European countries with centrally planned economies) far surpasses other industrialized countries.[48] Women are 50 per cent of the paid labor force. A survey of working-class Soviet families showed that in slightly more than half the families, women's earnings equalled or exceeded their husbands'.[49] Though there are still greater numbers of women in 'female' job categories, women do every kind of work. Women are 30 per cent of the engineers, 72 per cent of doctors, and one-third of all judges. The decline of women in medical schools and increases in engineering schools are creating a tendency toward equalization in numbers. Wage increases in service and consumer industries where women are concentrated have helped close the gap caused by the previous emphasis on heavy industry.[50]

Women's strong position in the labor force can be partially explained by the fact that there were twenty million more women than men in 1970. The State needed women's labor to reconstruct after the war. Without great efforts by women who were used to hardship, the Soviet Union would not be in its position of strength.[51]

Women may be important figures in their industries, but women in leadership roles usually act as individuals. Since the State controls resources, women as a group do not have control over the decisions in any sector. Fewer women have positions in the decision-making bureaux than in other areas. In 1970 women were 31 per cent of the members of the Supreme Soviet, and 14 out of 360 members of the Central Committee of the Communist Party.[52] And the powerful military is almost exclusively male. Many women who are nominated for political offices withdraw from candidacy because they do not have enough time after their jobs and household duties to do all the work involved.

Household chores are very time consuming because of the long queues in shopping, the scarcity of goods and of labor-saving appliances. A Soviet sociologist estimated that women spend 40 hours a week doing housework, while men spend only 15 to 20. Lydia Litvinenko, a mother and doctor of economics says 'For women spare time is almost non-existent. . . We women spend two or three times as many hours as the men on home and family. *In other words, a woman works for her husband too.*'[53] The spiralling divorce rate (ten times greater now than twenty-five years ago) and plummeting birth-rate are attributed to women's double workload and disappointment at men's lack of help and support.[54]

Because women have less leisure time than men, they also have less time to take the free courses which upgrade their jobs and increase wages. The tremendous changes which have taken place since the revolution make it easier for women to overlook this. Many women say they would like to have part-time jobs that would allow them to keep up in their field while managing the household. They would prefer, of course, that men do more housework, but many men do not want to do it.[55]

Women form many social networks but they have few independent political networks. A government agency lobbies for women's rights, but an organization in which women are recognized as a separate political entity has not existed legally since the *Zhenotdel* was abolished.

Sweden

In Sweden the extent of the legislation giving women token representation places it close to negotiation power in potential, but these reforms have not had their full effect on women's position in society. These reforms help free women to take part in the paid labor force, which has been short of skilled labor, and make it easier for women to have children. Although the current proposed changes are increasing women's status, they are being initiated by a male-dominated government that could deny these rights as fast as they are being given.

The Social Democratic government, in power until 1966, took a pro-woman role in the discussion of the role of women and men in the home known as the 'sex-role debate.' Its legislation is at the forefront of the reforms in the support of women which have been accomplished by the coordinated effort of many political organizations.

Women's fertility has been given great support through many social programs from extensive maternity benefits to family allowances, including single mothers, and increasing though still inadequate childcare facilities. The government has also run a campaign encouraging men to share parental duties and care of the home, and there is also tolerance of homosexuality in social agencies, indicating that the sex-role system is beginning to break down.

The entire school system has been redesigned, as well as the Family Code and welfare system. School children are being given new role models in order to foster less stereo-typed images of women's work. From 1966 to 1967 women were about 50 per cent of the students in the free vocational classes, and their salaries were 77 per cent those of men.[57] However, in 1975 only 30 per cent of all Swedish women had full-time jobs.

The attitudes of men, the socialization of children, and women's integration into the male sectors of the labor force have not caught up with even the state-defined goals of equality. The focus of the sex-role debate on human libera-tion tends to disguise the fact that men have privileges, such as greater leisure time, higher wages, and are the first hired. The mainstream debate does not recognize that men have gained these benefits from the work of women. It is true that men must be doing housework and childcare before women can reach all their goals in other areas, but it is sometimes assumed that men will sacrifice their privileges voluntarily, with encouragement. The vast majority of men in Sweden haven't.

A study of children's attitudes found that once they reached an age of social awareness, they forgot about the non-sexist role models they learned in their early years at school. Real social relationships had a much more powerful influence on them.[58] Women still do not have full economic independence, nor the social independence to define their futures for themselves.

The government's official vision of women's liberation is limited by their own interests as men who benefit from women's exploitation personally, and through the economy. Birgitta Wistrand, a feminist and government official, says that although there were five women in the Cabinet in 1979 women still have the least important jobs in government and almost no power in the upper echelons of businesses and unions. Women have more rights than in other countries, but no real power.[59] For the government women's 'equality' means a more efficient use of human capital, more incomes to tax, more skilled labor to fill their labor shortage, and greater support for their party from women. It is also in their interest that women produce children to end the labour shortage, that the family remains the basic social unit, and that men's status is not diminished. When men are deciding the path to equality, it is designed for their purposes. The greatest government support has been given to women to allow them to have children.

Women in Sweden do not have an independent power base from which to demand or control the flow of changes. All the reforms have been given to them by a government which is more liberal than the average individual in its attitudes towards women because of its need for their participation in non-traditional areas.

The increasing concern with high taxes and support for the conservative party, which feels that traditional solely male-supported families are discriminated against, could reverse many of the reforms that have been put into effect. Recently some women in Sweden have begun consciously to form feminist groups, and are attempting to make lasting changes in the lives of women. If they are successful, Swedish women might then have a basis for strength independent of the male-dominated institutions – a strength which would ensure the gains they have made.

The potential to lobby: negotiating power societies

We do not believe than any . . . system now in operation, or likely to emerge in the next generation, will grant full equality to women, although throughout the world the general position of women will improve greatly. The revolutionary philosophies which have accompanied the shifts in power in Communist countries or in the Israeli kibbutzim have asserted equality, and a significant stream of philosophic thought in the West has asserted the right to equality but no society has yet granted it. Nor does the movement in Western countries, including the Communist countries, suggest that the future will be greatly different. We believe that it is possible to develop a society in which this would happen, but not without a radical reorganization of the social structure.

W.J. Goode, 1963
World Revolution and Family Patterns[60]

Negotiating power occurs in societies in which women have an independent power base from which to control or fight for control over aspects of their lives.[61] However this in no way constitutes equal power. *In no contemporary society do women have the rights, privileges, or leisure time that men do.* In negotiating power societies, women are still responsible for home maintenance and childcare, and the magnitude of this job means that women have much less leisure than men. It is considered their 'role' to service the men and children in their families for free.

In a society with negotiating power, women have influence within certain spheres that cannot be taken away at will by the male hierarchy. Their relative economic and political independence is based on this access to and control over important resources, respect for their reproductive powers, and the strength of their networks. In these societies, being a woman gives one a place in the world that commands a certain amount of respect and some advantages.

But this respect and the power that women do have belongs not to women as women, but to their *function*. If and when their function changes, so too does their status. The support does not exist for women's culture, independence or equality, but only for their continued healthy subsidy of the male economy. Women's networks don't have equal power, simply the potential to lobby in women's interests.

Women have achieved a degree of autonomy in some traditional societies through economies where their labor and resources have remained key throughout development, but many of these societies are being destroyed by the more powerful societies surrounding them. The Iroquois people and their traditions were almost destroyed during colonialism. The Ewé culture is also rapidly losing many of its traditions that were supportive to women.

Women also may experience a great increase in status when revolutionary changes have allowed them to organize themselves and demand changes in the patriarchal structure. We include the Women's Associations in China as an example, though recent changes are rapidly pushing China into the token category. Institutional supports can allow women more control over their own affairs through protection of women's rights and the potential for communication among women that they provide. When the needs of the patriarchal structure infringe upon women's traditional or newly won rights, women have a basis for contention that has formal recognition within the system. This ability to voice grievances and be heard is in contrast to what exists in token power societies, where women operate outside the established system, and may face ridicule, jail sentences or beatings and still not be heard.[62] However, if the basis for women's separate organization is eradicated, if the needs of the patriarchy and its underlying values change, the foundation for the high status of women can swiftly crumble, as it is currently doing in China.

Even in times of vast social transformation, there are so many social and economic institutions which are oppressive to women that are integral to a society, that it takes years of profound change in social priorities to reverse the process. Most socialist societies, for example, have not experimented with their model of industrialization. Since industrialization itself involves a centralization of human labor, its structure makes it difficult to decentralize decision-making and economic control. Only China was willing to place priority on the quality of social interaction over the rate of production, a policy which was not integral to the new society, but dependent on the views of the leaders, and has been rapidly reversed since the death of Mao Tse Tung and the rise of Teng Hsiao Ping. A woman-centered model of industrialization would require the socialization of women's work in the home. Since this 'invisible' and unpaid work makes possible the high productivity of male workers and the immense profits gleaned by industry (whether owned by private interests or the state), no country has yet been willing to do this. As a result, there are no industrialized nations where women hold negotiating power.

China

Within a few decades since the 1949 revolution, the lives of women in China changed from blatant and horrifying degradation to among the most progressive of any patriarchal culture, and then began to decline until they virtually have only token power. For this reason, it is a useful example of how women's power can increase and diminish through changes in male priorities.

Prior to the Communist revolution, pain, suffering and servitude were the norms for Chinese women. Domestic problems, the largest motivating factor in suicide in China, were responsible for 26 per cent of all suicides, and 72 per cent of these suicides were women.[63] Women owned no property, had no access to education, and worked as slaves for their husbands and their husband's landlords. Prostitution was prevalent, and 10 per cent of the population in rural areas and 5 per cent of the population in urban areas suffered from syphilis.[64] For over a hundred years many women actively participated in a number of rebellions, protesting against footbinding, traditional marriage, and demanding suffrage at the time of the Republican Revolution of 1911. Not until the Communist Party began to organize in the countryside and support women's struggles for liberation, were some of these more fundamental changes made possible. As C.K. Yang pointed out, 'The Communists from the beginning recognized the potential political strength of the women's movement, and during the thirty years of their struggle for power consistently nursed its development to augment their political force.'[65] The Chinese Communist Party encouraged drastic transformations in women's lives to enable their greatest possible participation in the national development process after the Revolution, and not from a commitment to the liberation of women itself.

When the government consolidated its power in the mid-1950s, 'stability' was stressed, much of which demanded a 'harmonious' family life. The Women's Associations were discouraged from acting independently, and women were encouraged to put more of their energies into the home. With the expansion of agriculture and the development of People's Communes in the late 1950s, women were again encouraged to enter the labor force to increase agricultural production.

Fundamental changes were made in the areas of birth control, marriage law, and ownership of property. Houses of prostitution were closed and other jobs found for the women (though the prostitutes were given no say in this decision). Abortion (not subject to a husband's approval) with up to a month's sick leave and contraception became free.[66] Late marriages (around the age of twenty-six) are advocated, both as a means of birth control and to enable women to work longer outside the home before marriage. Marriage is now a free choice, divorces are possible at either person's request, and women retain their family names after marriage.

Prior to the 1949 Revolution, wife-beating was not only condoned, but any man refusing to beat his wife every night, against the order of his father, could be thrown into the magistrate's or the landlord's dungeon. With the Revolution, wife-beating was prohibited. As one man said:[67]

> All my friends beat (before the revolution) their wives, so
> I was only observing custom. Sometimes I didn't have any
> reason except that I hadn't beaten her recently . . . . Right
> after liberation it was difficult for me to beat her anymore.
> I would sometimes lose my temper and raise my elbows
> to beat her, and she and the children would restrain me,
> reminding me that Chairman Mao wouldn't permit it, so
> I refrained. . . . They maintained a spirit of revolt and if
> we mistreated our wives they would all protest. It was
> impossible.

Many of the changes that took place during and after the Revolution were due to the strength of the Women's Associations. Women came together to 'Speak Bitterness' and develop alternatives and support systems. They confronted their husband's privileges and abuses of power, holding public meetings in which men who refused to give up their old oppressive attitudes and behavior towards their wives were beaten up by the crowd of women until they promised to respect the new ways of the society.[68] If this process had not been supported by the revolutionary government, the women might have been punished rather than the men.

Most Chinese women consider access to crucial resources and to paid work to be responsible for the most significant changes. 'The right to own land and property in their own name was the key to the liberation of women, according to all the cadres who reported. On many other questions the women were divided. . . . On one issue they all agreed, however. Women should be able to get and keep a share in the land.' One village woman was quoted as saying, 'After we get our share we will be masters of our own fate.' Another said, 'When I get my share I'll never look for a husband again. A husband is a terrible thing.'[69]

However, there are still many areas where women are not equal in China. They do not receive equal work points for equal work in the communes. Work points are allocated on the basis of productivity for socially recognized work so women who are physically weaker receive fewer work points. Even though daycare facilities are very accessible and mothers often leave work in the factory to see to their child twice a day, women are responsible for meal preparation and child-care in the home, for which they are not given work points. Their work in the home is still mystified, as is evident by the common assumption that 'women are better with children,' and the remark that although men increasingly share house-work in the home, women 'prefer' to do cooking. Homo-sexuality is implicitly condemned by being ignored and denied by the dominant culture, reflecting a serious resist-ance to examining and fighting sexual politics and oppression on a basic level.

Though many of the Women's Associations sprang from already existing networks between women in the villages, they were incorporated into the Party as soon as they were formed. This meant working for goals defined by the Party rather than goals formulated independently by the women themselves, though women sometimes initiated discussion about problems not defined by the Party. In 1976 women began to demand that men share the housework, and since the women remained strong and vocal, the party supported them and men began to share the work.[70]

Less than 50 per cent of professional workers are women, and far fewer than that are represented in the leading bodies of those institutions.[71] In 1972 the Central Committee had 13 women members out of 170 and 10 alternate members out of 139.[72]

There have been changes in China's internal economic policy since the death of Mao Tse Tung and Teng Hsiao Ping's rise to power, which are having an extremely negative effect on women's status. At the time of the Revolution the Chinese made the conscious choice not to base their economy on a model of uneven growth (growth for its own sake), but rather to decentralize industry, and to insure full employment, the eradication of class divisions and the formation of work situations which provided everyone with the maximum input into decisions affecting their work lives. 'Efficiency' and a higher standard of living were sometimes sacrificed to the quality of social life being created, and a more equitable distribution of goods and resources. The economy became extremely labor-intensive and work did not become as specialized and hierarchically structured as in other industrialized countries. The economy was structured on the assumption that people as individuals and the economy as a whole would be more productive if motivated to work for the growth of the collective whole rather than for private profit.

Now China is either forgetting or ignoring the lessons learned from the effects of industrialization on the west, which according to feminist China scholar Lisa Rofel is in keeping with its historical patriarchal priority of becoming a major world power. It is shifting away from the socialist economy that made its model of development so unique and effective. Socialism was seen by those now in power only as a means to achieving that patriarchal goal, not as an ethical imperative, and could thus be abandoned when it no longer seemed the most effective way to achieve it. Along with bonuses in cash instead of work points for extra work performed and the distribution of certain goods through the market instead of the state-planned distribution, fashion magazines are now pushing the latest Western styles for Chinese women. With the development of the market and the corresponding centralization of people and goods, the breakdown of the extended family into the nuclear family, a more mobile and consuming unit is necessary, women must be reintegrated into the home to disguise their future unemployment in a less labor intensive economy.

Women are being 'refeminized' leading them to see their role in the family as a crucial aid to national development. Whereas previously shared housework and the building of childcare centers was a constant issue, it is now seldom mentioned. Women's traditional role as mothers is more frequently held out as women's useful patriotic contribution. And attitudes towards sexuality are becoming less puritanical which, when not accompanied by women's control of their sexuality, paves the way for a new form of female subservience.[73]

Although Chinese women's access to resources, networks and leadership positions have increased greatly in the past thirty years, women's teetering negotiating power has already declined. This has been largely because women's networks were not strong enough independent of the Party to impact major policy change and broaden and reinforce women's power. When the type of female participation needed by the Party shifted, women-centered priorities were compromised. Only if women redevelop networks independent of Party policy and create and maintain independent visions and struggles for change will they be able to make more fundamental changes in their lives and work towards equality with men.

Ewé society[74]

In the Ewé culture of Togo and Ghana in West Africa, men's privilege is maintained by women's labor in the home, symbolized by women's serving food to their husbands, then retreating to eat in another room with the children. Women's services enable men to enjoy far more leisure, and with colonialism, a higher standard of living. Nevertheless there are a number of supportive institutions that women have been able to use as tools in bargaining for power in their society, (though since colonialism even these have been disintegrating).

Men's work in Ewé society has traditionally been viewed as the more prestigious, but women's work has been so crucial to the economy, and women have been so collectively well organized, that they have been greatly respected for their work by men as well as other women.

As in many other West African countries, women are very active in trading, 'and the market is largely a woman's world.' Women sell crops they raise and all kinds of other goods. Their operations range from roadside stands to large warehouses or fleets of small trucks travelling to up-country villages.[75] Women control 90 per cent of the distribution of goods, including importing, in Togo and Ghana and it is said no government can function without their support.[76]

In the pre-colonial division of labor, men were responsible for hunting and fishing, defending the village, clearing the fields, and growing the staple crops – yams and corn. Women were responsible for home maintenance and childcare, food preparation, growing garden crops, growing supplementary crops such as manioc and peanuts for home use and for sale, and trading their own and their husbands' crops in the market. Women were given access to, and control over, their own portion of the community fields upon marriage. But much of this has changed. There is little game left to hunt, the military is responsible for defense and many men grow cash crops, such as cocoa and coffee, on their land for export. Others leave the villages to seek work in the government or private corporations. Unemployment is high and cash-cropping seasonal, but there is a great stigma attached to men doing 'women's work.' Consequently, women are left doing all their own and some of men's traditional work, plus extra trading or waged work to supplement their incomes, with little help from men or technology. Men's modernized work has acquired even more status and authority and women's increased workload has made women's status as unrecognized sustainers of the economy, far more blatant and oppressive.

Market women, even the wealthiest, have also been hard hit by colonial development. There are now increasing numbers of middlemen, mostly male and often European, intervening in their trade. In 1976 severe shortages and rapidly inflating prices caused the Ghanaian government to stop market women from selling essential commodities. They charged the women with hoarding, creating artificial shortages and pushing prices up. Yet, as one of them explained:[77]

'The traders can't be blamed for the shortages because the shortages are real.' 'It came about,' said another, 'because central importing and distributing organizations involved three or four middlemen, each of whom demands a bribe. By the time it reached me it already cost more than the controlled price. . . . It had to be hidden and sold only to trusted customers.'

In the area of education women have much less opportunity. Only one-quarter of Ghanaian women had been to school in 1960.[78] The gross enrolment ratio for females in primary school in 1975 was 68 per cent, versus 129 per cent for males. This indicates that education was considered important enough for older boys to attend primary school but older and younger girls already have many responsibilities. At the secondary school level the ratio for females was 9 per cent versus 29 per cent for males, and at the university level, 0.33 per cent for females versus 2.10 per cent for males.[79]

In spite of the increasing pressure on traditional institutions women still have some access to supportive institutions built into their everyday lives, especially in rural areas.

Women often work together in their own fields, or as family members preparing meals together, village women meeting at the stream to do the wash, or family, friends and neighbors, walking five to fifteen miles a day to market together, sitting near each other in the market, and setting the day's prices together. They share childcare, news, and looking after each other's market stalls. In addition to making the time more pleasant, this shared work enables women to share information and in fact serves as an integral and vital part of the village communications system. Consequently, they have a tremendous sense of solidarity when it comes to acting in their collective interest.

Just as the village chief serves as the representative of all the village people, many villages still have a queen mother who serves as the representative of, or advocate for women. This role is one of negotiator and go-between and carries no power in and of itself. She sits on the council of elders (otherwise all male) and is the primary negotiator when there is a problem between women, or women and men in the village. Her token position in the male council is backed up by the economic power and collective consciousness of all the village women.

Each woman is supported in her interactions with her husband by a strong female support network within the family, and strictly enforced social norms. Many men have left their villages to seek work elsewhere but the husband who remains is still held responsible for provision of the staple crop, maintenance of the family compound, buying the children's school uniforms and books, etc. If a husband does not hold up his end of the family responsibilities his wife goes to an older female relative who brings the matter up with the husband and acts as an advocate. If he refuses to cooperate, the matter is brought before a family tribunal, comprised of extended family members of any age or sex who wish to attend and his behavior is severely admonished. Under no conditions would he be supported in behaving irresponsibly, a phenomenon which is increasing in the urban centers as the extended family network breaks down.

The extended family network is also used against women, however, in support of the ultimate male prerogative. A man who wants more children or whose wife does not become pregnant after several months of marriage is supported in taking on more wives who may compete with her for status and benefits, as long as he can fulfill his responsibilities toward all of them. A woman involved in extramarital relationships must be surreptitious, (though they are common and a well-developed system of fines exists to punish those discovered indicating social recognition of 'covert' behavior).

A last source of support and authority that needs to be mentioned is that of the traditional religion, still practiced by many people, especially in rural areas. There are as many female as there are male divinities and they are worshipped by both men and women. There are as many priestesses as priests, and many women possess spiritual and psychic skills, for herbal healing and the performance of crucial ceremonies. There is a generalized respect, sometimes tinged with fear, towards women's skills with the 'supernatural,' and their resulting exercise of power outside the 'formal' (male-dominated) political process.

Men in Ewé society hold ultimate authority. Nevertheless, traditional Ewé society insures that women have structured support systems so that the power that men hold cannot be abused outside of male-defined limits. As the traditional division of labor breaks down rural women are burdened with extra work and enjoy few of the benefits of technology, making these support systems more necessary to women's survival, while they decline in strength. Hopefully the potential exists for women's support networks to be used to prevent further deterioration of their status and to forge new sources of power and control over their lives, if Ewé women perceive this as a need.

The Iroquois[80]

Iroquois women of the eighteenth and nineteenth century held very high status and broad-based power in their communities, more so than Ewé women or Chinese women have held, yet still not equal to men's. Although the institutions which afforded Iroquois women this power have been largely decimated by white American intrusion Iroquois women continue to enjoy a higher position within their culture than their white counterparts.

Much of Iroquois women's authority stemmed from the fact that the public and private spheres were traditionally far more integrated and women's major role in residences meant authority in the community at large. Iroquois women presided over the residences and the Longhouses, and ultimate authority over the household was held by the matron (an older woman chosen by all the women). The matrons selected the male council of elders, deposed them if they behaved inappropriately, and influenced their decisions, including the decision to go to war or establish treaties. The matrons also co-ordinated female clan members' economic activities, including their agricultural work and contributions of food for charity and public festivals.

Some anthropologists believe that women's authority was due to their extensive economic participation.[81] Work groups of women were responsible for the planting and cultivating of the fields and the harvest, though sometimes the men helped them. They also gathered food and fished (as did the men) and sometimes went on hunting expeditions with the men.

The passage of descent through the female line, inheritance by women, and habitation upon marriage in the home of the wife's mother, also contributed to women's high status.[82] Marriages were arranged by the mothers of the concerned persons, and either husband or wife could obtain a divorce with little ceremony. Husbands who did not fulfill their share of responsibilities could be forced to leave by the woman's family.[83]

The control that women held over the crucial resources and distribution of the goods gave them their power. Yet this control was exerted as a form of service to men. For example, although the wife controlled the food supply, whenever her husband returned she had to set his meal in front of him. The double morality for men and women was reflected in the fact that if a woman found her husband had visited other women while on a journey, she shouldn't cause him problems because as a 'good wife' she would go to heaven but her husband would go to the house of the 'wicked one.'

Women's sway in the community was not the formal power held by men. Women's extensive economic role probably subsidized leisure time for men, although outside observers did not record it. The women owned the objects of the household, the house itself, and the land and 'the husband, in ancient times, could regard as his own, only his weapons, tools and wearing apparel.'[84] Women also controlled most of the wealth of the clan in the form of stored food, withheld at their discretion when necessary to influence major decisions.

As the male and female spheres of work become more separate, and the household is less integrated with the community, women's status is declining. Iroquois women still hold a relatively high status on the reservations with clan mothers appointing chiefs and descent is still traced through the female line. Carolyn Matthiasson notes that 'Onondaga is one of the few places in the world where a comment about a family with only one child would probably be that they are "lucky it's a girl." '[85] But this is because of the female function as a conduit for inheritance, and not because women are valued more than men.

The authority Iroquois women hold will probably last as long as their institutions are allowed to exist as alternatives to Western mainstream society. The future of Iroquois women lies in their power to organize and exert influence within their communities and to prevent the erosion of their culture.

4 *The personal is economic*

Most of us rarely think of social institutions such as the family, or a particular culture's educational system, as having an economic value, or even an economic base. Even less do people think of institutions which are usually considered to be personal matters – such as standards of beauty, love and romance, prestige, social ideals, or violence against women – as economic in nature. Yet all these social phenomena are either outgrowths of economic institutions or help to form and create such institutions. At the very least social and economic institutions closely affect each other, and they are often inseparable. Jessie Bernard, in her article 'The Status of Women in Modern Patterns of Culture,' gives the following example:[1]

> If the mores had forbidden women to follow their work into the mills and factories, the technologies which depended on their work would have been retarded. But if the technology had not created the wage-paying jobs for them, the status of women would have continued to be one of universal dependence. It is a nice theoretical point to determine, in any one case, which way the influence operates. The emphasis for the most part has tended to be on the effect of material culture on the status of women rather than the other way round. And the effect, it has been found, has been great.

Many aspects of women's social and emotional life regulate their participation in the economy to insure the greatest benefit to the dominant male economy. In some cases women have found particular methods of adapting to social norms which serve as survival mechanisms.

Education: gaining control over the means of reproduction

Social conditions such as the birth-rate and level of female education, are directly related to women's economic participation. In a 1965 survey of 89 member states of UNESCO (United Nations Educational, Scientific and Cultural Organization), it was estimated that 43.4 per cent of school-age children, most of them girls, did not attend school.[2] There are a variety of reasons for this, stemming from social conditions and cultural attitudes towards women, and some of these factors are changing. In many countries, child marriages traditionally prevented most girls from attending school, but now more girls are getting married at an older age. Sex-segregation, symbolized by the veil in other societies, prevented girls from being educated with boys, and consequently from being educated at all, when facilities were not built, and teachers provided, specifically for girls. Many families have not had the means to send all their children to school, and normally it has been the girl's education which was sacrificed. Even when schools are free, the cost of books, clothes, etc., is often prohibitive. In addition, many families feel that they could not do without the help of their daughters at home, where they usually have more responsibilities than boys, and at a younger age. Another problem is that classes are often conducted in a national language which is different from the children's own language. Boys, generally more mobile, have by school age developed a greater facility with the foreign language, but girls, who stay closer to home and compound with their mothers (who also do not usually speak the language), do not have that opportunity.

Girls are also far more likely to drop out of school. Marriage, and the economic needs of their families, which require girls to work at home, are the two largest factors that pull them out of school. Because they don't have the same access to elementary and secondary education, and drop out earlier than boys, very few ever obtain advanced degrees. In 1960, out of 70 countries responding to a UNESCO inquiry on advanced education, in 11 countries there were from 0 to 14 per cent female students, in 32 from 15 to 29 per cent; in 23 from 30 to 44 per cent and in only 4 were there 45 per cent or more.[3]

It is clear that, in spite of official propaganda to the contrary, most countries around the world still have not made female education a priority. Doing so requires a vast restructuring of economic and social institutions. Substantial change in this area is not desired by many countries because education encourages women to try to better their economic and social standing beyond what is possible within the limitations of the male-dominated society.

Author Nicole Frederich questions the priorities of most countries:[4]

> Many contemporary thinkers say 'to teach a man is to teach an individual; to teach a women is to teach a family and a nation.' Those who proclaim this truth are no less likely, with regard to providing the means for this instruction, to provoke the question of the financial benefit derived from the education of women. Logically, since the ultimate goal is certainly the education of the nation, absolute priority ought to be given to the education of women. No country, as yet, appears to have attempted this experiment.

There are a few societies where the education of women is considered important, usually because it will help further a goal that is important to men. Phyllis Ntantala has written that in apartheid in South Africa, where she comes from, black families greatly encourage their daughters' education but the government gives them little support:[5]

> That there has never been any free, compulsory education for Africans has never deterred African parents from giving their children, especially girls, education . . . . The girls were not left behind, for as the parents put it, education was the only inheritance they could leave their daughters who had no rights of inheritance under Customary Law. Writing on this subject: 'The Education of Women,' Mrs. Jessie Herslett . . . . suggests as a reason

that African parents feared education made people soft and as they did not want their sons turned soft, they sent their daughters to school instead. Whatever the reason, it has borne good fruit for the African people.

South Africans make great efforts to educate female children even though the government provides them with an educational system that is unequal in its treatment of blacks and whites, and which costs the parents money. The education of girls has thus become part of an overall survival strategy and therefore a priority for black South Africans struggling with racism and severe exploitation.

There are many ways in which the degree of female education affects women economically, aside from the more obvious facts that with a better education women have access to more jobs and greater economic and social independence. The higher the level of female education (and, therefore, of women's income and occupational status) the lower the birth-rate. This fact was used as an argument against women's economic independence in the nineteenth century, stating that it 'would detract from motherhood, or, worse still, lead to "race-suicide".'[6]

A study done in Thailand in 1970 found that women had about half as many children if they had received even five years of education than if they had received none. Though this could relate to a difference in class or income, all the women in the study were asked what they believed to be the ideal number of children, and all of them indicated that they would rather have had fewer than they had.[7] Access to education also meant access to information about birth control, and greater economic independence, career aspirations, and responsibility and participation in activities outside the home. All of these combine to create viable economic alternatives to compulsory marriage and constant child-birth, and make a woman less dependent on having many children to help around the home or farm. Conversely, the more children a woman has, the more her access to education, work options and general status is limited.

As countries industrialize, there is often a decrease in the death-rate, which sometimes heightens women's status. For example, during the Industrial Revolution in the west, as the infant and child mortality rate decreased, women were no longer required to bear many children to insure the survival of some. Other work, such as weaving, that women had combined with their household responsibilities was now performed outside of the home. Their need to go outside the home for income and the rising costs of raising a family, led women to bear fewer children. Women were then more able to work outside the home and increasingly enjoyed a greater level of economic independence.

A social phenomenon known as the 'marriage squeeze' can also facilitate women's economic independence and alternatives to marriage and children. Since women traditionally marry men older than they, females born during a period of increased natality find fewer men available for marriage. The result in monogamous societies is more single women, late marriages and a decreased birth-rate. This happened in the USA in 1962, when there were 13 per cent fewer men than women of 'marriageable' age, and in Malaysia in the mid-sixties as well.[8]

In the west in the late nineteenth century, the proportion of single women was partly responsible for changes in the status of women and their increased economic independence. Middle-class parents became concerned with adequate education for their daughters, who might have to support themselves. Wealthy families became concerned with inheritance rights. These concerns were reflected in changes in educational institutions and laws concerning the property rights of women. Daughters of working-class and poor rural families were a major part of the industrial work force during this period. They often preferred gruelling factory conditions, long hours and low pay, to lives of economic dependence on family or husbands.

The economics of prestige: from survival in scarcity to conspicuous leisure

Prestige (by which we mean one's standing in the eyes of one's community, whether judged by one's actions, position, values or wealth) operates economically to motivate people to accumulate or give away surplus goods, or to live according to certain standards.[9] Women's prestige most often comes through their relationships with men or through their support of male-dominated social and economic institutions. This sometimes forces women to change their life orientation several times to correspond with society's changing needs. At different times in the history of the Soviet Union, women have been highly regarded for roles as varied as the 'hero mother' and the hard-working factory woman. The economic basis of prestige means that women may take a position more supportive of male supremacy than many men, because of their dependence on male approval for survival.

Prestige is often the mechanism through which the needs of an economy affect child-bearing. In the west (especially in white Anglo-Saxon Protestant families) having a large number of children is often looked upon as an anomaly and a sign of lower status, while for an Ewé woman the bearing of many children is highly prestigious because of the support they bring in old age.

Sometimes recognition is given to women's multiple roles through prestige, glorifying women's burdens rather than recognizing their price. The West Indian woman is often referred to as 'my mother who fathered me,' which implies a certain level of societal recognition in the West Indies of her responsibilities. Yet it is still a form of idealization that is clear from the following statement made by a West Indian man in the course of a talk on women and development:[10]

we look to you women to bring a new dimension of
concern. You have proven resourceful in mothering
and fathering our Caribbean societies; there is no doubt
that you will rise to the occasion now.

Not only have West Indian women risen to the occasion of being supermoms, but he would now superimpose a new responsibility on women – that of concerning themselves with taking the initiative in development efforts. Why did he not ask the Caribbean male to take a greater role in development efforts, as well as in the home, which would relieve women tremendously?

In many cultures, especially where women have no other access to prestige, age is a major source of respect. It is often the views of older rather than younger women that are sought for, listened to and acted upon by men. In Bangladesh, for example, where women enjoy little other authority, an older woman's views will sometimes be heeded. In pre-revolutionary China, though wives were treated as slaves by husbands and mothers-in-law alike, older women benefited from the only source of authority they would ever have: age with a son. The fact that all women hoped that they, too, would one day be mothers-in-law served to help make them think their experience of their exploitation was personal. If each woman looked forward to that day, then she focused less on the current conditions under which she suffered, and was less likely to rebel. The prestige accorded to older women served the economic function of keeping women in their place, doing household labor for long hours without remuneration and often inadequate food and clothing.

In each society lack of prestige may cut us off from goods and services necessary for survival. Within the USA women of different economic classes are rewarded for different feminine functions. The black welfare mothers described in Carol Stack's book *All Our Kin* gain prestige within the community by sharing surplus goods and time with each other. Caring for others' children is also a mark of great esteem within their system.[11] In white middle-class society asking a peer to do childcare might be thought an imposition, nor would these women be as likely to give each other a favorite dress or piece of furniture.

This difference reflects the different economics of survival of the two groups. The first group relies on reciprocity between women's networks, sharing occasional surplus as a means of ensuring that something will come in at one's own time of scarcity. The second depends almost exclusively on the resources of the isolated nuclear family unit. This reflects not only differing survival responses to very dissimilar economic situations, but a cultural difference in attitudes towards women's activity. While white middle-class women in general have only recently been trained to be resourceful and contribute to their families' cash income, a study of black professional women in New York in 1973 showed that there were proportionately more black than white women in the professions in that area because these women 'from early childhood on . . . . had the image of woman as doer fixed in their minds.'[12]

Among any group of women from middle-class or wealthy families who have consistent surplus money or time, prestige is usually held by those who use that surplus to consume more goods. This reinforces the present economic system by providing a market for goods and some material benefits to the buyer. The consumption serves individual husbands for whom it represents wealth and the possession of a wife who can make choices with 'taste'. The men, as greater income producers, ultimately dictate the patterns of consumption while their wives do the work of purchasing.[13] Wives who do not perform these functions well are subject to rejection.

Even women who have spent their lives as housewives catering to male expectations can sometimes find themselves out of a job. The 'new' couple of the middle class is one in which the man and woman both have professional jobs. These men prefer 'interesting' wives who can make money, while still doing the chores, and bring them more prestige than 'just a housewife.' Rich men may gain prestige from their ability to maintain wives who do not lift a finger in any useful occupation. Called 'conspicuous leisure' by Veblen, this provides evidence of a man's wealth to his peers.[14]

The subtle whip: ideal as norm

> Men are in charge of the women because Allah hath made the one of them to excel the other . . . . So good women are obedient, guarding in secret that which Allah hath guarded. As for these from whom ye fear rebellion admonish them and banish them to beds apart, and scourge them.
>
> Koran, Chapter 4, Verse 34[15]

Every society has ideals that are often confused with norms of behavior although they are quite different. The tension produced by the difference between what is considered the best behavior, the ideal, and the way people actually live, the norm, functions economically by exerting pressure on individuals to strive for a standard they think is the norm and produce more in their work.[16] An ideal in some western societies, as another example, is that people, including women, can choose their lifestyles freely. This disguises the fact that there are few options available to women, and makes women feel inadequate when they aren't able to live as they'd like to.

A multitude of stereotypes operate in conjunction with all these ideals. They serve to keep women economically dependent. By keeping them unemployed or underemployed, on the most basic level the 'norm' of heterosexuality and associated feminine behavior serves to channel women into unpaid work for men. Outside the home such stereotypes maintain women's exploitation as well. A representative of Bell Telephone in Canada says that they hire women for their numerous low-level, low-paying jobs because women get pregnant, get married and quit their jobs, and so are more satisfied with these jobs than men would be.[17] In Japan women are traditionally laid off first because 'they don't have families to support' so their employment is not considered important.[18]

This economic stereotype is sometimes used to force women to live in the style that is most advantageous to the business employing them. For example, non-Canadian women (mostly Caribbean, South American and Indian) are required to sign a humiliating declaration, which is currently being protested by women's groups, in order to be 'allowed' to emigrate to Canada as domestic workers. They have to be 'single, widowed, divorced, without minor children or the encumbrance of common law relationships and the issue thereof'[19] – in other words, they should have no life of their own. The desire for economic opportunities not available to them in their own countries compels many women to lie about their family life.

In many societies menstruation is thought to be physically or spiritually harmful to men and is used to justify work segregation.[20] Almost everywhere women are called weaker and less intelligent than men, or they are told that their sexuality would distract men from more important work. One Russian woman in a high position in industry has said that when a woman changes a decision she has made, the attitude of men is that it is a feminine flaw, while if a man changes his mind, he is considered to be making another decision.[21]

All such sex-role stereotypes serve the function of justifying in men's eyes their exploitation of women. From women's perspective, such stereotyped norms are detrimental to their self-respect and discourage attempts to move into new spheres that might lessen their exploitation.

Motherhood

The ideal of men as heads of households ignores the large number of households all over the world that are headed by women. In Africa, for instance, one-third to one-half of farms are run by women, and in West Africa one-third of households in the towns are headed by women.[22] Governments can avoid dealing with these women and their economic problems since no one believes in their existence as a group.

The role of motherhood, especially in the west, is idealized and mystified to make people believe that the nuclear family where mother stays at home is the norm. Adrienne Rich notes:[23]

> Motherhood is admirable, however, only so long as mother and child are attached to a legal father. Motherhood out of wedlock, or under the welfare system, or lesbian motherhood, are harassed, humiliated, or neglected. In the 1970's in the United States, with 26 million children of wage-earning mothers, 8 million in female-headed households, the late 19th century stereotype of the 'mother at home' is still assumed as the norm – a 'norm' that has, outside of a small middle-class minority, never existed.

The illusion that women are not heads of households has a variety of economic functions, from justifying lower salaries for women, to paying them less-than-subsistence welfare benefits, a punishment for the transgression of a norm that is not really prevalent. It also makes women not living in stereotypical nuclear families internalize guilt and a low self-image, impelling them to work harder to show that they are truly 'fit' mothers.

The role of mother is an ideal that contains so many social identities[24] that women are simultaneously deprived of their own physical and emotional health and leisure, and constantly obligated to others. They cannot keep up with the many demands of their role, which include sacrificing their own needs to provide refreshed, functioning men who will be better workers.

Most women around the world work long hours and are on call twenty-four hours a day, seven days a week with no vacation or weekend time off, and little or no monetary reward. They are required to do a multitude of different tasks each day, including paid work outside the home because they receive no money for their work in the home. They have very little time to themselves, and often feel terribly guilt-ridden if they aren't always dedicated to their children. Women who don't work outside the home often feel that they are at fault because they can't become the ideal woman who is fulfilled by motherhood alone. Where the patriarchal system is most powerful, it has thus created a constrained being, narrowly defined by sex, whose feminine role makes great demands on her.[25]

The idealization of motherhood is often used to blame women for social problems. In the following excerpt from a speech by a Jamaican man concerning male and female roles in Jamaica, a common myth is revealed: that women, alone, are responsible for poor male behavior because of bad mothering:[26]

> I have already referred to a fairly prevalent feature of Jamaican family life where many men (competent in their business careers) may be domestically immature, making mothers of their wives, avoiding responsibility for child caring, and avoiding personal, tender extra-sexual socializing with their wives by persistently coming home late. Fears are expressed of being called a 'sissy-man'.

Duties about the home are neglected . . . . How did this get
to be so? Is it part of a tradition? – handed on surprisingly
enough by mothers themselves, who often make daughters
into thoughtful, caring, responsible creatures but let the
boys play their way into and through life, at least where
domestic responsibilities are concerned.

What he overlooks is the fact that children's education and
socialization does not exist in a vacuum. Children the world
over are exposed to social reinforcement of roles through
their playmates, adult behavior, school, and the media. In
addition, fathers and close male friends and relatives often
have a great deal more influence over boys' socialization than
do mothers and other females. Although the women perform
the chores associated with child rearing, it is an unstated
assumption that the boys will emulate their fathers and other
men's behavior, and learn the standards of behavior from them.

In bringing up boys to conform to domineering sex-role
stereotypes, women are actually doing their job as it is
understood and defined by men. Men define how children
should behave and women are carrying out their orders,
which often are unstated assumptions about male and female
sex-role behavior. Rhona Baptiste presents the female perspective behind the Jamaican man's assertions:[27]

> the Caribbean woman has had to 'appear' weaker or lesser
> in the face of a western society which promotes the
> masculinity and liberation of man. Thus it has been the
> Caribbean woman's lot to have to tolerate an errant man
> 'for the sake of appearances,' or, as often happens in the
> upbringing of a boy child, to allow him an early freedom
> 'because he is a boy' and therefore entitled to certain
> freedoms, even irresponsibilities.

The same author who blamed Jamaican women for men's
failings in family life also mentioned a set of demands that
women encounter when entering formerly all-male domains:[28]

> women, too, in our culture, require a dimension of
> affectional relationship in such occupations that men do

not require. In addition, the movement back and forth
between the roles of career woman and homemaker calls
for a switching of gears that many women find difficult.
Such a woman may have to be assertive at work but
protective and receptive at home. Some women can't
manage the switch in role, may neglect the one or the
other, and may remain perpetually at odds with their
environment. Awareness of the problem will help to
combat it.

In his view, women are expected to shoulder the responsibility for balancing a cut-throat work-world, with their
traditional role in the home. Rather than suggesting that men
become less hardened in their dealings in their work world,
or that men accept half the responsibility in the home,
thereby facilitating new roles for men and women, he suggests
only that 'awareness will help to combat it.'

Beauty

'Her looks had been her only capital.'
> From a description of a southern
> Italian woman by Ann Cornelisen.[29]

Beauty is also thought to be a pure ideal, but in reality it is
very much a part of the economy. Standards of beauty
constantly change over time and across cultures, making it
unattainable for women, and making millions of dollars
for cosmetics and clothing manufacturers.

Advertisers in the United States spend billions of dollars
annually for beauty products in an attempt 'to control
our responses, arouse our anxiety and stimulate our needs
. . . women are desperate to conform to an ideal and impossible standard, and many go to great lengths to manipulate
and change their faces and bodies.'[30] In the effort to reap in
the megabucks, inessential 'beauty' products are sold that are
not only useless, but dangerous. In the USA, feminine hy-
giene sprays, for example, must now be labelled 'CAUTION:
the use of these products is hazardous to your health.' Yet,
due to artificially created needs, twenty-four million women

spend $50 million annually for beauty products.[31]

Personal appearances must be maintained as part of the work of wives, receptionists, waitresses, etc. Catherine MacKinnon has observed that 'for women, "attractiveness" – meaning an ingratiating, flattering and deferential manner which projects potential sexual compliance – has economic consequences.'[32] Men hire, promote and fire women on the basis of their perceived 'desirability,' a heterosexual standard of potential accessibility which is influenced by class, ethnic and racial factors as well as sexual factors. One American woman put it this way: 'Not being attractive enough does have an economic effect ... you know you can't get really well-paying jobs. If you ever go to the top floor of an office building, you know the women look a certain way.'[33]

Women are defined by sex and channelled into hetero-sexual roles in almost every society, beginning with the early distinctions in children's clothes. Later they must dress themselves up, emphasizing their sex to catch a husband, or to keep many of the jobs that are available to women.[34] The cost of fashionable clothing and make-up comes out of women's income and time rather than that of the employers who expect it. Even if some women can play the game successfully for a while, everyone gets older, so that women must fear the loss of influence based on such transitory powers.

In Vietnam during the American occupation many prosti-tutes underwent surgery in order to make their facial features more western and their breasts larger, as well as making more superficial changes in their appearances, to please American men who provided their only means of living.[35]

In the Soviet Union, women were encouraged to pay more attention to their appearance when the cult of motherhood was being paraded to get women back into the home and producing more babies. Ilya Selvinsky, a male Soviet poet, wrote in the Literaturnaya Gazeta:[36]

> We need an art which educates young boys to admire the miracle of beauty in women, and young girls to aspire to imitate the examples of such beauty. For a barbarian woman is simply a person of the opposite sex ... but art

teaches men to idealize women. This distinguishes civilized people from primitive ones.

The attempt to have women aspire to a pedestal is in reality an effort to keep them out of the male world, a transparent ruse to isolate women from the work-place and from other women, and to put them back into the home.

For ten centuries Chinese women's feet were bound in order to fulfill a male fetish in the name of 'beauty.' When girls were six or seven, mothers began to bind their feet. The feet of women born into upper-class families were bound so tightly that they could not walk at all, while peasant women's feet were bound so that they could just barely walk. Immobilized women were a symbol of the wealth of the upper-class male, imitated by other men. Girls without crippled, decaying feet three to four inches long could not marry, and had no place in society.[37] They had no means of escaping their forced marriages, because they could not support themselves with their work. Though footbinding (and corseting in the west), stopped in this century, such fashions as high-heeled shoes and tight skirts in the west, or restrictive kimonos in Japan, continue to meet male demands for female vulnerability.[38]

When women have some economic independence, their clothing tends to be less restrictive. In modern China women and men alike wear loose-fitting pants and jackets and comfortable canvas shoes (though attempts are now being made to start a fashion industry there). In the traditional Ewé society women's clothing is certainly not restrictive or unhealthy, though there is far more sexual differentiation of clothing than in China.

Racism

In most third-world countries, as well as in white-dominated western countries, white society has been held out as an ideal, through the media, advertisements and educational systems. While racism, the justifying philosophy, is experienced interpersonally, its economic base runs deep in the structure of most political, economic and social institutions.

As a social theory, it has been developed and used to rational-
ize countless social horrors, from colonialism and slavery to
forced sterilization. Though the rationale expressed is usually
some form of paternalism (similar to many common attitudes
towards women) – such as 'what would the poor ignorant
people do without our benevolent aid in creating jobs, family
planning, and more viable social structures' — its motivation is
largely economic. Racism within societies and much of
foreign aid comes down to exploiting labor and resources and
maintaining white skin privilege. Racist attitudes compare
other cultures and value systems to the 'norm' of white
western culture. When people living according to different
value systems fail to meet white western standards, racist
generalizations (they're too slow, child-like, incapable of
responsibility, etc.) are used as a justification for firing
people rather than questioning the economic system or
understanding people's behaviour as a form of cultural
resistance.

The effects of such thinking on non-white women and men
are devastating, and they inevitably have economic consequences. When such racist stereotypes are internalized, they
prevent people from identifying the domination of white
culture as the problem: people experience their oppression
on a personal level, as resulting from their shortcomings. This
both encourages them to accept hard work for little money
and under poor conditions and discourages them from
questioning or trying to change the system.

In an article in *The Black Scholar*, Elizabeth Hood explains
the effect of white cultural supremacy on black women in
the USA:[39]

> Society, infested with racism, compares black women
> unfavorably to white women . . . Black women who,
> because of racial discrimination, require many times more
> strength to cope with family life alone, are often the
> recipients of harsh criticism and negative labels.
> Unmotivated, lazy and immoral are adjectives frequently
> applied to the black woman forced to accept public
> assistance. Yet, these women are merely adapting to the
> conditions forced upon them by a racist society.

Women bear the brunt of many of the social and economic policies that are motivated by racial exploitation. Hood summarizes many of these policies:[40]

Racism is the linking chain which binds all the master plans designed to destroy black people: psychological tests to establish mental inferiority, the unequal distribution of wealth to ensure poverty, inadequate diets which may cause physical illness and mental retardation, sub-standard housing in communities lacking clean air, shortages of dental and medical care, unequal educational opportunities, and federally-subsidized involuntary sterilizations.

It is women who must, on a daily basis, absorb the effects of racism in the form of sub-standard housing, and inadequate medical care and education for their families. They must try to make do for their families, struggling at all times with the gap between their reality and that of the idealized white middle-class family presented to their children at school, on television, and in the movies.

In addition, third-world women are the special target of sexist policies and actions of the dominant culture. It is mostly third-world women, not white women, who suffer from sterilization abuse (described in the Violence Against Women Section): a population program that blames the victims of poverty instead of changing the conditions of poverty. A study in Washington, D.C., showed that black women have one and a half times greater chance of being returned to jail after an initial hearing than white women.[41] Because of the double economic burden imposed by racism and sexism, and because of the racist nature of the pay and status of hierarchy for most blue-, white-, and pink-collar jobs, third-world women often have differing economic priorities. Michele Russell, in a speech on Sexism and Racism asked:[42]

What makes the black registered nurse resist hospital unionization drives which the white Croatian woman orderly welcomes? . . . . What prompts black women to

say, 'Please, Lord, let me have the luxury to stay at home
and be a housewife? . . . black women voluntarily take pay
cuts in order to have white collar jobs associated with
gentility.

Thus the degrading effects of racism on the job make some
black women aspire to low or no income jobs due to their
prestige value and/or relief from the gruelling conditions of
most jobs that have been available to them.

Although these examples concern black women in particular, racism affects women from other cultures in similar
ways. The racism inherent in the acceptance of white culture
as a social norm has economic effects on women all over the
world. It negatively affects women's self-image and encourages
them to work harder to meet aspirations imposed on them
from a different culture. Racism also exacerbates the exploitation of women, and it takes on a form of its own which
affects third-world women in ways that neither white women
nor third-world men experience.

One of the effects it has on white women is to give them
the illusion of acceptance by the dominant culture. Racism
as an ideology and institution creates the distorted notion
for white women that they truly belong to, and thus have a
stake in, male-dominated institutions that thrive on racism's
inequities. The extent to which white women internalize
racist thinking blinds them to their common exploitation as
women and thus diverts them from acting on their own and
women's behalf.

A progressive vision of change for all women which inspired
earnest and sincere confrontation of racism, occurred in the
history of the Abolitionist and Suffragist movements (and
later in the Civil Rights and Feminist movements) in the
United States.

Many of the early suffrage activists had also been active
in the abolitionist movement and often spoke publicly
about the parallels between the position of women and
black people. In 1860, Elizabeth Cady Stanton said:[43]

The prejudice against color, of which we hear so much,
is no stronger than that against sex. It is produced by the

same cause, and manifested in much the same way. The Negro's skin and the woman's sex are both prima facie evidence that they were intended to be in subjection to the white Saxon man. The few social privileges which the man gives the women, he makes up to the (free) Negro in civil rights.

Yet when white men drafted the Constitutional amendments to give the vote to black people, they excluded black women. It was, as Sojourner Truth so aptly put it, 'a great stir about colored men getting their rights, but not a word about the colored women.'[44]

When the National American Women's Suffrage Association (NAWSA) was formed in 1890, their commitment to the civil rights of black people began to be watered down by those anxious to obtain the vote. Women who had been active in the abolitionist movement were no longer in leadership positions in NAWSA, and some women were encouraged to become involved due to the hope of 'enforcing white supremacy in the South by securing the vote for white women.'[45]

In the classic collision of sexual and racial politics, black women have often been the primary losers, even when they were active participants in both struggles. Fannie Lou Hamer describes how women lose out in this process, in 'The Special Plight and Role of Black Women':[46]

In the past, I don't care how poor this white woman was in the South she felt like she was more than us. In the North, I don't care how poor or rich this white woman has been, she still felt like she was more than us. But coming to the realization of the thing, her freedom is shackled in chains to mine and she realizes for the first time that she is not free until I am free.

Racism on the part of white women is still a part of political reality. However, another part of women's history has often been forgotten: many women have successfully formed alliances across racial, ethnic and class boundaries.

As early as 1800 women were publicly articulating their commitment to work together with women from other classes and races. The historican Barbara Berg tells of the work of urban white women, during the first half of the nineteenth century:[47]

> [These women] formed hundreds of associations
> dedicated to helping the aged, infirm, impoverished,
> and deviant (sic) female in cities across the nation
> . . . . Female benevolent societies . . . transformed the
> imprecise perceptions of women throughout
> America into a compelling feminist ideology. The
> members postulated a community of women. They
> continually emphasized the similarities between
> themselves and Black, Indian and immigrant women.

This tradition continued as a part of the struggle for the vote for women. In an article called 'Bridging the Gap' Ella Gross also draws on the suffrage history:[48]

> we cannot forget that the women who helped
> [Susan B. Anthony] organize moderate, liberal and
> radical women to participate in the first women's
> conference were women of all colors. The burning human
> rights issues provided the fire that ignited Susan Anthony's
> motivation to protest. Sojourner Truth pointed out the
> relationship between freedom for the slave and equality
> for women of any color when she came to the aid of
> Greces Dana Gage at a women's conference in Akron,
> Ohio in 1951 . . . . When Sojourner came to the front of
> the group and described her oppressive situation as a
> non-recognized being, she clearly demonstrated to white
> women the connections among all oppressed people's
> struggle for liberation and called for the sharing of spirit
> and determination amongst women to accomplish both
> human liberations.

That women came together, in spite of male hostility, disapproval and punishment to form close personal and political bonds, is as vital a part of women's history as the complexity of forces pulling women away from each other.[49] Many women today are learning from the past and working hard to cross the male-imposed boundaries of race and class in their political work. Some feminists are forming racism and classism study groups, and writing of such problems in the feminist movement.[50] But the awareness of classism and racism is still small and must become worldwide for the necessary changes to take place in the lives of all women.

Love and emotions

A wife's love is measured by her headaches.
Italian proverb quoted in
Antonioni's film, *Story of an Affair.*

Even the differing male and female ideals for levels of emotional intensity serve an economic function. Women as a group are socialized to be supportive and sensitive to the needs of others; and partly as a result of this socialization, women give and look for in others a high standard of emotional giving and intensity. Men, to the contrary, learn not to verbalize or express their feelings, because they are afraid of being vulnerable. Since information gives power, they often keep personal information to themselves. This opposite emotional training means that when dealing with men, women as a group give constantly in situations with little hope of having their own needs met. The fact that both men and women are aspiring to the social ideal mystifies the interactions. A woman who's not getting what she needs emotionally from a man or her family usually feels that *she* must be the problem, that she's not giving enough or making them feel secure and happy enough. In attempting to fulfill unrealizable ideals, women constantly give more and more of themselves, in the form of material, social, personal and emotional services. These services, as we shall see later, have economic functions, which are made all the more profitable to the recipients by the fact that women consistently try harder and harder to meet unattainable ideals.

The social ideal for men's behavior in heterosexual love relationships does not require sacrifice. The reality of how men operate is usually a mixture of love and exploitation. One anthropologist describes the behavior of men in a low-income community in the USA that is true for most men since they are frequently insecure about their masculinity. He says: '. . . in a world where sexual conquest is one of the few ways in which one can prove one's masculinity, the man who does not make capital of his relationship with a woman is that much less of a man.'[51]

The ideal of love also allows women to be convinced that their nurturing work should be done for free. The demand for wages for women's work in the home is seen as cold, mercenary, and unwomanly. Those extensions of this work for which women can earn money, such as domestic work in other's homes, sexual services, childcare, and nursing, are paid very little, because it is done for free in the home and is supposedly part of women's nature. Male-dominated nurturing professions, such as medicine and the ministry are often well paid and respected. In most economies money provides the main recognition for value, and whatever falls within male spheres receives that recognition. When women work for money it is mercenary; when men earn money they have a career. When women work without pay it is condescendingly perceived as volunteer work, though it makes possible much of the social and cultural work in many societies, while the volunteer work done by male professionals has the prestigious title of 'pro bono' (and they rarely go entirely without pay).

Blaming the victim: the bad woman/good woman dichotomy

In most cultures, women who do not conform to social ideals, however far such ideals might exist from the norm, are considered 'bad women' and often stigmatized or ostracized. When women are forced by social circumstances to vary their role from the ideal they must absorb the costs alone. In Japan, for example, mothers who work outside the home face disapproval at home and among their friends. If childcare is available, it dramatically reduces their salaries.[52]

Worse than familial and social disapproval is the tendency to 'blame the victim,' prevalent worldwide as an excuse for sexism. (We use the word 'victim' not in the sense of a passive recipient of abuse, but simply as someone who has had a crime perpetuated against her.)

Apologizers for violence blame the victim, to insinuate that women are not the victims of a larger social order, but active participants in their own victimizations. In other words, if women are oppressed by men it's their own fault because they don't stand up to it alone or, because they have raised men to behave that way. They subtly shift the responsibility from perpetuator to victim. This thinking is so internalized in many cultures, that it is commonly believed that women are inherently and biologically masochistic.

There are many reasons for blaming the victim. For those who don't want to believe and admit how horrifying conditions are for women, blaming the victim is a convenient means of dealing with one's emotions. Rather than dealing emotionally with the kinds of horrors that men and society perpetrate on women, one says that the victim brings it on herself.

Since sexual inequities and the abuse of women are considered to be the norm and taken for granted, the victims are seen as the deviants.

An extreme example is found in Arab culture, when a woman's honor – her chastity – has been questioned or violated (through adultery or rape). To restore her own and her family's honor, a male family member will kill her with total impunity, to pay back the 'honor debt.'[53] This also happens on a social level, when women as a group are blamed for society's problems, instead of being seen as its victims.

Blaming the victim in this way serves several other important social functions. We discussed earlier two widely used examples of blaming mothers for society's problems: the case of mothers being held responsible for the behavior of their sons, and the problem women have coping with the double demands of family and job. Blaming the victim obscures the true source of the problem, by diverting attention from its most visible component, the victim. And it absolves all those contributing to the problem from their responsibility in the matter. In so doing, it prevents the questioning of the fundamental social issues which need to be dealt with. Finally, by diverting energy and attention away from the real issues, it heaps more work and responsibility on the victims, instead of offering concrete support and change in the social dynamics. Blaming the victim helps to ensure that the status quo will remain intact.

When women appear to be stepping outside their assigned behavioral pattern, labels are slung at them, another form of blaming the victim. Through the use of socially unacceptable stereotypes and labels, women are compelled to conform to social norms through fear and threat of ostracization, loss of jobs in or outside the home, etc. For example, in many cultures, a woman who never marries is called an 'old maid' and ridiculed. A woman who sleeps with more than one man is called a 'whore' and scorned. A woman who lives with and relates primarily to women is called a 'dyke' and ostracized. If a woman can't stay single, see more than one man, or socialize primarily with women, what option is open to her other than to 'settle down' with one man? Other terms with which we are all familiar and which are astonishingly similar across cultures, such as 'bitch,' 'slut,' etc. similarly constrain women's sexual behavior, aggressiveness, outspokenness, etc. In this way, the 'bad woman' syndrome continually directs women's behavior, putting constant pressure on women to behave in a manner acceptable to men. The role of the 'good woman,' on the other hand, is perhaps best summed up in the words of Marabel Morgan, author of *The Total Woman*: 'It is only when a woman surrenders her life to her husband, reveres and worships him, and is willing to serve him, that she becomes really beautiful to him.'[54] The combination of these two extremes in sex-role stereotyping serves the economic purpose of confining women to undesired marriages, unpaid agricultural work and housework, and underpaid jobs, in the service of men.

In Ethiopia, for example, a woman cannot go into a restaurant without being considered a prostitute.[55] A married woman even suspected of sleeping with a man other than her husband can be returned to her family and ostracized.[56] These same norms are prevalent, though in different form, throughout the world. The following example of Hispanic culture (that of Latin and Central Americans in the USA) illustrates the same underlying assumptions:[57]

> This hispanic woman, contrary to what's acceptable for
> the man, must gain the respect of others by keeping her
> virginity if she is single and by staying away from
> extramarital relationships if she is married.
>   A respectable woman must not go out alone with
> men, she must not walk the streets late at night. The
> control of the man over the woman is such that many
> hispanic women must ask permission of their husbands
> to go out or to attend any activities. The women who
> break these rules of conduct are devalorized in the eyes
> of the hispanic society and seen as 'bad women.'

In some situations false distinctions are made between
women. These, again, serve both to divert attention away
from the real cause of the problems, and to make women
identify more closely with the ideal they are trying to live up
to than with each other. The distinction is made between the
woman who is raped and has a prior sexual history, and the
woman who was a virgin. The former is considered more
deserving of the rape, even to have brought it on. Children
kidnapped into sexual slavery are considered less culpable
than older women who are kidnapped. The prostitute who is
raped and beaten by a client is seen as more deserving of the
assault than is a middle-class suburban housewife who is
raped and beaten.

Karen Lindsey has pointed out how prostitution as an
institution helps to separate women from each other, encourages women to identify more closely with men than with
each other, and thus facilitates the 'divide and conquer'
strategy's success:[58]

> *We are taught that prostitution is a deviation from the*
> *social-sexual norm. In fact, it is the most blatant*
> *manifestation of the norm itself* . . . . To survive . . . . all
> of us, all the time, in some way or another, sell ourselves
> to men . . . . To say that some of us don't sell ourselves
> is like saying that some of us don't breathe polluted air –
> it simply isn't possible. Our degradation may be more

successfully disguised in one occupation than in another, but it is always there. Why do we ignore it?

We ignore it because we've been carefully taught to. The myth of the fallen woman is a vital part of our education. Prostitutes themselves serve as easy gratification to men, but the *institution* itself has a far deeper purpose in the maintenance of male supremacy. *By creating a class of women for other women to despise, the patriarchy blinds the rest of us to the reality behind our own condition.* Whether we condemn, pity or 'tolerate' the hooker, we isolate her from the rest of womankind, and ascribe to her alone the degradation under which we all live. Our acquiescence to the myth gives men a little more power over all of us – the threat that if we get too far out of line, we'll face the same punishment.

In an article on right-wing women, Andrea Dworkin describes women's investment in identifying their husband's wishes as the ideal, and women who live different lifestyles as dangerous. In speaking of the predominance of violence in the family and women's fear of their anger towards the men in their lives, she says:[59]

Fear of a greater evil and a need to be protected from it intensifies the loyalty of women to men who are, even when dangerous, at least known quantities. Because women so displace their rage, they are easily controlled and manipulated haters. Having good reason to hate . . . women require symbols of danger which justify their fear. The Right provides those symbols of danger by designating clearly defined groups of outsiders as sources of danger.

Distinctions between 'bad' and 'good' women also help to keep the problems of the 'bad women' invisible. If it is only something that happens to 'bad women,' who bring it on themselves, then society need not concern itself with it.

These distinctions are also an ill-disguised way of expressing men's hostility towards women. Because men speak of the 'good women,' they are able to vent their hatred unchecked towards those they define as 'bad women' and pretend that they don't hate all women. The police can ignore the pleas of 'bad women,' and husbands and rapists can continue to abuse them with impunity.

The broad framework of men's hatred and fear of women, and women's economic dependence, exploitation and power-lessness are themes which remain the same across most cultures, though the specifics vary. Violence against women is a 'hidden' crime. The violence is not generally recognized for what it is – a cultural pattern of abuse of power over women – or it is understood and accepted as such. Its social acceptance serves to actively support or covertly permit the perpetrators to continue their crimes. Whether or not they use violence themselves, all men benefit from women's enforced power-lessness in the home, the streets, and at the workplace.

The economics of marriage and the family: love's labor or institutionalized slavery?

Kyeseke kana sakutwa	Let me try to pound.
Kyeseke kana sakutwa sana	
Kyeseke kana sakutwa telela.	Let me try to pound the
Kyesekeyo nakitwanga	way I used to.
Kyesekeyo nakitwanga sana	
Kyesekeyo nakitwanga telela.	
Mumuji wama banana	My village has many
Mumuji wama banana sana	bananas.
Mumuji wama banana telela.	
Mabele saka hankanka	When my breasts were
	firm
Mumome bitwa kamwale.	Young men looked at me
Ba mama basa bakana	To watch me pounding.
Mwanani iyi mucheche	My mother sent them
	away;
Waluba kuteka meme	'My child, you are still
	young,
Wayuka kutwa maluku	You don't know yet
	how to heat water
Nakoma naba rubemo	You only know how to
	pound fingermillet.'

Balume sanga baila	I am grown up now and have forgotten,
Nakuka bakeya kesha	Since my husband left me long ago.
Balume kebe tukane	I think he will come back tomorrow.
Kebasake bakapenta	My husband is divorcing me;
Nakebo kubwela kwetu.	He likes street girls more than me.
	I want to go back home.
	Kaonde song, Zambia[60]

Heterosexuality

The social institution most commonly viewed as 'personal' which has the most profound underlying economic ramifications is that of compulsory heterosexuality. The need is so great on the part of patriarchal societies for women to unquestioningly internalize their role as unpaid laborers in the home that the male/female union is mystified, romanticized and taken as the norm, while other life-styles are either trivialized, scorned or condemned. All the 'bad women' stereotypes we spoke of earlier refer to women who have strayed from this heterosexual norm, whether by choice or by default. Such energy is put into belittling those viewed as deviant because it is crucial to the dominant culture that people do not question heterosexual coupling and marriage. Adrienne Rich, in her article 'Compulsory Heterosexuality and Lesbian Existence,' discusses the various forms that this compulsion takes:[61]

> we are confronting not a simple maintenance of inequality and property possession, but a pervasive cluster of forces, ranging from physical brutality to control of consciousness, which suggests that an enormous potential counter-force is having to be restrained.
> Some of the forms by which male power manifests itself are more easily recognizable as enforcing

heterosexuality upon women than are others. Yet each one I have listed adds to the cluster of forces within which women have been convinced that marriage, and sexual orientation toward men are inevitable, even if unsatisfying or oppressive, components of their lives. The chastity belt, child marriage, erasure of lesbian existence (except as exotic and perverse) in art, literature, film, idealization of heterosexual romance and marriage – these are some fairly obvious forms of compulsion, the first two exemplifying physical force, the second two control of consciousness.

Women across cultures are socialized from birth to view heterosexual coupling and marriage as not only ideal, but necessary. Women in alternative life styles are impoverished, harassed, ostracized, threatened and even imprisoned and killed. In the same article, Rich gives examples of the forcible rape of a lesbian in a health sanatorium in Norway when she expressed an aversion to sleeping with her husband, and of the lesbian from Mozambique who chose to live in exile rather than renounce her sexual preference or be sent to rehabilitation camps. Women's 'choice' of heterosexual coupling is so important that a vast array of social forces across cultures exist to ensure that women will indeed 'choose' such a lifestyle, and that if they don't they will face such severe social criticism that few other women will dare take the same course.

The inducement to heterosexual role-playing in the service of men exists outside the family as well. Many women who work for pay outside the home confront expectations that part of their job is to service their employers and other male employees as surrogate wives: from the making of coffee to demands for sexual 'favors'.

All this coercion is necessary because it represents not merely a life 'style', but a worldwide institution whereby women service men for free within and outside the home. Once it is understood that an enormous social conspiracy exists to mystify and enforce women's slave labor, the economic base of many misogynistic institutions becomes clear, from pornography and wife-beating to genital mutilation and the killing of widows and 'adulteresses' (all of which we will be exploring in further detail).

Marriage and slavery

> There is a Chinese word for the female I – which is 'slave'. Break the women with their own tongues!
>
> Maxine Hong Kingston,
> *The Woman Warrior*[62]

> Our class is slavery. Within that category we are treated relatively well or badly. Most of us are poor.
>
> Leah Fritz,
> *Dreamers and Dealers* [63]

Women's duty to love and obey men to whom they are attached is part of a contract for which they hope to be supported financially, or reimbused with an exchange of services. In reality, women have little recourse in most societies when men don't fulfill their part of the bargain. Men can prosecute for desertion, return women to their families and reclaim their bride price, beat, rape or even kill women with social authority if they are not satisfied with their merchandise.

Women have been traditionally defined in terms of the nature of their economic relation to men. A daughter or girlfriend is unpaid, while a mistress receives possible room or occasional board and gifts with no legal claim to them. A wife has recognized legitimate access to room and board, though rarely more, and additional responsibility for all household services, while a prostitute receives an hourly or piece-work wage for one specific purpose.

The rewards that women receive are unreliable income because they are only favors from men that benefit from their labor. Gloria Steinem has compared the good treatment of some women by their masters to the status of house slaves in the United States, who were treated better than field slaves and sometimes developed loyalty to the families they worked for (though many of the house slaves found ways to rebel, and so do many women within their families). Marriage in most societies is not an equal contract, but one that gives a man the rights to use a woman as a slave.

The analogy between marriage and slavery holds true on more than the contractual basis of marriage. In pointing out some of the similarities here, we are not trying to say that all marriages are like slavery as black people, for instance, knew it in the United States. Rather, we are trying to point out some of the similarities in the institutions, and the ways in which they give absolute power and control to one set of people over another. Whether or not this arbitrary authority is maliciously used against the powerless individual in all marital situations is beside the point. That the husband has this authority is what's important here.

The equation of marriage with slavery dates back centuries and across cultures. It can be traced, in western civilization, through the English and other Latin-based languages. The word 'family' comes from the Roman 'famulus', meaning a household of servants, indicating the patriarchal relationship of the father to his wife and children as of man to servants. The word 'slavery' is defined in Webster's dictionary as 'continued and wearisome labor, drudgery; the condition of moral and mental bondage, servitude, the loss of control of oneself, freedom of action, etc.' Certainly from the previous discussion of women's work and status throughout the world, it would be hard to distinguish the feminine role from 'slavery.'

The basic rules for women's behavior in Hindu culture, first expressed and written in the 'Laws of Manu,' written around 200 AD, read much like Webster's definition of slavery:[64]

Nothing must be done independently, even in her own house by a young girl, by a young woman, or even by an aged one. In childhood a female must be subject to her father, in youth to her husband, and when her Lord is dead to her sons, a woman must never be independent . . . . Though destitute of virtue . . . . or good qualities, a husband must be constantly worshipped as a god by the faithful wife. . . . If she violates her duty towards her husband, a wife is disgraced in this world.

When slavery was outlawed in certain parts of Africa, men who had formerly kept a household of female slaves preferred to marry them rather than lose their labor. The contemporary form of buying and selling of women is that of the exchange of a daughter without a bride price, but with the cancellation of a debt. Mothers and daughters are also sent to work for free in the fields of creditors to pay off a man's debts in many societies, such as the Ivory Coast in 1959.[65] In the Bangladesh parliament, during the discussion of legislation abolishing slavery, there was great consternation over the fact that the abolition of slavery would hurt wealthier men less than poor men. Wealthy men could afford several wives, while poor men who could not would be denied the privilege of buying women's services as slaves. The question debated was not the morality of the use of women's unpaid labor through marriage, but that of the poor man's rights. The women's rights were not considered on any level.[66]

In 1869, John Stuart Mill wrote this concerning men's rights in marriage:[67]

Marriage is not an institution designed for a select few. Men are not required, as a preliminary to the marriage ceremony, to prove by testimonials that they are fit to be trusted with the exercise of absolute power . . . . The vilest malefactor has some wretched woman tied to him, against whom he can commit any atrocity except killing her, and if tolerably cautious, can do that without much danger of the legal penalty . . . . When we consider how vast is the number of men, in any great country, who are little higher than brutes, and that this never prevents them from being able, through the law of marriage, to obtain a victim, the breadth and depth of human misery caused in this shape alone by the abuse of the institution swells to something appalling.

Marilyn French describes the underlying power relations in the contemporary middle-class American family, in her novel, *The Women's Room*:[68]

> The unspoken, unthought-about conditions that made it
> oppressive had long since been accepted by all of them:
> that they had not chosen but had been automatically
> slotted into their lives, and that they were never free to
> move (the children were much more effective as clogs
> than confinement on a prison farm would be) . . . .
> Husbands were rarely discussed, but were always in the
> background. They were usually brought up to illustrate
> some absurdity or some constriction . . . . Husbands were
> walls, absolutes, in small things at least. The women often
> would howl and cackle at them, at their incredible
> demands and impossible delusions, their inexplicable
> eating habits and their strange prejudices . . . .
> But no one ever suggested that the situation could be
> changed, no one ever challenged the men's right to demand
> and control . . . . Husbands, like children, had their
> eccentricities, and women had to put up with them.

Wives, like slaves, do not receive pay for their work, only
room and board and some fringe benefits over which they
have no control. Full-time houseworkers work long hours,
never retire from having to work for the family, and receive
no pensions, overtime benefits, or vacations away from their
families (except in Sweden and the USSR, and some women
married to wealthy men).

Their work is crucial and often the basis of the economy,
but it is devalued and considered menial. They have no control over their hours or working conditions because they have
no strong bargaining position. Wives are not organized into
unions. Like 'house slaves,' some women are isolated from
each other, such as upper-middle-class housewives, or Asian
women working with their husbands in the fields; often,
(as with some 'houseslaves') they identify more closely with
their masters than with each other. They and their children
bear their masters' name. Wives can be beaten if they
disobey, and they must be sexually available at their husband's whim. They may be raped and also psychologically
abused by their husbands. They are often valued only in their

capacity as 'good breeders' or as sex objects. If they attempt to leave, they sometimes must escape through an 'underground railway' network of 'safe homes' and shelters for battered women. There they are hidden as fugitives so they won't be killed when found or beaten again and forced back to their labor.[69]

They usually have no other lifestyle options, not always because they would be beaten or killed if they tried to run away, but because few options exist that enable a single woman to support herself and her children. (It is debatable whether institutions such as welfare in the United States can be seen as a real option, due to the poverty and lack of control that recreates women's powerlessness and dependence. The average monthly welfare check for a mother with three children, in Massachusetts in 1979, was, for example, $379.30.)[70]

Even those women who are not full-time unpaid housewives are affected by the slavery of marriage. As Leah Fritz notes, a woman who freely contracts to be available for a limited time and for a definite amount of money is not a full slave, but a 'freed slave.'[71]

A slave who has been 'freed,' whether by her own efforts or through some special dispensation of a master, can never be truly free while female slavery is an accepted fact of society, for there is no badge or sign she can carry - not even a credit card - which will protect her in the world at large.

The elements within the slavery of marriage can be seen more clearly by comparing it to the slavery of women's forced prostitution. We are referring here to women *forced* into prostitution, not to women working independently of pimp overseers who take most of their profits. The analogy has been made many times: is it better to get paid for one's services directly, as in prostitution, or in the form of room and board with a marriage contract?

Prostitutes, married women and non-participants alike have resisted the analogy. It strips marriage of the romanticized veil which allows women to divide themselves into good women and bad women. It clarifies the economic and social relations and underlying men's relationship to women as it is institutionalized in marriage.

Men's needs are taken as the norm, and entire cultures are built around the 'naturalness' of their getting their needs met by force or coercion. Yet women who do most of the work involved in meeting men's needs whether as housewives or prostitutes are despised precisely because they are in a menial, subservient role, a role men put them in.

The labor of many prostitutes is expropriated by pimps or organized gangs, just as the wife's unpaid labor is expropriated by her husband and by the society that refuses to recognize and reorganize the services she performs. Both can be beaten and/or sexually abused when the man they are servicing is displeased with their services. Both depend on the men they are servicing for their livelihoods.

The Indian woman who asked, 'Why does a girl get married? For some protection, some security . . . I was married through a marriage bureau,'[72] had the same need for a source of income as the Indian prostitute who said:[73]

I was married off when I was a child. My husband never liked me. He said I was too dark. He was always telling me to go back to my father's house. If I said I wouldn't go, he would get drunk and beat me up. I put up with this hell for a long time. One day he got drunk and tried to amputate my leg with an axe . . . . That's when I left his home and came to Nanded.

I looked for a job for a long time, and finally found work as a plumber's hand. I was paid Rs 2 a day. I had to survive on these two rupees!! And work was not always available. Some days there was no money. Whoever I approached to get work would ask me to have sex with them. Finally I decided that if I could not get work with dignity this dignity was no use. But then I found I had lost my dignity for the same measly two rupees. I lost my pride and still remained starved. That's how I joined the meat market and started selling my flesh. I've been at this for ten years now . . . . Now they have sucked my youth away, and my price has gone down. Each time, I sell my body for two rupees. But customers are still scarce. Just to survive, I have to go looking for customers till midnight.

A survey of 100 prostitutes and call-girls in Bombay showed that this woman's experience was not unique. More than 90 per cent of the women were illiterate, and most of them were single, separated or widowed, having nowhere to go when separated from or deserted by their husbands.[74] Here we can see how the 'bad woman' threat might encourage many women to stay with abusive husbands.

The process pimps use to procure women for slavery in prostitution, described by Kathleen Barry as 'befriending or love' is similar to the complex emotional, social and economic forces that shape the life of an engaged or newly married woman:[75]

> Procurers who employ the strategy of befriending or love and romance use both tactics together. They may begin by befriending a forlorn runaway and then calculate a romantic connection. The strategy of befriending and love is designed to fit the needs and vulnerabilities of its potential victim. A procurer's goal is to find naive, needy teenaged girls or young women, con them into dependency, season them to fear and submission and turn them out into prostitution.

The pimp and husband both see the woman they are taking in as objects for them to make useful. One pimp wrote:[76]

> Most potentially beautiful women arrive at the age of 17 or 18, for all intents and purposes a shell . . . . like an unfinished house which is potentially a mansion, while the structure may be there, it needs to be finished on the outside . . . . a woman who is potentially beautiful must also be finished, inside and out.

Husbands also try to make wives unto their own image. Wives are given a new name and accompanying set of expectations to fulfill. They are expected to be fulfilled by their new identity as appendages to their husbands.

Pimps make women feel glamorous and important at first, then once the women are dependent, they make them feel indebted and fearful. By cultivating women's low self-image, the pimps make them believe they couldn't survive alone, that they need 'protection'. The process of 'seasoning,' is one 'meant to break [the woman's] will, reduce her ego, and separate her from her previous life.'[77]

The pimp promises protection in return for obedience and good behavior. He controls the hours and conditions of a woman's work, which he, for the most part, benefits from. If she tries to leave, he threatens her, tracks her down, tries to sweet-talk her back, or holds her child hostage. She has no place to go and is considered free game for all other pimps.

These are all elements of marriage, though they may be more subtle. For example, although the occupational hazards are the same [physical, verbal and sexual abuse], prostitutes are exposed to more of it from more people and from the social system. In Bombay, for example, 40 per cent of the prostitutes die before they reach the age of forty.[78]

There are probably few married women in this world who could not identify with at least one, if not most, of the preceding changes that they went through in the process of their own 'seasoning' to marriage. Although it may not apply to every woman, the analogy is extremely useful in helping to see the underlying economic and power relations in the marriage arrangement as it occurs in most countries.

Same-sex marriages

The concept of love also hides the economic relationship of marriage. Because relationships between men and women are romanticized, especially in the west, it is sometimes difficult to see through what we consider 'personal' to the underlying economic relationships. In many cultures around the world, relationships between people of the same sex help to illustrate the underlying economics of relationships which, when heterosexual, are usually mystified and idealized.

In a few societies, same-sex marriage exists as a supplement

to heterosexual marriage for some women. Its primary
purpose is economic, and sometimes it is to insure the
lineage for the children of a woman who does not want to
marry a man but to remain 'free,' and sometimes there is also
a great deal of affection between the 'husband' and 'wife.'
A Nigerian Igbo anthropologist, Victor Chikenzie Uchendu,
describes his own culture, in which the basic household unit
is woman-centered, by saying that two or more of these
households are connected to or share a husband, 'who may
be male or female.' He goes on to say that a large compound
consists of brothers, their wives and children, plus some
sisters or daughters, and their 'wives' and children, and that
a rich man or woman might have several wives and many
children. All a woman must do to be a 'husband' is to pay a
bride price to buy the right to another woman's labor. In
describing his own childhood, he says: 'My mother was then
a "big" trader and she needed someone to help in our house
and so she "married" one wife after another.'[79] Thus women
can be bought and sold by wealthy women as well as by men,
indicating the degree to which wealth gives women some of
the privileges of men. These 'privileges,' just like the privileges accruing to men who benefit from women's free services
in marriage are obtained through the exploitation of the
woman functioning as 'wife.' Thus, it does not matter *who* is
is the role of 'husband,' but rather what the underlying
power relationship is in the marriage, and the fact that one
person's labor and the product of their labor belongs to
another person.

In an article in *The Black Scholar*, Audre Lorde notes that
the Fon of Dahomey have twelve different kinds of marriage,
including:[80]

> one which is known as 'giving the goat to the buck', where
> a woman of independent means marries another woman
> who then may or may not bear children, all of whom will
> belong to the blood line of the other woman. Some
> marriages of this kind are arranged to provide heirs for
> women of means who wish to remain 'free,' and some are
> homosexual relationships.

The love that may exist in same-sex marriages does not negate the underlying economics of the relationship any more than it does in heterosexual marriages. In non-marital primary relationships between people of the same sex, although the motive of the relationship is love, it also has economic ramifications and the people enter into economic dependency or interdependency. Audre Lorde quotes the following statement made by a 92-year-old Efik-Ibibio woman of Nigeria who tells the story of her life:[81]

> I had a woman friend to whom I revealed my secrets.
> She was very fond of keeping secrets to herself. We acted
> as husband and wife. We always moved hand in glove
> and my husband and hers knew about our relationship.
> The villagers nicknamed us twin sisters. When I was out of
> gear with my husband, she would be the one to restore
> peace. I often sent my children to go and work for her
> in return for her kindnesses to me. My husband being
> more fortunate to get more pieces of land than her
> husband, allowed some to her, even though she was not
> my co-wife.

Lesbian relationships in western countries also often involve economic interdependence. Yet because lesbians constitute such a threat to the male power structure by symbolizing women's ability to function happily independent of men, they are ostracized and experience severe discrimination. Because lesbians do not live up to society's ideals, they usually have even fewer economic resources than women in heterosexual relationships. The occasional economic support and implicit social support that heterosexual women receive is in itself a kind of privilege.

The extended family

Family structures are social institutions which develop and are encouraged by other elements within society to fulfill economic functions. Types of families such as the extended family, nuclear or polygynous family, represent different social mechanisms for organizing women's slave labor.

Ultimately it is individual men and/or the male-dominated power structure that benefit from women's economic contribution to the family, but within that framework the particular family structure has a tremendous effect on women's power and access to resources.

An extended family with the presence of many relatives living in close proximity to a woman can be beneficial or oppressive, depending on such factors as whether it is her family or her husband's family, and the degree of power held by women. If women are respected and supported to some degree, then the presence of relatives can serve to keep husbands 'in line', to insure that they hold up their part of familial responsibility. However, if women have an extremely low status and are viewed as little more than sources of unpaid labor, the presence of relatives simply represents more demands made on women's time and energy. If the dominant social structure serves to pit women against each other, ranking them according to age or marital status, an extended family can be a source of conflict and resentment. In other cultures the presence of other women in the household can serve as a source of shared responsibility in home maintenance, cooking and childcare, and emotional support.

Marriages within extended families are usually seen as mechanisms for uniting two families, thus expanding each family's social and economic networks. They are often arranged by women's fathers, or sometimes by older female relatives. Arranged marriages are common within these family networks.

In one type of extended family, the Matabele society of Rhodesia, children have one mother with whom they usually live and several 'little mothers,' who share responsibility for them. Male children may have another mother in the city with whom they stay in order to go to school.[82] This gives the women greater flexibility in their work while it benefits male education, and also provides services the state would have to provide in other societies.

The multinational economy takes advantage of women's work within the extended family structure to support men when they are sick or unemployed, as in the case of women in developing countries discussed earlier. Children and the elderly occasionally take part in home production, but are basically supported by the women's work.

The nuclear family

Within the nuclear family, as in other family structures, women sustain the family and its economic functions. The structure of the nuclear family is ideally suited in many ways (from the point of view of the dominant culture) for industrialized western economies. The small unit of wife, husband and their children provides a greater number of consumption units than an extended family or any other living situation, since each family strives to buy one or even two of many household appliances that could easily be shared by a few households. This isolated unit is also being promoted as an ideal by multinational firms and neo-colonial interests within the third world to provide new markets. Isolation makes each family more dependent on the job of one or two breadwinners, fostering job loyalty. The small family is more easily relocated according to the needs of business and it isolates women from each other, preventing shared work and support.

When women shop they act as the 'purchasing agent' for the family, holding authority over minor purchasing decisions within a qualitative and quantitative economic framework defined by their husbands. Ironically, this function is accompanied by the image of women as frivolous beings who spend hard-earned money, which tends to limit the control of money that their husbands allow them.

The position of children within the nuclear family is one of even more dependence than that of women. As people without economic independence, they, like women, have few rights and are told what to do and when to do it. Children's powerlessness serves as a preparation for future obedience to those with more power both in the workforce and, for girls, within their own families.[83]

Polygyny

While polygynous marriages seem to be a social or religious

institution, an examination of women's work within these marriages brings to light its economic foundation. Polygyny is most common in societies in Africa and South-east Asia where women do agricultural work and are responsible for supporting themselves.[84] In those societies where there is still collective or family land tenure, an additional wife means additional land and another worker. Here the husband usually must pay a bride price. Their children, both female and male, are valuable assets as future laborers. The women often cultivate the fields, and their older sons prepare new land for cultivation, while the husband supervises their work.[85] This diminishes or eliminates entirely the need for hiring labor. In the traditional African marriage of this type, women produce food for the entire family and supply other household necessities from the sale of their crops. It is easy to see why in much of sub-Saharan Africa, one-third to one-quarter of all married men have more than one wife.[86] Table 2 shows the distribution of work among men and women in Yoruba society in Nigeria in West Africa. (The term 'family aid' refers to non-domestic labor, mostly agricultural.) A full 19 per cent of the women receive nothing from their husbands; only 5 per cent receive food, clothing and cash, and only 28 per cent receive all their food from their husbands. It is clear that in this polygynous society, women's labor and income as housewives, family aids and self-employed workers are a definite economic asset.

Table 2 Rights and duties of Yoruba women[87]

Percentage of women with the following rights and duties:

Wife contributes to household:

Wife receives from husband	*as self-employed, family aid and housewife*	*as self-employed, and housewife*	*as family aid and housewife*	*as housewife*	*Total*
Nothing	8	11			19
Part of food	32	16			48
All food	15	11	1	1	28
Food, clothing and cash	1		3	1	5
Total	56	38	4	2	100

The additional labor provided by several wives allows the husband leisure time in many societies. In one study of a Gambian village in Africa where women produce rice, men with several rice-producing wives produced less millet (a crop traditionally grown by men) than did men with one wife. In the Central African Republic, village men with two wives found more time for hunting, a highly-valued spare-time activity.[88]

In addition to time, the institution of polygyny enables men to acquire more property, in the form of wives, land under cultivation, and increased crops, which can then be converted into more material goods, homes, etc. One man explains how the labor of one wife can be converted into the acquisition of another wife: 'He says to the first wife, "I like such and such a girl. Let us make a bigger farm this year." As soon as the harvest is over for that year, he sells the rice and so acquires the additional wife.'[89] A village woman in Upper Volta described how she became a second wife: 'I was very young and only knew that my older "sister" (woman connected by blood or marriage) who was married to Aliru wanted me to come and live here and help her cook and fetch water. I didn't know I was to be her co-wife.'[90] Ester Boserup describes the ways some male farmers can expand their cultivation: 'three possible ways of development present themselves to the farmer: expansion by technical change (the plough); expansion by hierarchization of the community (hired labor); or expansion by the traditional method of acquiring additional wives.'[91]

It is also said that to maintain optimal control over women, the ideal number is four. This is because the labor of one is considered to be like none at all since she works for her family as well as her husband, two are said to compete and three may form coalitions.[92]

A late seventeenth century account of polygynous marriages among the Carib Indians in the Caribbean islands shows the overt economic basis of their marriages, which is not dissimilar to many polygynous relationships the world over today:[93]

It frequently happens that a man will marry 3 or 4 sisters

at the same time and they claim that an arrangement of this kind makes for more peace since they were brought up together. This is an advantage to men, who see wives as servants and no matter what affection they may have for them, the husbands never forgo the attention that their wives have to give them, or the respect which they insist must accompany their services.

What do women think of the institution of polygyny? In rural areas many women prefer a polygynous arrangement, because they can share the domestic work, cooking and caring for the husband and children. On isolated farms wives also provide valuable companionship. In Ivory Coast one opinion study showed that 85 per cent of the women preferred polygynous to monogamous marriage, citing such economic and domestic reasons.[94]

However, many women dislike their polygynous marriages. In many cultures where colonial regimes and later neo-colonialism recruited young men for construction, mining and plantation labor, there has been a scarcity of younger marriageable men. During such periods, young women are often married to older men. Many young women who are required to do difficult work while married to older men attempt to earn the necessary money to pay back the bride price their husbands paid for them, and thus buy their freedom from their husbands. This gives many men an incentive to keep bride prices high, and to prevent young wives from earning money, as a way of keeping them and their free labor.[95]

If a husband manipulates the relationships between women to pit them against each other, thus preventing the possible development of networks between them, the presence of polygyny in that household will work against women. If, on the other hand, the women involved are conscious of his attempts to separate them, and don't let it happen, then their numbers can be a source of support and strength.

Another concern that many women share concerning polygyny is whether the children of all the wives will all be treated equitably with respect to schooling, material advantages, and other opportunities. One Ghanaian woman dealt with this problem individually by helping to educate the daughters and sons of her less-educated sisters herself, after her sisters had helped her go to school, thus strengthening the women's networks by sharing advantages that were individually acquired.[96] However, many women cannot or will not help each other in this way, and so the children receive vastly differing degrees of attention and support, depending on their mothers' marital status.

With colonialism, social customs have deteriorated in many cultures, and with them have gone strong family networks, often resulting in the greater vulnerability of women in the family. Men's duties and obligations with respect to their children are becoming less and less well defined, as are their relationships to their wives. The distinction between the rights of and obligations towards wives, concubines, and girlfriends were clearly established and upheld in traditional Ghanaian culture, for example. But today, especially in urban areas, men have many children by different women, with whom their relationships are less defined. The mothers may receive little material or in-kind support for themselves and their children. In addition, with the super-imposition of European law, mothers of children born 'out of wedlock' have no recourse when fathers renege on support, as they would have had in traditional society. (The term 'illegitimate' is never used, since no child is considered illegitimate, regardless of the marital relationship of the parents.) As a consequence of growing male irresponsibility in this area, women's groups such as the Ghana Assembly of Women began a campaign in 1956 to strengthen customary marriage, to clearly define women's rights in the law rather than to abolish polygyny per se.[97]

Florence Dolphyne, vice-chairman of the Ghana National Council on Women and Development, feels that if polygyny were legally abolished it would simply continue in extra-marital relationships, where women had no social recourse if men weren't upholding their responsibilities. But if men were held legally responsible for all their wives and children, the financial pressures alone would prevent many polygynous marriages. And Dolphyne feels that polygyny sometimes works to women's advantage if the husband can provide support for more than one wife.[98]

Other women's groups, composed mostly of younger, more urban women, are actively fighting polygyny. Feeling that 'polygamy would lead to the degradation of female dignity and respect . . . . (and that) most rural communities would use polygamy to provide a labor force for the men, hence degrading women's position in society.', the UWT National Council of Women in Tanzania, fought the proposed 1969 marriage laws allowing conversion of monogamous to polygynous marriages by consent of both parties, and won.[99] In general, it has been through the efforts of educated women, who themselves have refused polygynous marriages, that the institution has been fought, which may in itself reflect an underlying difference in women's attitudes and resources on the basis of their class backgrounds.

Regardless of the class and ethnic identities of those speaking for or against polygyny, the issues have more to do with women's power in different situations than with polygyny itself. The efforts by the Ghana Assembly of Women were important in that they addressed the division of power and responsibilities within the family, and fought to insure that women's status was not further eroded with the deterioration of social institutions that would traditionally have been supportive of women's interests.

Female seclusion and the veil

In societies where fewer women work in the fields, polygyny is usually less widespread (2 per cent in Algeria, 3 per cent in Pakistan and Indonesia, 4 per cent in Egypt).[100] Only wealthy men can afford to support more than one wife when women do not grow their own food or earn much cash.[101] In many of these societies women are secluded in the home and covered with the veil and long garments. In some cases, women are allowed to leave the home but they must continue to wear 'the veil' wherever they go. They are seen as an economic burden, because their domestic work is not valued. There are an estimated 200 million veiled women in the Arab world alone.[102]

By isolating a woman in the home, purdah defines her

relationship as property to her father or husband. In maintaining the illusion of non-productivity, it justifies her
treatment as a household slave and the expropriation of her
labor entirely to the male's benefit. As one Moroccan woman
described it:[103]

> The veil, so talked about by tourists seeking exotic
> excitement around the Mediterranean shores, is the symbol
> of our slavery. The veil means that the woman belongs to
> a man who possesses her body and worries about its being
> seen by others. To a veiled woman, seclusion is the only
> rational way of life. Her only reasons for being are to
> provide sex, children, and good cooking.

In many of these cultures, women married to the wealthiest
landowners are often prohibited from leaving their home
compounds at all. Although these women do no agricultural
or waged work, they serve both as domestic slaves and as
status symbols of the husbands' 'conspicuous leisure'.

This role is important enough to their husbands to sacrifice the economic well-being and possible prosperity their
family would enjoy with women's added wage labor. In the
Sudan, it is considered 'a mark of distinction and sophistica-
tion' for a woman to go into seclusion upon completing her
education.[104]

Yet even though it has become a point of male honor for
women to remain secluded within the home, many thousands
of women throughout the Middle East still bring in cash
income and sometimes even support their entire family,
through sewing, cooking and doing childcare for other
families, raising animals or vegetables and selling them, and
operating as midwives or religious specialists.[105] In Moroccan
cities, for example, women have done craft work, although
competition from European machine-made products has
greatly decreased the possibility of women earning an independent income through crafts.[106] Their lack of options
forces them to accept very low reimbursement for the goods
they can make for sale outside the home.[107] Clearly, women
must bring in an income out of necessity, but the mythology
that they are worth nothing and produce no value justifies

their continued enslavement.

In cultures where women cannot bring in much cash income, such as Hindu culture, a woman's family is usually expected to pay a dowry when she marries. While women's status is largely dependent on the production of children, sons are especially valued because they will require no dowry.[108] The dowry is seen as a mechanism for assuring that the daughter's position in her new family will be secure. In Thailand, in the nineteenth century, a man could sell a wife for whom he had paid a bride price, but not one whose parents had paid him a dowry.[109] However, this is no guarantee of a woman's security, as shown by the hundreds of 'dowry murders' in India, for example, by husbands and in-laws dissatisfied with new wives.

In some societies where women are in purdah, it is the husband who makes a payment to the family of the bride. Fatima Mernissi points out that in Morocco:[110]

> In fact the marriage contract is a bill of sale. The dowry is the price the man pays. The woman's duties toward her husband are stated in article 36 of the Moroccan code: fidelity; obligation to breast-feed the children; good housekeeping; obedience; deference toward the father, mother and relatives of the husband.

The man's payment of a dowry might also be explained by the fact that although women are perceived to be economic dependants, many women in rural Morocco (where 80 per cent of the population lives) go unveiled and do as much (unpaid) agricultural work as domestic work.[111]

Polyandry and matrilineal inheritance

Polyandry – or one woman having many husbands – might seem on the surface to be more appealing to women. But polyandry is rare, and as it exists within patriarchal societies it does not insure that women have equal power to men. In fact, it comes from quite the opposite set of assumptions. While 16 per cent of all societies have monogamous marriage and 83 per cent polygynous or a mixture of monogamous and polygynous, only 1 per cent have polyandrous marriage.[112] In the latter cultures, some of which also practice female infanticide, the institution functions to provide men with wives who would not otherwise have access to women's slave labor.

In the polyandrous Nayar society in India,[113] for example, women's role still benefits the male-dominated economy. Women collectively take responsibility for childcare, so that children have a variety of close relationships to women they call 'auntie'. Although a woman has several husbands, there are clear lines of responsibility governing each father's relationship to 'his' child. Every child has a father who claims responsibility for paternity. If no man claims a particular child, the mother can be banished or killed.

In Nayar society there is also matrilineal inheritance – inheritance passed down through the female instead of the male members of the family. It is far more common, and like polyandry, it can appear on the surface to be a form of female economic control, but in fact, women rarely benefit from it.

Most matrilineal societies are like the Nayar, in that a woman's brother takes the responsibility for the financial and emotional care of the children that patriarchal cultures would expect a father to provide. He exercises the kind of power over his sister that a husband would over his wife in a patrilineal society. Therefore, though inheritance is determined through the female, it is controlled by men.

Inheritance, according to some people living in matrilineal societies such as the Ashanti in Ghana, represents the male's concern that men retain complete control over their lineage which requires that the family line and blood remain intact.[114] While the identity of a child's mother is always known, that of the father is open to question. Only by enslaving women, in purdah or in a variety of other repressive social institutions can they be kept away from extra-marital sexual relations. This is difficult in agricultural societies where women's labor is needed and they are not secluded. Matrilineal inheritance is one way to solve this problem. The child is of the same blood as the maternal uncle and thus the family lineage is maintained. Although this gives biological fathers a lesser role with respect to the child's identification in the family, each man identifies with his nephews.

Residence

> It was said, 'There is an outward tendency in females,' which meant that I was getting straight A's for the good of my future husband's family, not my own. I did not plan even to have a husband. I would show my mother and father and the nosey emigrant villagers that girls have no outward tendency. I stopped getting straight A's.
>
> Maxine Hong Kingston,
> *The Woman Warrior:*
> *Memoirs of a Girlhood Among Ghosts.*[115]

A factor which greatly influences the amount of power that women hold within most families cross-culturally is whether the newly-married couple resides with the husband's family (patrilocal), the wife's family (matrilocal), or independently. This is further influenced by whether marriage is exogamous, meaning that one marries only outside one's village or area, or endogamous, meaning marrying within. When a woman is forced to leave her family's home or compound, and often her village of birth, to go to live with her husband's family, she loses crucial access to friendship networks and family members who could support her in times of need. She is often at the whim of her husband and his family. When husbands live with their wive's families they are held accountable for their behavior, and the wife has greater access to sympathetic help.

An interesting study of the families of Turkish men who migrated as 'guest workers' to western Europe showed how the position of women changed enormously as their role within the family changed. Before the men's long-term absences, the home was defined and controlled by the husband and his family. Women were dependent and in a servile role. After their absence the wives became the nucleus that held the family together, and their homes became the homes that men came back to. The women controlled the flow of cash as it came from Europe, made all the decisions concerning the household expenses and the children, and dealt with institutions such as banks and post offices for the first time. Consequently, they became increasingly sophisticated and developed new skills which made them less dependent on their husbands when they returned. It is interesting, also, to note that when some of these women migrated to Europe, they adapted far more rapidly than the men, perhaps because they had had to learn how to adapt to new and hostile situations after moving into their husbands' families.[116]

Thus residence plays a large part in determining women's ability to develop networks. The strength of women's networks, in turn, can have a tremendous effect on women's ability to get support and to change their lives. Among cultures and within each culture, there is a great variation in how these institutions combine and how they affect women's access to resources and ability to change their lives. What is more important to ask, in looking at any family, is who controls women's lives and the work that they do, and who is benefiting from the underlying power relation?

Familial v. Social power

In some societies (such as those that are less class-stratified or where families produce most of what they consume) there is no great separation between family and community. In these societies authority held by women in the family represents authority in the community.

In most societies there is a separation, but the authority women hold within the family can also affect the power women hold in their communities. Power within the family can enable women to learn new skills and to form support networks that can be used to advocate for women's needs and rights on both an individual and collective basis outside the home. For example, in describing the lives of women in southern Italy, Ann Cornelisen notes:[117]

Alone, the decisions are theirs. They farm the land, sell what they judge should be sold and blackmail the authorities into supplying what they feel is their right.

Their husbands will be very conservative about the use of
any money left over from what they have sent home . . . .
Like land, a house is 'real' and will always have a value.
The women may be less cautious. I have known some who
became entrepreneurs in a small way, buying bits of land
and hiring men to work it at day wages. One of their great
pleasures is being able to fire the men and replace them
with others more willing to work.

Cornelisen feels that women's authority over day-to-day
existence in many western and Catholic peasant societies
gives women such power that they live in a 'matriarchy', felt
by everyone if not formally recognized.[118] Yet she does not
examine the implications of life outside this sphere.

It is important to distinguish between power exerted
within the family which is part of a woman's job in the
home, and power to affect the forces which ultimately
govern her life. In men's absence, whether they live and work
in areas away from their homes or simply during their daily
absences from the home, women exercise a great deal of
authority over their children and in household matters. Yet
the authority wielded in men's absence does not always
prevail upon their return, nor does it enable women to
exercise authority over their husbands or the Italian government or Church. Men maintain control over the relationships
with the institutions that affect their village from the outside.

What this power in the home comes down to is that women
carry the burden of sustaining the family and have decision-
making power over those tasks that comprise their workloads, whether it consists of disciplining children, budgeting
money sent by their husbands, or investing it in potentially
lucrative projects. But only when the skills and networks
developed by women within the family are converted into
resources valuable to the society outside the home, do they
amount to real power within their communities. As one
Italian woman replied to Cornelisen's theory:[119]

As for the women. Put any label you want on it. It
amounts to the same thing: we do whatever no one else
has done. That's what we're taught; that's what we're

supposed to do. Men work and talk about politics. We
do the rest. If we have to decide, that's fair too. Why
should we do all the work and not decide? We decide, but
we don't have to talk about it in the Piazza. Call that
power, if you want to. To us it's just killing work.

These women do the same killing women's work that
keeps every society going though it gives them some advantages in men's absence. But nowhere does this burden translate
into equal power in all spheres – to the contrary, it represents
women's servant status in relation to men across cultures.

Slavery's underpinnings: rule by force

With No Immediate Cause [120]
        by *Ntozake Shange*

every 3 minutes a woman is beaten
every five minutes a
woman is raped/every ten minutes
a lil girl is molested
yet i rode the subway today
i sat next to an old man who
may have beaten his old wife
3 minutes ago or 3 days/30 years ago
he might have sodomized his
daughter but i sat there
cuz the young men on the train
might beat some young women
later in the day or tomorrow
i might not shut my door fast
enuf/push hard enuf
every 3 minutes it happens
some woman's innocence
rushes to her cheeks/pours from her mouth
like the betsy wetsy dolls have been torn
apart/their mouths
menses red and split/every
three minutes a shoulder
is jammed through plaster & the oven door/

chairs push thru the rib cage/hot water or
boiling sperm decorate her body
i rode the subway today
& bought a paper from a
man who might
have held his old lady onto
a hot pressing iron/i dont know
maybe he catches lil girls in the
park & rips open their behinds
with steel rods/i cant decide
what he might have done i only
know every 3 minutes
every five minutes every 10 minutes/so
i bought the paper
looking for the announcement
the discovery/of the dismembered
woman's body/the
victims have not all been
identified/today they are
naked & dead/refuse to
testify/one girl out of 10's not
coherent/i took the coffee
& spit it up/i found an
announcement/not the woman's
bloated body in the river/floating
not the child bleeding in the
59th street corridor/not the baby
broken on the floor/
    'there is some concern
    that alleged battered women
    might start to murder their
    husbands & lovers with no
    immediate cause'
i spit up   i vomit   i am screaming
we all have immediate cause
every 3 minutes
every 5 minutes
every 10 minutes
every day
women's bodies are found

in alleys & bedrooms/at the top of the stairs
before i ride the subway/buy a paper/drink
coffee/i must know/
have you hurt a woman today
did you beat a woman today
throw a child cross a room
   are the lil girl's panties
   in yr pocket
did you hurt a woman today

i have to ask these obscene questions
the authorities require me to
establish
immediate cause

every three minutes
every five minutes
every ten minutes
every day.

While the bad woman/good woman dichotomy controls
women's consciousness to enforce their unpaid work, and the
family controls women's slavery economically, violence
against women is used as a form of physical coercion to the
same end. Violence is grounded in the need to keep women
working within the spheres determined by the dominant
male system. Violence is used worldwide as a threat and a
punishment for disobedience to that role. Women live in fear
of unprovoked attacks from strange men, verbal abuse and
beatings from male relatives, and forced institutionalization
in mental hospitals. All men, whether or not they use violence
themselves, benefit from women's enforced powerlessness in
the home, the streets, and the workplace.

The link between male violence and female independence
is illustrated by the statement of one senior police official
after the brutal beating of female Jawaharlal Nehru University students who were protesting against an increase in
the bus fares of the Delhi Transport Corporation: 'You see,
women students from JNU deserve to get their legs broken . . . . they drink coffee in the morning and smoke pot in

the evening.'[121]

Individual, interpersonal acts of violence against women are the lowest common denominator, the bottom line of male/female social relations in the sense that no matter what the social and economic standing of any male in any society, he can ultimately use physical force to try to force a woman to submit to his will. Though most rapes, for example, occur between people of the same class or race, sexual harassment is also perpetuated by middle- and upper-class men on women who work for them. But upper-class women are certainly not invulnerable. A rich woman is as subject to beatings from her husband, street harassment and pornographic descriptions of her life as any other woman. Her class privilege hasn't freed her, nor does it 'protect' her from any man, no matter what his class status.

Rape

Susan Brownmiller, in *Against Our Will: Men, Women and Rape*, aptly called rapists the 'shock troops' of male society.[122] Because one woman can be raped, all are controlled by the fear of rape.[123] Women's mobility is thus limited, and they are excluded from many night jobs and parts of town that might give them more economic opportunities. In Brazil the Mundurucu men threaten to punish with gang rape any woman who walks unaccompanied by other women. This is not considered 'rape,' because it is not done by 'force.' From their point of view, a woman knows her socially ascribed limitations and has no choice but to submit to her punishment if she oversteps these limitations. Women's social conformity and collective productivity is reinforced by their need to travel to and from the fields in groups to avoid this punishment.[124] In Chapter 3 we mentioned that the method in Ethiopia of obtaining wives through kidnap and rape limits many women's mobility even more severely, since many women live on isolated farms where there are no other women with whom they could walk. This results in severe immobility in other areas of their lives as well because the few opportunities that exist for the training and education of young women are usually miles away from their homes.[125]

Rape has been used cross-culturally to single out women with reprisals for their independent behavior which directly or indirectly threatens the male economic power structure, and as retaliation against the property of other men. In Andhra Pradesh in India, gang rape was used by landlord's lackeys to try to suppress peasant organizing in which women were deeply involved. The Sanghams, or peasant organizations, were agitating for higher wages against illegal land-holdings, bribes, fines, and compulsory labor extracted by the landlords. One young woman, Kankamma, the president of the Sangham in her village, described the effects of the threats of rape by the landlord's lackeys and even by relatives and friends opposed to the organizing:

> The dora's [landlord's] goondas of our own caste have
> vowed to rape us, to beat us, and to ransack our houses.
> They are not letting us live in our homes. Nor are they
> allowing us to enter the village. After the Ryotu Mahila
> Sangham was formed, Kondiah, my own cousin, took an
> oath that he would rape me whenever he got the chance.

Sudesh Vaid, in her article, 'Breaking Fear's Silence,' in which the above incidents were cited, goes on to clarify women's participation in the Sanghams in 1978:[126]

> The Mahila Sanghams, however, meet a specific need
> of the women of the poorer classes who are sexually
> abused by men of the upper classes. There are districts
> in this region where it is customary to send a girl to
> the landlord when she attains puberty. Village women
> are also made available to the landlord when his wife is
> pregnant. Over the years, this sexual exploitation by the
> upper class men has become part of the daily life of the
> poorer women. But now women are beginning to resist
> and revolt.
>   The Attacks on Rajavva and other women activists are,
> on the one hand, part of the repression of the movement
> of the poor peasants. They are also specifically directed
> against these women as women who are defying 'old
> customs' and practices which are degrading to the female

sex. The repression has taken the form of sexual violence, either threatened or actual – from molestation to rape.

The women have no recourse when raped. Family members who try to intervene in their behalf are beaten as well. The police, working in the interests of the landlords, themselves often beat, rape and gang rape the village women. In Bihar, in late 1978, the Central Reserve Police Force and Bihar Police forcibly entered the homes of people living in a village where peasants had been cultivating the land of a local landowner. The police beat, gang raped and sexually tortured the women, and opened fire on some of the men and used their bayonets. The incident, however, was denied in Parliament,[127] indicating state sanction of such tactics.

When violence towards women is socially accepted, it reinforces women's tendency to believe that things will only get worse than they already are if they behave independently. Women often internalize the dominant view of recipients of male violence as 'bad women', who are overstepping their boundaries, and blame themselves for acts committed against them. This is especially true in cultures dominated by the Catholic church:[128]

> The idea of rape as God's punishment for some previous
> sin or the equating of rape with the sex act arose directly
> from the teaching of the Church, and its emphasis on
> virginity and purity of mind and body. The Hispana who
> is raped then feels that she should not have ventured
> out into a negative and hostile world, that she has
> committed a sin by having sex with an inappropriate
> partner, and that she is either being punished by God for
> something terrible that she has already done or she is
> going to be punished because she was raped.

A virgin who has been raped faces further male disapproval, and many a man will not consider her for marriage, since she 'has been used.'[129]

> The Puerto Rican woman learns, from a very early age,
> that in her virginity are represented her dignity, honor,

respect and femaleness. At the same time, when a woman is dishonored, the family as a collective suffers the public humiliation, shame and disgrace.

In western cultures, and especially the United States, everyone is familiar with picking up the newspaper and reading stories of the rape, maiming, dismemberment and murder of women. In the winter and spring of 1979 a series of fourteen brutal murders, all but one of black women in the Boston area, were covered by the media in such a way as to blame the victims. Women involved in community response to the murders were appalled by the coverage and felt that:[130]

> They wrote about the women as though some deserved what they got and some didn't. The women who were killed got no respect. What they didn't write about was what kind of life is this where women, any woman, can't walk on the streets anymore.

The false distinctions the coverage made between the victims feeds into the common myth that some women provoke and deserve their abuse:[131]

> Black people, especially older blacks, are now believing that this only happens to women who are or have been in trouble and that it could never happen to them - that if you are a 'good girl' it won't happen.

Men's power over women makes tham treat women as objects on which they can act out any of their feelings. Rape is punished only to the extent that women have power in the society at large. In the USA an estimated one out of three women are raped in the course of their lives. More than 95 per cent of men arrested for rape are found to be 'psychologically normal' by testing. According to FBI statistics, in 1973 47 per cent of those arrested for rape were acquitted, and of 36 per cent found guilty, only 2 per cent served terms for rape, and 17 per cent for lesser offenses.[132] By contrast, in traditional Ewé society, rapes occur rarely and only in large towns. Because in small communities everyone is known, rape could only occur if sanctioned by the community since women's reproductive capacity is respected and women's familial and friendship networks serve to uphold their status such as it is. Rape is not tolerated.

Contrary to popular belief, most rapists are not strangers, but acquaintances, family members and friends. In the United States, for example, 45 per cent of reported rapes occur in the home, and 67 per cent of rapists are known by the victim.[133] One out of four women are sexually abused before the age of eighteen (some statistics say before twelve), 75 per cent of the time by someone they know, and 38 per cent of the time by a family member.[134] In addition, married women are often raped by their husbands, though few countries consider this a crime. The dynamics of wives' and daughters' economic dependence on their assailants highlights the relationship of economic control: women are property to be used by their owner as he wishes. It also makes clear the relationship of economic dependence to social and inter-personal dependence, maintained through control of financial resources as well as violence, fear and intimidation.

Hispanic women living in the USA who are not USA citizens, face the additional problem of fear of deportation. Because of their social and legal status, the pattern of rape is different than that for most other American women. They are raped most often by gangs, supervisors and immigration officials. For them, the phenomenon of blaming the victim, so common in instances of violence against women, takes on a triple jeopardy. Along with social and familial ostracization, and enormous feelings of guilt, women encounter hostility from the authorities or services to whom they go for help, and fear of deportation if reporting rape by a supervisor or immigration official.

Sexual assault and harassment

Eve-teasing (physical and verbal molestation of women) and rape are manifestations of the same attitude which denies us our humanity, which reduces us to mere objects: mere bodies to be used or abused.

If these bodies are not on piecemeal sale for a few rupees, or life-time sale with a dowry thrown in, then they can be trespassed on, and sampled at will. If they are not the well-guarded property of one man, then any man is free to buy them if he can, or to grab them if he can't.

And this man is not necessarily a pervert, a 'goonda.' He could be the respectable elderly gentleman edging closer to you in the cinema; anonymous hands pinching you in the bus; a boyfriend who expresses his love for you by 'screwing' you or any girl who comes his way, while his father keeps a virgin bride ready for him. He is often our employer, whose molestation we have to put up with to hold the job; the landlord whose fields we cultivate, the policeman we go to for help. And quite often, 'it's all in the family' – an uncle, a cousin, a father-in-law. There was a recent report from Delhi of a father who raped his 15-year-old daughter. And of course our own husbands, thanks to whom sexual violence and rape have become a part of our lives . . . . Eve-teasing . . . . is a way of spitting out contempt at us for being women. And this is true whether the remark hurled at us is 'Hello, Sweety' or an obscenity. It is an act of aggression, psychological and physical, to humiliate and terrify us . . . . It is a systematic attempt to destroy our sense of self . . . . sexual violence is a conscious process of intimidation to keep women oppressed and in a permanent state of fear.

Editorial by Manushi, *A Journal about
Women and Society*, New Delhi[135]

Harassment and sexual assault are used to influence women's behavior in a constant, more generalized, way than actual rape. It may be used by men at any time to express their opinions that women 'belong in the home,' that they should serve all men at all times, or that sexual services are part of any employment a women might have.

Street harassment reinforces this dynamic each time a woman steps out of her house in most societies. In her article, 'Sexual Assault' Norma Boujouen wrote:[136]

The hispanic woman, wherever she goes, finds herself a subject of verbal abuse by the man. 'Piropos' or little phrases that insult the dignity of the woman as a person provide strong proof of the daily humiliation suffered by many women . . . . The street behavior of the hispanic men indicates the acceptance of sexual harassment as part of daily life. Even when this behavior is totally unacceptable to the woman, she chooses not to take action for fear of retaliation.

A Moroccan female University student describes male hostility towards female independence when she and six other women were harassed on their way to their dormitory at midnight, by two drunk men who tried to force some of them into a car:[137]

Scared to death, we started fighting back. For if a woman loses her virginity, no matter under what circumstances, even rape, she will dishonor the entire family, and will have a hard time convincing a future husband - if she ever finds one - of her innocence. A police car stopped at first. We welcomed the police and asked for protection. The police looked at us and then walked over to the men. They started a conversation about the indecency of 'modern girls' who are bringing shame on the society, violating traditional rituals, challenging the Koran rules, and 'screaming for help after all that' . . . . A growing number of educated women, who come mainly from the middle and upper class, can afford to go to school, discard the veil, and get a job. But they will never be liberated (by that alone). Any police officer, obnoxious judge, or mildly capricious head of state, could at any moment withdraw their liberties by bringing forward the necessity to respect tradition.

Sexual harassment of female students also occurs within universities, perpetuated by professors with the promise of good grades and recommendations in return for sexual favors (and conversely, punishment for refusal with bad recommendations).[138]

When this dynamic occurs at the workplace, women who are economically dependent on their assailants have little recourse other than giving up their jobs. Nine out of ten women responding to a survey in the United States said that they had received unwanted attentions on the job, from fellow employees as well as supervisors and employers.[139]

Catherine MacKinnon has observed in her book, *Sexual Harassment of Working Women*, that verbal and physical harassment from employers is predictable with women's present status:[140]

> Specifically, if part of the reason a woman is hired is to be pleasing to a male boss, whose notion of a qualified worker merges with a sexist notion of the proper role of women, it is hardly surprising that sexual intimacy, forced when necessary, would be considered part of her duties and his privileges . . . . women tend to be economically valued according to men's perceptions of their potential to be sexually harassed. They are, in effect, required to 'ask for it.' . . . . the very qualities which men find sexually attractive in women they harass . . . . are the real qualifications for the jobs for which they hire them.

The fear of reporting sexual harassment can stem from the fear of losing a job or job benefits, or of worsening one's working conditions. Waitresses are especially vulnerable to workplace harassment because their income is so dependent on tips. One waitress explained:[141]

> [Men think] they have a right to touch me, or proposition me because I'm a waitress. Why do women have to put up with this sort of thing, anyway? You aren't in a position to say 'get your crummy hands off me' because you need the tips. That's what a waitress job is all about.

When another waitress served a customer who reached up her skirt, she asked her manager for protection in future incidents, and he also harassed her. 'They put me on probation, as if I was the guilty one. Then things went from bad to worse. I got lousy tables and bad hours.'[142] In this example, the power of male bonding and sanction of sexual harassment is particularly overt, though it often takes place in more subtle and institutional ways. Men may pretend they haven't seen, that nothing has happened, or that a woman is making something up out of nothing. Men's interest in allowing harassment to continue is rooted in the implicit assumption that women are put on earth to service them and their needs, including their sexual desires and fantasies.

Because women usually have fewer economic resources than men, men are often in the position to take advantage of their economic privilege. MacKinnon observes that this female vulnerability actually arouses sexual desire in men. It's a part of the male code that women are defenseless, so men know they can get away with it.[143] Much of what makes rape and sexual harassment so hard to prosecute, she points out, is that it is so similar to 'normal' heterosexual encounters. Rather than view this similarity as an indictment of such 'normal' encounters, men see it as a reason why harassment can be condoned:[144]

A crime of sex *is* a crime of power. Sexual harassment (and rape) have everything to do with sexuality. Gender *is* a power division and sexuality is one sphere of its expression. One thing wrong with sexual harassment (and with rape) is that it eroticizes women's subordination. It acts out and deepens the powerlessness of women as a gender, *as women*.

The link between women's vulnerability and male sexual arousal is the clearest in pornography, a four billion dollar annual industry in the USA alone.[145] In the music industry, record album covers depicting violence against women (rape, women bloodied, in chains, etc.) are designed to sell records to boys from the ages of 13 to 17.[146] This advertising, in capitalizing on violent pornography, is socializing the next generation of rapists and woman-beaters. This is also true of parts of the fashion industry: mannequins in store windows depict women being brutalized in 'witty' and 'sophisticated' style.[147] The volume of pornographic literature and movies attests to the number of men already socialized to equate their eroticism with women's objectification, submission and abuse.

Wife-beating

> Disobedient wives were to be soundly thrashed, but not 'straight on the face or on the ear', since the husband would be sorely disadvantaged should his spouse thus become blind or deaf or otherwise incapacitated. 'Keep to the whip,' enjoined the Code, 'and choose carefully where to strike.'
>
> Sixteenth century Russian domestic code[148]

Women who are beaten by their husbands or lovers are blamed implicitly for not being good wives and mothers and conforming to men's expectations of them. Wife-beating exists in almost every culture on earth: A woman is beaten every eighteen seconds in the United States alone, and there are as many cultural variations of the North African expression, 'Women and camels need to be beaten,' as there are countries. In France, it's 'Women, like walnut trees, should be beaten every day.' An old Chinese saying goes, 'A wife married is like a pony bought; I'll ride her and whip her as I like.'

The economics of wife-beating can be seen clearly in an example from Bangladesh. There women are considered economic liabilities because their work in and around the home rarely brings in wages. Consequently, women, forced to rely on their husbands for economic support, are terrified that their husbands will divorce them. The stigma of divorce, and most parents' inability to pay a second dowry, make it extremely difficult for women to remarry. Husbands also threaten their wives with polygyny, though this is so expensive that few can afford it. Widows and divorced women are often reduced to begging for food and travelling from village to village, a constant reminder to married women of the fate that could await them. Most women choose, out of necessity, to remain obedient to their husbands and are powerless to do anything about beatings they receive. When one woman was beaten by her husband with a stool after she refused to tell him if the rice was ready, she could do nothing but share her anger with a neighbor, 'In this country men beat you over nothing at all.'[149]

Though the circumstances of women in other parts of the world are different, the same economic and social factors combine to sanction men's violence towards their wives, and to keep women tied to the home. Wife-beating is used to 'punish' wives for alleged, suspected, or actual acts of independence. It is thus both an overt manifestation of women's slavery in the home and a mechanism for maintaining that slavery. The cross-cultural assumption of women as property is most overt in many Arab countries where men are considered to be within their rights in murdering a wife believed to have been unfaithful. In France, such a murder is considered a 'crime passionnel' and husbands often receive lenient sentences.

It is not surprising to find that wife-beating and other forms of violence against women are most prevalent in cultures where women have minimal and token power. In cultures where women have negotiating power, violence against women is far less prevalent and usually not sanctioned by the community.

Sexual slavery

The sexual enslavement of women (known by the racist misnomer 'white slavery') forces women to perform, involuntarily and without pay, labor that lines the pockets of men all over the world. Kathleen Barry provides a structural framework for understanding seemingly disassociated acts of violence against women as sexual slavery.[150] The international slave trade, prostitution rings and syndicates, pimping, pornography, rape of women and girls, wife-beating, genital mutilation and purdah and polygyny, all fall within her definition of sexual slavery:

> *Female sexual slavery is present in all situations where women or girls cannot change the conditions of their existence; where regardless of how they got into those*

conditions they cannot get out; and where they are subject to sexual violence and exploitation. Sexual slavery, whether it is carried out by international gangs or individual pimps, is a highly criminal and clandestine activity, as is the slavery carried out by fathers and husbands in secret and tolerated. Its setting may be an Arab harem, a German eros center, an American pimp pad or a suburban home.

Barry points out that there is little distinction between local procurement by pimps and international prostitution rings when it comes to many women's arrival in a life of prostitution. (Some women are not controlled by pimps and may choose prostitution for a number of reasons, including disgust with their low-paid and unpaid jobs as nurses, typists or housewives, because it pays better.) Some are lured by the glitter and glamour of the riches they believe will be theirs. Others turn to it out of desperation for employment, sometimes responding to phony employment agencies offering exciting foreign work, only to find out the nature of their work once they get there. In many countries women are sold to slave traders by parents believing the prospective husband's story that he is taking her off to his home in the city. Others are kidnapped, then drugged, beaten and tortured until they comply with their captors. Wherever a woman's enslavement falls along this continuum, Barry states that:

Together pimping and procuring are perhaps the most ruthless displays of male power and sexual dominance. As practices they go far beyond the merchandising of women's bodies for the market that demands them. Pimping and procuring are the crystallization of misogyny – one of the fullest expressions of male hatred for femaleness. Procuring is a strategy, a tactic for acquiring women and turning them into prostitution; pimping keeps them there.

The trade in women has touched most countries and crossed every ocean and continent, and the variations in the prices for women are just as great. European women are sold in Zanzibar for as much as $10,000, destined for Middle Eastern harems. Ache Indian women from Paraguay are bought for $2.00 and sold for slave labor, and Paraguayan peasant girls bought from poverty-stricken families or promised work in the cities, are sold to brothels in Asunción, Paraguay, Europe or the United States.

Female sexual slavery wouldn't be such big business if there wasn't such an enormous demand in many societies. The largest demand occurs wherever large numbers of men live away from their families: in the military, among travelling businessmen, sailors and immigrant laborers.

Although the British-based Anti-Slavery Society has been bringing word of cases before the UN, and INTERPOL (the international police organization) conducted an international survey on the problem in 1975, international traffic in women for prostitution remains a hidden crime. No one has been able to estimate the total volume of women being sold into prostitution around the world. Yet if the number of gangs and syndicates and the presence of organized crime are any indication, one can assume that it's big money and a booming business.

Institutional and reproductive violence

Nothing's private in a one-room house . . . . I had nine children in that room, back there, and I suppose I'll die there the same way – with all the men in the family sitting around the fire muttering, 'Why doesn't she hurry up about it' . . . . My father, my brothers, my husband's brothers, they all sat there by the fire and drank wine and waited. If you make a sound, if a pain catches you by surprise, or the baby won't come out and you can't stand it and you moan, you've disgraced yourself. You keep a towel shoved in your mouth, and everytime it hurts so bad, you bite down on it and pray to God no noise comes out. I always tied a knot in one end so I could bite real hard, and my sister had a way of crooning and stroking me that made it better . . . . So many times it was all for nothing too. Six of nine died. I could have wailed then – that's all

right – but there are some hurts that stay inside . . . .
Nothing's private here, not birth, not death, not
anything. No matter what any one says, though, you
never get used to it.

Ann Cornelisen,
*Women of the Shadows: the Wives
and Mothers of Southern Italy*[151]

Many women whose behavior defies male boundaries wind up
in institutions where they are 'treated' in the name of health
care. Women in mental institutions and prisons are stigmatized, and given even less respect than women outside of
institutions. Female prisoners in many countries around the
world are subject to special forms of harassment. They are
forced to give birth in prison, their children are taken from
them, and they are sexually tortured and raped. The case of
the North Carolina prisoner, Joan Little, who killed her
jailor as he attempted to rape her, showed clearly that
women are commonly and continuously sexually assaulted
by prison guards in the United States, under the threat of
physical harm or death.[152] In some prisons, up to 80 per cent
of the women are given thorazine, librium, or other drugs
daily to keep them 'manageable.'[153]

Similar abuse of women also takes place in mental hospitals.[154] They are treated worse than male inmates are, because
they are expected to conform to the role of docile woman.
Women who refuse treatment, who fight back, who express
their anger can then be sent to a third institution, the violent
wards of mental institutions or prisons.[155] Thus, women who
don't accept traditional forms of oppression and express
anger, can end up in repressive environments geared to knock
all their anger out of them and thus 'rehabilitate' them to
society's purposes.

Reproductive violence stems from men's attempts to control women's sexuality and production of children to men's
economic advantage. One form seldom publicized is that
of genital mutilation. Fran Hosken, who has extensively
researched the problem, states that it ranges from sunna
circumcision, involving removal of the prepuce and tip of the
clitoris, to clitoridectomy and infibulation.[156] Women who

have been infibulated must be cut open to permit intercourse and child-birth, and are often sewn up again after each birth. All these forms of genital mutilation are found throughout Africa and in parts of South America, Australia and Southeast Asia, and clitoridectomies were common in the west as a form of 'therapy' until recently ('love surgery' is the contemporary version – whereby the angle of the vaginal opening is changed to increase penile/clitoral contact). All forms of genital mutilation result in a high risk of infection, hemorrhage shock and death due to loss of blood, as well as the possibility of death in child-birth for both woman and child. It is estimated that between 25 and 30 million women in Africa alone are subjected to one form of genital mutilation or another. Its intentions are clearly to reduce and control sexual response in women for the maintenance of male imposed morality and 'faithfulness' of daughters and wives. Since genital mutilation, especially its severest forms, is most frequent in cultures where women are highly segregated from men, it is very probable that it is intended not only to restructure women's sexuality to men's pleasure, but to limit women's sexual relations with other *women*. In a biographical account of one woman's life in a Turkish harem, lesbian relationships are referred to, and are probably prevalent in many other cultures, though not yet widely documented.[157] In thus attempting to limit female sexuality, genital mutilation helps to maintain women's relationship as property to men.

The issue of who controls women's bodies, from standards of health care to reproductive rights, has historically been pivotal to demands by women for control over their own lives. Husbands, like cultures at large, have used violence and control directly or indirectly to insure that women remain pregnant, and therefore tied to the home, where they perform free services.

The ultimate violence – murder – is often used against women who cannot be controlled in other ways. In Europe during the Middle Ages, at least seven million women were burned at the stake as 'witches' by the Catholic Church and developing European nations, for the 'crimes of healing, birth control, midwifery, and peasant organizing. Before the massacre groups of women met, travelling all over Europe to participate in rituals and learn skills from each other.[158] The incredible number of killings helped to wrest the traditional control of medicine away from women into the hands of the rising male medical profession and scientific establishment. They have been making money hand over fist and controlling women's health care ever since.

Men's control over women begins with their control over women's *existence* with female infanticide. In many cultures where women are seen as financial burdens, female infants are killed at birth (as in pre-revolutionary China where a box of clean ashes was put next to the birthing bed to suffocate the child if it was a girl) or slowly through the withholding of nutritional foods (as in India). And later in life, in cultures where women are seen to have no function except through their relationships to their husbands, they must kill themselves upon their husband's funeral pyre. Men's attempts to control the means of reproduction are manifested in a variety of institutions, from church doctrines and health care systems, to socially sanctioned abuse and brutality. Because many men only value women as producers of children, their negative feelings toward women are often expressed in violence towards their reproductive organs. The violence used by men in many societies against women who are pregnant or who have recently borne children shows this ambivalence towards women's reproduction. In the USA female slaves were violently abused as *women* by slaveholders to keep them hard at work, as well as being raped by overseers and plantation owners. One slave, for example, told of how women with suckling children they'd left at home were beaten across their breasts which were full of milk, because they couldn't keep up with the other hands.[159]

Keeping women 'barefoot and pregnant' has been used historically and cross culturally to control women's mobility, to keep them economically dependent and to use them as mere producers of workers and heirs. Leah Fritz noted in her book *Dreamers and Dealers, An Intimate Appraisal of the Women's Movement* that one basis of patriarchal economies is that:[160]

human life has no intrinsic value, ... the purpose of
labor is not to sustain human life . . . . people are valued
only for what they can produce. (The ultimate corruption
of this product-worship is the preference for an embryo
over the woman, the denial of a human being's right.
not to produce.)

A West Indian woman with 14 children described what
a life of child-bearing had done to her:[161]

If I had my life to live again I would not have one single
child . . . . You know what it is to lie down every night
and try to get into a comfortable position to sleep. Year
in, year out. You know what it is to be heavy on your
feet, dragging yourself around, feeling hot and sweaty,
your stomach big and heavy, year after year . . . . You
know what it is to have six children round you in the
house . . . . Lordy, they round your foot . . . . Then you
send them to school, and before you make two turns in
the house and hustle and prepare something for them to
eat, they come home for lunch. Lunch. What lunch. You
could never have enough to feed them all. I tired with
children. Tired. Tired.

Control over women's reproduction has been exerted by
male institutions that deprive many women of their ability
to produce children, just as others have been forced to bear
children. Many population control programs in recent years
have responded to women's requests for help in controlling
pregnancies through massive sterilization programs rather
than making the range of birth control methods accessible to
women. Though ostensibly a response to women's real need
to exert more control over their reproductivity, such programs have in fact wrested the control away from women and
put it in the hands of doctors, social scientists, and governments who determine at what point a woman will be unable
to bear children. Women seeking help with birth control are
sometimes told that the sterilization operation is reversible,
and consent to an operation that they barely understand.
    Sterilization abuse has also occurred without any desire for

birth control on the part of the woman. In many parts of the world, women are sterilized unknowingly, during clinic visits, or immediately after a difficult childbirth. (In such cases women may be asked during or just after the birth whether they want to endure that kind of pain again. When the response is 'no,' they are asked to sign a form without knowing its intent, to 'ensure' that this pain won't happen again.)

The violent methods used to control women's function as producers of children are understood to be an essential part of the economy by men in positions of power. The number of children produced determines the number of people that are at productive ages relative to 'unproductive' ages. The distribution of children within races is also very important to those in power, since it can increase disparities between groups, strengthen the political position of minorities, etc. Poor women, especially third-world women, in the USA have been systematically prevented from having children.[162]

20 per cent of married black and Chicana women under the age of 45, and 14 per cent of all Native American women have been sterilized (often without their consent) compared to 7 per cent of married (poor) white women.[163] (In contrast, white middle-class women often have to fight for their right to sterilization as those in power try to encourage them to have greater numbers of children.)[164] The policy of sterilization rather than birth control has become frequent in recent years and has been extended by the USA to many other parts of the world. In Puerto Rico over one-third of the women of child-bearing age have been sterilized. In Brazil more than one million women were sterilized with the help of money from the United States Agency for International Development.[165] Between 1965 and 1975, the USA government spent $732.4 million on 'assistance to population programs in developing countries.'[166]

This 'aid' takes place at the same time that traditional forms of birth control have become obsolete with increasing westernization, and other alternative forms of birth control are not made available. Traditional forms of birth control, though often extremely oppressive to women, did serve to limit the birth-rate without taking away women's reproductive abilities. Taboos on sexual intercourse (including intercourse during nursing), prolonged lactation, herbal and sheath birth control, infanticide and induced abortions, all served to limit and sometimes reduce the birth-rate. Population planning programs which choose to provide permanent sterilization (rather than also making available safe forms of birth control such as the diaphragm, or less safe methods such as the pill and IUD) take the control of reproduction away from the women themselves.

Reproductive violence also occurs when women are denied access to safe abortions. Abortions in the USA, for example, are becoming harder for poor and third-world women to obtain. Up until 1978 the Department of Health Education and Welfare paid individual states 90 per cent of the costs of sterilizations for poor women and only 50 per cent of the cost of an abortion[167] (and now in the wake of the anti-abortion movement, many states have cut off all abortion funding).

These activities are not needed as the result of a 'population explosion.' Studies show that improvements in women's status are more effective in lowering birth-rates than are population programs.[168] When women have greater access to resources and a higher income, children are less necessary as current workers and insurance against the future. With more education, women are more aware of birth control options and, with a higher status, they are less dependent on producing children to prove their own worth. Funds for the education of women would do more to raise standards of living equitably and lower the birth-rate, than sterilization programs.

Like other forms of violence against women, this physical coercion keeps women in the economic position men have defined for them. As slaves, women have no more control over the numbers and spacing of their children than they do over the conditions of their work in the home, or freedom of movement outside the home. Men control women's behavior, individually and institutionally, to maintain their economic productivity at the optimum level.

5 *She who sows does not reap*

Behind every great man stands a woman.
> Anonymous

A poster made in China says that women hold
up half the sky. I find this slogan both
condescending and untrue. The execution of *all*
the real needs of humanity has been our burden.
> Leah Fritz,
> *Dreamers and Dealers*[1]

If women are really doing work, people have argued smugly,
then what do they *produce*? To answer this question we must
reconsider what we mean by work and productivity, and
closely examine who is benefiting by the work that women
do. As one sociologist pointed out, 'while there are no ready
measures to analyze women's contributions through their
"nonproductive" labor to a family's or a nation's ability to
produce, no one expects to get along without these unmeasure-
able contributions.'[2]

Services: those unmeasurable contributions

Teeleza, mwan'a ka, ni ku laele
Ona koo ko ya u tiise lubasi lwa munn'a hao
Lutimbo lu maswe, Lusebo lu maswe ku ba manyalo
Muta ni ta shwa u ta ni nahana
Makete, mwan'a ka, Ku fiyela mwa ndu ki nto ya niti
Mikeke ya hao, Libyana za hao u no li tapisa
Ki bona bupilo bwa kwa manyalo.

> Listen to my advice, my child;
> The marriage you are going to enter
> Requires you to respect your husband's family.
> Hatred is very bad.
> It is also bad to gossip about your husband's family.
> When I die, you will remember me and my advice.
> Tidiness is very important,
> Keep your husband's cloth clean,
> Dishes and household utensils should be clean also,
> Do not forget to sweep your house;
> These are the responsibilities of a married woman.
>
> Lozi folk song, Zambia[3]

Housework

> What bothered her was not that the tasks that had to be
> done were exerting. It was not even that they were
> tedious. It was that she felt that the three others lived
> their lives and she went around after them cleaning up
> their mess. She was an unpaid servant, expected to do a
> superlative job. In return, she was permitted to call this
> house hers. But so did they.
>
> Marilyn French, *The Women's Room*[4]

Much of what women do is service work; yet because it is
done within their homes or compounds for members of their
own family, it is not considered to be service work in the
traditional sense of the word. It is considered 'personal' and
no compensation is given. Even though most of what women
produce is used by others, no exchange is visible outside the
family. When a woman prepares meals for her own family,
it is seen as an act of love as well as one of duty. If someone
were to do this same work for non-related people in a restaurant or fu-fu bar (where pounded yams and stew are sold
in West Africa), then it would be seen as productive work by
male standards and paid for – either in the form of a wage
by the restaurant owner, or by the profits of the fu-fu bar
(although it may not be registered in national production and
census statistics, unless women earn a regular salary there).

When a woman cares for sick family members, it is seen as a natural response to a personal or family crisis. Done in a hospital, this would be seen as work and paid for with a wage. When a woman teaches her children how to talk or how to take care of themselves and begin to help with family and social responsibilities, or when she teaches them the customs of her culture, it is seen only as a natural extension of her ability to give birth to, and nurture, the child. When this same work is done in a daycare center for other women's children, or when it is expanded to include reading, writing and other skills in school, then it is seen as work for which money is paid.

Home maintenance work done for one's family is not seen as work. Such work is paid for in others' homes, yet then the wage is poor, since the job is viewed as an unskilled extension of unpaid work in the home. The domestic worker in many countries works all day in others' homes, then returns to her own at night to do the same work free of charge for her family. This work is so despised, and domestic workers are treated so badly, that there is even an international slave trade in domestic workers. Many women acquired in third-world countries are sent to Europe and the United States to work as domestics. The Paraguayan peasant women discussed in Chapter 4 are recruited for prostitution at weekends and forced to do domestic work during the week.[5]

And yet the value of women's unpaid work for their families is, in reality, so high that in the United States alone a 1970 survey of Wall Street employees' families found that women spent an average of 99.6 hours a week at housework. (Women from poorer families spend even more). Based on wages that professionals receive for each task, it was estimated that the women's work had an unpaid value of $257.53 each week as shown in Table 3.[6]

In 1979 Evelyn Kaye estimated the same job to be worth about $700 a week, $35,000 a year. To arrive at this figure, she included 98 hours of on-call time for childcare each week, valued at $294, and managerial work, budgeting and planning time, in addition to the kinds of work described below.[7]

The mythology of housework, whether in terms of the

Table 3 Value of women's unpaid work for their families in a 1970 survey of Wall Street employees

Job	Hours per week	Rate per hour	Value per week
Nursemaid	44.5	2.00	89.00
Housekeeper	17.5	3.25	56.88
Cook	13.1	3.25	42.58
Dishwasher	6.2	2.00	12.40
Laundress	5.9	2.50	14.75
Food buyer	3.3	3.50	11.55
Gardener	2.3	3.00	6.90
Chauffeur	2.0	3.25	6.50
Maintenance man	1.7	3.00	5.10
Seamstress	1.3	3.25	4.22
Dietician	1.2	4.50	5.40
Practical nurse	0.6	3.75	2.25
Total	99.6		257.53

maintenance of a western-style condominium or an African compound, declares that housework is a personal service. In all nations the state has 'higher priorities' than paying for women's agricultural or domestic work because they benefit from the present arrangement. (In the USA, for example, if all women were paid for their work in the home at the 1970 survey's rate, the figure would equal between $500 and $650 billion annually, more than half the Gross National Product, and five to six times the military budget of the mid-70s.[8]) Male power structures everywhere thus consider it 'ridiculous' to pay women for their 'natural work.' Objectively, housework is an endless, usually thankless, job encompassing many areas.

In India there is an expression, *aurat ka dukh*, which means 'the sorrow of women.' One 'happily married' woman defined it as follows:[9]

> [It means] having to do the same thing, the same routine
> every day, without any chance of a change. Sometimes
> I just long to get away. Get out and away and just not
> cook and clean for a week. But I can't go . . . . I suppose

it's just our lot. It's a woman's lot to suffer.

Society outside the family benefits economically from this work through the education and care provided for children and through the maintenance of male workers which allows them to return to work clean, fed, clothed and rested at minimal cost to the employers.[10] And there are indirect benefits everywhere.

In 1898, Charlotte Perkins Gilman pointed out this economic relationship:[11]

For a certain percentage of persons to serve other persons, in order that the ones so served may produce more, is a contribution not to be overlooked. The labor of women in the house, certainly, enables men to produce more wealth than they otherwise could; and in this way women are economic factors in society.

In addition to the multiplicity of tasks that women perform in the home, they must coordinate all these services with the needs of their husbands and children – in effect, acting as home managers – a job that increases with modernization.

A woman in India described her experiences living in an urban environment:[12]

In the old days, people would get up, wash, eat and leave. There was no elaborate routine, no tea drinking, for instance. Now the woman has to keep supplying cup after cup the whole day. You have to lay the table in a certain way; you have to prepare all kinds of new-fangled dishes.

In all cultures women share the same general responsibilities, though the specific tasks differ. The preparation of food often involves everything from the cultivation of fields to the gathering of food, firewood and water, pounding, chopping, preserving, and cooking and serving.[13] Women are responsible for childcare, though children may have their own tasks to perform. Younger children are brought to the fields to be watched as the women work. In West Africa, women are responsible for much of the trade that distributes food, clothing and household items. In industrialized countries they iron curtains, decorate houses, help with children's homework and search for bargains. In Kenya, they are responsible for the maintenance of their thatched roofs after the men have done the one-shot job of building them.[14]

Women are responsible for being sensitive to the emotional, as well as the physical needs of their families, nurturing their members, and supporting them in times of trial or conflict, – in essence, supporting the family and keeping it stable. Thelma Awori, the National Secretary of the Uganda Association of Women's Organizations, comments on this demand as articulated by a male African leader in his speech to a women's seminar:[15]

A statement of this nature shows a strong unwillingness
to take responsibility for one's own behavior. In effect
it says, 'My role is to succeed in employment and business,
but you too must get a job or go into business because I
cannot do it alone. And if I fail it is really your fault
because you have made conditions at home so unpleasant
for me. You must also always be prepared to cover the
tracks of my failure by keeping a smiling face and an
appearance of financial and psychological well-being
regardless of what I do.' The woman, therefore, becomes
the scapegoat for all his failures, and not being fully
aware of her situation she fights for equal rights and
thereby becomes a better scapegoat.

The African woman today must get rid of this man-
child on her back. This is the responsibility, the burden.
Equal rights will not rid her of this burden.

Here Awori has gone straight to the heart of the matter: that women's burden comes not from their lack of access to men's world, but to the separation and division of power, benefits and responsibility between men and women, which is rooted in women's role and work in the home.

Agricultural work

The agricultural work that the majority of women around the

world do almost every day is an extension of service work in the home or compound. In some cultures (such as the Ewé culture described previously) where women traditionally held negotiating power, their childcare and agricultural work have been highly valued as work. But increasingly, this perception of women's work and contribution is being eroded, as colonialism and development have superimposed western standards, and economic relations onto these cultures. Women are 50 to 90 per cent of the agricultural labor force in much of sub-Saharan Africa, South-east Asia and parts of Latin America. They do much of the agricultural work on their families' land that sustains each family, and consequently the economy. Yet even when they are producing most of the family's food, it is not considered productive labor because the exchange takes place within the family. In these parts of the world the system of cultivation is called 'shifting cultivation,' and there is enough land per household to let some lie fallow after it decreases in productivity, while cultivating another piece of land in its stead. Ester Boserup points out that here the agricultural work is done largely by women and is difficult, repetitious and enjoys little help from newer technological methods. For example, women in Uganda work 450 per cent the number of hours that men do in agriculture. In Gambia, the percentage rose from 168 per cent in 1949 to 213 per cent in 1962.[16]

In much of Asia, North Africa, the Middle East and Latin America where the population is denser, and shifting cultivation is no longer possible, the use of the plough and domesticated animals is the main form of agriculture. In these cultures where land is far more scarce, the landowning class is often a minority of the population, there is far more class stratification, and much of the agricultural work is done by hired laborers rather than family members. Throughout Asia from 15 to 70 per cent of the agricultural workers are hired laborers.[17] Boserup also points out that in these cultures, most of the agricultural work done within landowning families is by men, and women's work is confined mostly to harvesting and caring for domestic animals. Yet women from poorer and landless families are often obliged to work for the men of wealthier, higher caste families to help with the subsistence needs of their own families. Women comprise as much as 44 per cent of the hired agricultural workers, yet are paid far less than men for the same work.[18]

The fact that men's work usually increases dramatically in all the cultures which move from shifting to plough agriculture is largely held responsible for men's reluctance to change in response to encouragement from many 'development' programs. The view inherent in the old Arab saying that 'a plough never enters the farm without servitude entering too'[19] exposes clearly the male concern that they might be forced to work on other men's farms, totally disregarding the existing servitude of women which makes men's comparative leisure possible.

In very highly populated areas such as Egypt and China, where male labor alone cannot meet the demands of intensive irrigation cultivation, women again do much difficult agricultural work in addition to home maintenance.[20] The economic power this gives women varies with other factors, such as their access to land and income and the degree of power held by women in their culture to impact economic and social policies affecting them. In China, for example, women today have much more economic power than women in societies with the strict division of labor that goes with plough agriculture, which prohibits or impedes their access to land and income.

In industrialized societies, agriculture has become so mechanized that it permanently employs only a few skilled workers. Additional labor is only needed seasonally and is very poorly paid. Less than 5 per cent of farmers or farm managers are women and female agricultural workers earn only half that of male farmers.[21] In Mississippi, USA, for example, black women are paid only $2 and $3 a day for clearing fields.[22]

Additional income

In all societies women are responsible for the work of making ends meet financially, as well as emotionally. The women in non-industrial societies often sell goods they produce, such as woven clothing (Peru) or provide services such as wood gathering (Ethiopia), or meals for travelers (West Africa), all to provide the extra cash necessary to feed and clothe their children if their crops and/or husbands' incomes are not sufficient.

In the Jewish areas of Eastern Europe in the Middle Ages, women:[23]

> had in many cases to furnish a part or the whole of the domestic budget. They thus engaged in all kinds of commercial operations and occupations, [including] money-lending. Noblemen and farmers in need of money frequently applied to them for loans on interest . . . . Congregations as well as private families did not hesitate to appoint them as trustees; communal funds were entrusted to them for administration and investment at their sole discretion.

In the Russian *shtetl* women did work in the home during the early stages of industrialization; they also sold their wares in the market and, according to one study, in the early part of the twentieth century, 15 per cent of Jewish artisans were female. They sold hand-made clothing to neighbors, and dairy products in the market, though this was not noted in census reports because it was inside the ghetto, and involved small quantities.[24]

When Jewish people emigrated to the USA in the late nineteenth century the women continued their traditional work, and expanded into other jobs. 'The businesses of the Jewish community often depended on the unpaid labor of the woman who "minded the store" to relieve her husband,' says Charlotte Baum, adding wryly that:[25]

> women are considered to be 'minding' the store (a passive role) while men are considered to be 'working' in the store (an active role). [While they worked outside the home,] housekeeping chores were taken over by female relatives . . . . These women were also unpaid workers, receiving room and board in exchange for their services but probably not considering themselves employed.

And, like many Gentile women, they often took in boarders to earn money – something rarely regarded as 'work,' since it entailed cleaning, cooking and housekeeping, women's 'natural work.' The Jewish women, because of their poverty, often did this not in large boarding houses but in order to afford three- or four-room apartments. 'Only with the aid of lodgers or boarders could the monthly rent be sustained.' Baum quotes a 1914 study which states that 'the economic area is more nearly an extension of the woman's domain than that of the man. To bustle about in search of a livelihood is merely another form of bustling about managing a home.[26]

In Bangladesh village women do all the hauling of water, childcare, cooking and house-cleaning, as well as the cleaning, drying and husking of rice, which is extremely time-consuming and difficult work. Many women, whose husbands own and work their own land, work long days, even through the noon hour when their husbands rest. But they eat last and receive the least food because their work is not considered an economic contribution. One Bengali mother of six complained to a foreigner living in her village,[27]

> My work is never done. All day I have husked rice, now
> I have to collect firewood and cook. I have a fever and I've
> no time to rest. I'll work until I die. Just work, work,
> work.

Bengali women whose husbands own little or no land have less work to do for their husbands and so try to find work husking rice for wealthier families. They are paid less than men for the same work, yet often enjoy a higher status within the family than do women in wealthier families, because they have their own income, which is sometimes the only income the family receives.

Women everywhere also try to make ends meet by cutting down on expenses, which usually involves increasing domestic work. Their additional work absorbs many of the male government's economic policies. In industrialized countries comparison shopping must be done to counteract the effects of inflation. Women spend more time mending and washing clothes, and learning 16 new ways to make hamburgers more

interesting. In an economic depression women help maintain
the family's standard of living by producing themselves goods
and services that previously would have been purchased.[28] A
1975 survey in Britain found that only 25 per cent of husbands had given their wives an increase in housekeeping
money, though prices and wages had both risen by 26 per
cent and the wives were still expected to make ends meet.[29]

Service work outside the home

When women do service work outside the home, they continue to play the same role of mother/wife, cleaning up after
and tending to the needs of others. Though women throughout the world do every kind of work imaginable, their work
is almost always work that needs to be done over and over,
the menial and repetitive, low-status work that bears little
prestige. Whether it's feeding men over the counter, or doing
laundry, housework, nursing or childcare, women's paid work
mirrors their unpaid role and responsibilities in the home.

The value placed on some women's jobs in the USA by
the government illustrates the low evaluation of the work
involved in comparison to some male jobs:[30]

Foster Mothers, Child Care Attendants, and Nursery
School and Kindergarten teachers supposedly require no
more training or responsibility than Restroom or Parking
Lot Attendants. What is even more appalling is that every
one of these parenting jobs ranks well below Dog Trainer.
The job of a Nurse who works in every major department
in her hospital and assists with surgery and birth is ranked
as slightly less demanding than that of a Hotel Clerk.
Only if she is also a Midwife, qualified to assume all of
the medical responsibilities of childbirth, does she rank as
high as the person who hands out keys behind the
hotel desk.

In Latin America low-income women who have few other
job possibilities available to them are usually obliged to do
domestic work in the homes of women married to wealthy
men. Fully 40 per cent of all non-rural female workers in

Latin America do domestic service work in other people's homes.[31] Similarly, women married to middle-class men who are in need of extra cash must go against social norms encouraging them to stay in the home, and do part-time work for others. Just as in the case of domestic workers, they do for others work which is normally done free for their own families: baking, embroidery, private tutoring and crafts.[32] The only difference is that, due to their class position, their work has higher status and is better paid than that available to lower-income women.

Paid service work mirrors women's traditional emotional work as well as physical work. Adrienne Rich explains:[33]

> When, in an oppressive hierarchy, women are trained for
> and given access only to certain 'service' positions
> (mother, nurse, teacher, social worker, day-care center
> worker – ill-paid, sentimentalized roles) it is chiefly
> women who find themselves facing, in the actual presence
> of living individuals (children, welfare clients, the sick,
> the aging), the consequences of the cruelty and
> indifference of powerful males who control the professions
> and institutions. It is women who are supposed to absorb
> the anger, the hunger, the unmet needs, the psychic and
> physical pain of the human lives which become statistics
> and abstractions in the hands of social scientists,
> government officials, administrators;

Women who are paid for doing secretarial work do much of the same work as wives of businessmen. Paddy Quick, in an article entitled 'Women's Work,' observed:[34]

> The job includes a concern not only with business work,
> but with her boss's social appointments outside the office
> hours, and with his family (remembering birthdays,
> covering up sexual affairs, booking vacations, etc.) She
> will also serve as a 'whipping boy' – someone on whom a
> man can vent his anger and frustrations, or demand a
> smile depending on his mood.

Secretaries also feel much the same way many wives feel

about the work that they do and their role in society. As one secretary said:[35]

> The people you work for make you feel demeaned . . . .
> We are the invisible force who do all the shitwork . . . .
> There's a real paternal attitude towards the secretary.

In the USA 80 per cent of women working outside the home do clerical work. Clerical workers comprise 18 per cent of the work force, amounting to fifteen million people. Yet only 9 per cent of clerical workers in the USA are organized into unions.[36] Because of the stigmas attached to clerical work which are similar to those attached to house mainten-ance work, women have internalized a low opinion of their own value.

Prostitution is another form of service work that carries a great stigma because of the kind of service performed. Although in most cases the service is simply sexual, it often involves massaging the man's ego as well, and both functions carry low social value because they are done for free by wives and the women are thought of as objects. Though the service can at times be well paid, it carries the same stigma, and much of the profit often goes to pimps, brothels or gangs. The Bombay brothels, for example, take away three-quarters of the women's earnings as maintenance charges.[37]

There are also many situations in which women do service work outside the home that is unpaid or paid at a rate well below the minimum pay scale. In the Church females do much of the service work necessary to keep it going – no matter what the denomination. Whether as nuns, active community women, or the wives of rabbis and ministers, women's unpaid labor makes the work of the Churches possible – a function of female religious communities that is seldom acknowledged by anyone other than the women themselves. In the controversy over a Vatican decision prohibiting nuns from distributing Holy Communion during Pope John Paul II's visit to Boston, on his United States tour in October 1979 Rene Smith, a regular distributor of Com-munion at a local community parish, spoke for many when she said, 'I find it very sad we can serve in everyday ways, but

on special occasions we're not good enough.' Rosalie Muschal-
Reinhardt of the national Women's Ordination Conference
summed it up, observing that:[38]

> In cities where archdioceses are asking families to give
> money [to help pay local expenses], they are taking
> women's money. For women to pay for their own
> oppression borders on the absurd . . . . Our outrage is the
> church being built on the invisible work of women.

The organization of all types of service work is such that
women place a low value on their own work and can't
imagine asking for more pay, benefits or control in their
workplaces. In the home women do stressful unspecialized
work and are responsible for co-ordinating a wide variety
of tasks. Outside the home most women do more specialized
service work — small pieces of huge puzzles — They have no
say in work which is not highly valued since it reflects the
unpaid service work in the home.

Children: income, security and the world's future

Kupula kuvava ngati ungaryanga waka
Ncembele e e e
Mwana wamunyako para wakulira mutole ubabe
Ncembele e e e
Ulimile wako wa cizungu cino ukamnonenku
Ncembele e e e

Pounding is tiring.
I would rather be eating than pounding.
Oh women
If you see another woman's child crying,
Don't neglect it – go to care for it.
Oh women
You modern woman without a child,
Go to care for other women's children,
You cannot wait for your own – it will never come.
Oh women
                    Timbuka pounding song, Zambia[39]

As this song illustrates, women's attitudes towards children vary dramatically as the economies in which they live make differing demands on their lives. But the bearing and raising of children is a common experience to women across cultures, and children are one of the most visible things that women produce.

Pregnancy and childbirth, in and of themselves, present health problems – an occupational hazard to women under all but the best of circumstances. The low regard for women's reproductive functions under patriarchal medical and social systems is especially reflected with respect to the birth process. In cultures where women have minimal and token power, there is often very little social support for pregnancy, in the form of lessened physical demands or time off from work with pay, maternity benefits, etc. In cultures where women hold minimal power and for women from low-income backgrounds and minority racial identities in token power countries, the birth process itself often takes place under extremely arduous conditions.

Table 4 reflects the higher death-rate from pregnancy as compared to various forms of contraception in North America.[40]

The death risk and the breakdown of women's health with repeated pregnancies is considerably reduced where the birth process is controlled by women instead of men. In cultures where women hold negotiating power and in token power cultures where some women have access to women-controlled health services, the toll on women's health is far less. This is because women are more informed, and are able to participate more readily in decisions as to the frequency of births and the conditions of giving birth.

Once a child is born a mother has 24-hour responsibility until the child is a self-supporting adult. This includes on-call time, while the mother is sleeping, for she must be available at any moment for a feeding, to soothe nightmares, or deal with illness or other emergencies.

The care of young children is in fact three full-time jobs, as was illustrated by the Norwegian man who requested three home helps from the Labor Exchange. When asked why three, he replied, 'My wife is ill and we have small children so

Table 4   Death rate from pregnancy compared to various forms of contraception in North America

Method	Pregnancies	Deaths due to pregnancy	Deaths due to method	TOTAL
		Women aged 20-34 years (1,000,000 users/year)		
IUD	30,000	7	unknown	7+
Oral con-traceptives	5,000	1	13	14
Diaphragm	120,000	27	0	27
Safe period	240,000	55	0	55
Pregnancy	1,000,000	228	–	228

she has to be on duty 24 hours a day as I am away all week. As each helper works only eight hours, you must send us three.'

Once children grow older, their mother educates them, teaching them language, survival, self-maintenance, social skills, norms, and traditions. If a child lives in a culture where she/he may never go to school, the mother is often responsible for further training the child, especially the girl child, with skills that she will later use to support herself. In many cultures, such as the Ga culture in Ghana, young women are apprenticed to their mothers, whether it be in trading, cloth-weaving and dyeing, or basket-weaving.

Government and business are often seen as being the main recipients of the fully-grown, socialized and trained workers that women have produced.[41] As we have mentioned, in many cultures where families own or have the use of their own land, and labor-intensive agricultural methods are used (such as sub-Saharan Africa and much of South-east Asia), children are highly valued as workers by husbands and fathers as well. In a study done in the Bwamba region of Uganda in East Africa, for example, it was found that men with only one wife cultivated 1.67 acres of land, on the average, while men with two wives cultivated almost twice as

Table 4　(continued)

| Method | Pregnancies | Women aged 35-44 years (1,000,000 users/year) | | |
		Deaths due to pregnancy	Deaths due to method	TOTAL
IUD	30,000	17	unknown	17+
Oral con-traceptives	5,000	3	34	37
Diaphragm	120,000	69	0	69
Safe period	240,000	135	0	135
Pregnancy	1,000,000	576	—	576

much, 2.94 acres.[42] Some of this additional labor and pro-ductivity was provided by sons and daughters, as well as wives. Clearly, in such cultures, a man with several wives and many children will be far more prosperous than a man with only one wife.

Children are not only a great economic asset, but in many cases, a necessity for the work they do around the home, income they bring in, and for financial support later in life in cultures where social security and job pensions are un-known. This is why birth control is seen by many women – in most cases accurately – as economic suicide and disaster, if it does not take place along with other provisions for women's income and security.

In those cultures with plough agriculture done largely by men (mostly Arab, Hindu and pre-revolutionary Chinese) the production of male babies is highly valued because females are not considered an economic asset.[43] Here, while males are current or potential sources of income, daughters are considered liabilities because they must be supported by fathers and husbands, and a dowry paid by the family to the future husband. In pre-Moslem North Africa and pre-revolutionary China, female infanticide and neglect of female children was common and resulted in an uneven sex ratio. In India, in 1921, there were 972 females to 1,000 males, and in 1971, only 930 females to 1,000 males as a result of the treatment of female children. One female sociologist described the importance of male offspring in India by saying, 'The Hindu desire for sons forces women into unwanted pregnancies and denies them control of their sexuality.'[44]

In Bangladesh, sons are so important as an old-age security for their parents that a woman loses her own name upon bearing her first son, and is thereafter called 'mother of so-and-so.' Since newly married couples live with the husband's family, women lose their daughters' help and companionship at an early age, while their sons stay on, working the family land, providing for their parents in old age and, significantly, for their mothers if their fathers die. Because health care is inadequate, women are worn down by bearing at least four or five children to ensure that one or more sons survive. A woman in one Bengali village who had borne eleven children (five of whom had died) exclaimed to a friend,

'Look at me. My hair grows thinner each year and my teeth are falling out. My body is weak. If I have another child, it will ruin me.'[45]

In many cultures, children are extremely important not only as laborers, but as continuations of family lineages. Where large families are extremely prestigious, a woman who produces many children has a far greater status than a woman who bears few or no children.

Men's varying responses to women's ability to bear children can be seen as differing attempts to control the means of reproduction. Either women are valued as producers of children, or control over their reproductive work is valued.

Of TVs and empty stomachs: a higher standard of living?

My husband said he wasn't going to be taken for someone dying of hunger, especially not now when he *almost* has a job. So – if you don't count the cafes – we have the first

(television) set in town, and I hope everybody's impressed
because those time-notes are going to rest heavy on my
stomach for thirty-six months.

> Ann Cornelison,
> *Women of the Shadows, The Wives and
> Mothers of Southern Italy*[46]

Women also produce a higher standard of living for their
families. They make goods which in effect serve as luxury
goods for families who would not be able to afford them if
they had to buy them. In most cultures these 'luxury' goods
actually serve to bring the family's standard of living up from
the biologically defined minimum standard of living – that
which is required to keep the family alive: food, shelter,
clothing, etc. to the culturally defined minimum – that which
is required either to meet social expectations (such as fashionable clothing or home decorations) or that which is required
to survive economically within the cultural context (i.e., a
car to get to work in Los Angeles, a bicycle for an African
man working in a big town). This minimum standard of living
changes from society to society and even within each society,
as the changing 'poverty level' cited by the USA government
shows.[47] For example, gas, electricity and running water,
which are part of the culturally defined minimum in the
USA, are at this time 'luxury' items for the relatively few
families in third-world countries who have them.

In most societies, it is women's and men's work both
which makes possible the biologically defined minimum,
but overwhelmingly women's work which makes the poor
and working-class families able to meet the culturally defined
minimum standards.

Women also make and alter clothing to keep up with the
fashions, covers to hide old and soiled upholstery, and
curtains or plant hangers. Although sometimes men also
contribute to the culturally defined minimum standards,
through doing household repairs or light carpentry, much of
what their energy goes into are items that raise their own
standard of living, which women benefit from less, such as
bicycles or cars used only by men or by women only to
chauffeur and do errands for men and children.

Women who withdraw from the paid labor force as their families become upwardly mobile take on new dimensions in their work, although it is widely assumed that their lives then become simply powder and frills. Their job becomes that of helping to acquire and maintain a higher class status and standard of living for their families. They must attend to their children's education and manage the increasingly complex family activities,[48] including entertaining their husband's friends and 'superiors' as a part of their new class standing. Some of these women do part-time paid work to provide additional income and further raise their families' standard of living. For example, many middle-class women in Mexico City run small shops or give singing or dancing classes.

Frequently, across cultures, women's work makes possible a higher standard of living enjoyed by men alone. Men eat out, drink with the boys, and have their own cars or bicycles, while their wives are at home keeping the household up and caring for the children. In *The Women's Room*, Marilyn French describes this process for white middle-class families in the USA:[49]

> For the men, of course, were experiencing life on a
> different level. Hamp flew around the country for his
> company, so he went first class and ate at expensive
> restaurants and was fawned over by stewardesses and
> waiters; Bill was a navigator for an airline and flew all
> over the world, staying at expensive hotels and resorts,
> eating at fancy restaurants, fawned over by stewardesses
> and waiters. And even Norm and Paul had a good share
> of expensive lunches out, 'company' dinners, and fawning
> over by nurses and secretaries. They brought their
> demands home; they began to see home and the women
> in them as provincial, small-minded, shabby. Increasingly,
> and perhaps inevitably, the equals they had married
> became servants.

Women's subsistence work in many African villages leaves men working in far-away towns freer to spend their wages on bicycles to get to work, radios to hear the news, western clothing to wear to work, drinking, recreation, etc. They also spend money for 'wifely' services in the form of meals out, prostitutes, laundry services, etc. Men enjoy a higher, more westernized standard of living, while the women and children live a more impoverished life-style in the villages. Most of men's wages go into their own consumption, while the total product of women's time goes almost entirely to support not only themselves but also their children, the elderly, and unemployed or retired men. A 1941 study done in Zambia found that 70 per cent of the men spent two-thirds of their adult lives away from their villages, and sent only 10 per cent of their wages back to their families, where three-quarters of the women lived.[50] In Zambia, as long as not more than half the adult men are away from the villages permanently, the farming system can 'function normally.' Around Lake Nyasa, women can sustain the work with 60 to 75 per cent of the men absent.[51]

When husbands leave their wives, alimony and child support payments often are not paid at all, or are quickly discontinued, leaving women with the total burden of child support. 90 per cent of child support payments in the United States are discontinued before the child is self-supporting, 75 per cent after five years and 80 per cent after 10 years.[52] When one considers that 22 per cent of USA households are headed by women, the magnitude of women struggling to support children with no financial help while their husbands usually earn higher incomes is staggering.[53]

So not only does women's work raise the entire family's standard of living to the culturally defined minimum when husbands are living with their families, but when husbands live apart from their families, women's work sustaining the biologically defined minimum often indirectly makes possible a higher standard of living enjoyed only by the absent husbands.

Slavery's profits: potential money

In my yard is a little money tree;
It flowers and it flowers, but none of it's for me.
I rake and hoe and water to keep the tree in health,

And all the neighbor women envy me my wealth.
But all the little dollars growing on that tree
Belong to Norm the Doctor, none of them to me.
                    Marilyn French, *The Women's Room*[54]

Women's work produces a great savings, both to the men
who don't have to pay for household services and to the
entire society which has been organized so that a huge
amount of socially necessary labor is done for free or is
vastly underpaid. The work women do free of charge represents a considerable saving in terms of money that would
have to be spent to maintain a household.

'Potential money' is a term we have developed to describe
that value which accrues to unpaid or underpaid services
performed or goods produced. Potential money represents
savings or profit to the persons or institutions not paying for,
but receiving the benefits of this work. In turn, this value
represents a loss to the person performing the work, though
it is not usually given a monetary value.

This savings is made possible through unpaid and underpaid work. Yet because the economy is structured without
taking it into account – treating it as non-work or less valuable
work – actual cash usually does not exist to pay for it. The
value of potential money exists, but in a latent state, it
can not be utilized without the intervention of an outside
force, just as potential energy exists as a latent force and can
not be used and is not manifested until it is transformed into
kinetic energy. It is a value that has never been monetized
but could be and the economy rests on top of it. The entire
economy is sustained by and functions as a result of this
'invisible' labor.

Traditional economic terms which approach this same idea
are 'goods-in-kind,' 'opportunity costs' and 'use-values.' Use
value does not express the fact that women perform these
functions for others, not for their own use. Potential money
differs from 'goods-in-kind' or Marxist 'use value' in that it
covers services as well as products, and embraces the notion
of benefit to one party and loss to another.

An example of potential money can be seen in the economic value of polygyny in traditional Yoruba society. One

study observes that:[55]

> wives contribute much more to the family income than the
> value of their keep and that the dignity and standing of the
> family is enhanced by an increase of progeny . . . . The
> Yoruba farmer argues that the increased output from his
> farms obtainable *without cash expense when he has wives*
> *to help him* outweighs the economic burden of providing
> more food, more clothing and larger houses (emphasis
> added).

Of course, as we saw earlier (in Table 2), one-fifth of the
Yoruba men provide nothing for their wives at all, thereby
increasing their profits to an even greater extent. The potential money with which Yoruba women provide their husbands
is a savings for the men who do not have to pay them or hire
help. This savings is then used by the men to reinvest in other
wives, land or property.

During and since colonialism, plantation owners in Africa
have made tremendous amounts of potential money through
the unpaid labor of women accompanying their husbands
to plantations, as well as those remaining in villages whose
subsistence agricultural work enabled men to work for less.
In the Congo the family accompaniment of male workers to
plantations has been encouraged since Independence because,
as the report of the Second African Regional Conference of
the International Labour Organization said:[56]

> on plantations and large farms . . . . the women made a
> home, helped to stabilize the workers, helped to feed the
> families by cultivating a small plot of land and were
> available to help in light seasonal agricultural work such as
> harvesting and weeding as wage-earning workers.

Thus, functioning both as an unseen (unpaid) and reserve
labor force, low paid and infrequently used, women's work
has directly contributed to the savings and greater profits
of plantation owners as well as serving their husbands. In
Asia, where solely male migration was not possible, since
the plough system of agriculture required men's presence in

the villages and wet-rice cultivation required both male and female labor, entire families worked in plantations. Here again, women's (and also children's) labor, remunerated at exceedingly low rates, made possible the under-paying of male workers who did not have to send money home. Women's two jobs of home maintenance/childcare and seasonal full-time plantation work make possible both men's leisure time when their seasonal work is finished and high profits by plantation owners by keeping wages down.

Women's unpaid services in the home produce potential money for the government and private industry, which are not required to pay for all the services that produce and maintain the workers that keep the society going. Added to such direct benefits in many countries are the savings from unemployment and retirement benefits not paid to women who have done service work for their husbands all their married lives. Many women then find themselves widowed or divorced without a penny to show for their labors. The Displaced Homemakers Legislation debated in the United States in the 1970s represents an attempt by women to get some of the potential money actually paid to them, but it would be limited to a woman's work after separation from her husband, omitting the many years she has worked for him.[57]

Throughout the world women's underpaid waged work further supplements these savings to the male economies, and in many countries is responsible for billions of dollars worth of profits and savings.

In many countries, women have done much of the least desirable, heaviest and lowest paid work. In Malaya women do the unskilled work of the building trade – moving earth, digging foundations and carrying heavy loads. In many countries women are used for transporting materials on building sites, and in India waggon-loading is traditionally considered a woman's job. In some Latin American and Asian countries women do 25 per cent of the work in mines and are paid less than the poorly-paid men.[58] The same has been true in the past.

In her book, *Woman, Church and State*, Matilda Joslyn Gage wrote in 1893:[59]

England claiming to represent the highest result of
christian civilization shows girls of the most tender years
and married women with infants at the breast working in
the depths of coal mines nearly naked, where harnessed
to trucks they drag loads of coal on their hands and
knees through long low galleries to the pit mouth . . . .
For the same kind of work men are paid three times more
wages than are paid to women.

In the 1970s a survey conducted in two state-owned
factories producing police uniforms in Kanpur revealed that
although the work is considered 'skilled', women are treated
and paid as unskilled labor, their wages falling below the
minimum wage because they are paid according to the
number of finished pieces they produce. There is no sick
leave or maternity leave, and because the women are hired as
'temporary' workers (even though some have been working
there for 15 years), they are not eligible for promotion.
Women attempting to organize unions have been fired, and
the remaining women, many of whom are old, widowed or
not in good health, are terrified of losing their job and so
never even talk about organizing.[60]
Women in prisons throughout the world are paid nothing
or next to nothing for performing services such as laundry,
stitching, and flag-making – work that is not recognized in
employment or production statistics. At the same time,
there exists almost no training to prepare women with skills
that can provide them with alternative sources of income
when they leave prison. Most women prisoners in the USA
are only given 'good time' off their sentences as an incentive
to do the work. And if they refuse to work, they are not
permitted to leave their rooms, and may be put into maximum security units or solitary confinement for their 'disrup-
tive' behavior. Here, again, as with prostitution, the nature of
the service work, the conditions under which it is done and
the stigma attached to the 'bad women's' lives all combine
to provide a justification for their slave labor. That prison
work is close to slave labor is illustrated by the fact that
women in the Ohio Reformatory for Women earn from 2 to
4 cents an hour. Women at the Federal Reformatory at

Alderson, Virginia, receive $15 a month, at the most, for industrial work making road signs, license plates, benches and tables for parks, uniforms, pajamas and bedding for state institutions, etc. Prisons, depending on the locality, and whether they're run by the Federal Government or the county, have different rules, regulations and wage scales, but the average wage for women in prison in the USA is 19 cents an hour, for six or seven days a week's work.[61]

In the USA Federal prison industries are run by a private company, which makes $2.5 million a year from one prison alone, the Federal Reformatory for Women at Alderson, Virginia.[62] The tremendous multi-billion dollar profits would be even greater if the items produced were sold on the open market where they would fetch far higher prices than those paid by the government, the sole buyer.

Low-paid or unpaid prison work, the international slave trade and sexual harassment of working women, all discussed earlier, provide more potential money through women's unpaid and underpaid work.

The production of potential money is also the norm throughout the world for other waged work that women do. In Canada, for example, a study of the trade unions showed that requirements of equal pay for equal work were avoided by systematic segregation of women into separate job categories with the lowest pay and least opportunity for advancement. Another study found that women were not able to attend union meetings where decisions could have been made to help them, because meetings were held at times when women had duties at home.[63] In industrialized countries, women's wages in 1972 were as low as 47.5 per cent of men's in Japan, 59.3 per cent of those of men in Britain, and in 1976 57 per cent of men's in the USA.[64] One study showed that 23 per cent of all United States manufacturing companies' profits – $5.4 billion in 1950 – were made by paying women less than men for their work.[65]

While men play, women pay

[Women's] time is completely absorbed in looking after their families, in child rearing, health care, subsistence farming, trying to earn money to help feed their family. It is the woman who is the beast of burden, who goes to the market to sell the produce, who goes four hours to fetch water, and another two to fetch fuel. She fills many simultaneous roles. For her, there is no time, there are no short-cuts.

Gloria Scott (of World Bank)[66]

In providing services for their children and their husbands, women are, in effect, producing time for them. That time can then be spent in the enjoyment of leisure, governance or creative pursuits, or reinvested to men's economic benefit, as when husbands use the time to increase their cash crops, take on second jobs, or overtime, or socialize with peers and/or superiors to further their career interests. Women perform personal services for men such as food preparation, laundry, and cleaning that men ostensibly do not have time to do for themselves. When the husbands have weekend or vacation time off, or retire, women's work in the home usually increases, and housewives never have vacations from cooking, cleaning or other domestic chores. One study showed that full-time housewives in twelve industrialized countries enjoyed 25 per cent less leisure time than men, and women employed outside the home as well had even less.[67]

The Ethiopian peasant woman described in Chapter 3 begins her day far earlier and ends it far later than her husband and children, in order to do all the work that permits men extra sleeping and socializing time. Asian women working on plantations must work full-time the year round as housewives, and as laborers during the growing season, while their husbands enjoy leisure time after plantation work is over. Women in the North Indian tea gardens work 2 to 4 hours more each day (not including their housework) than their husbands.[68] Husbands of Mazahua migrant women in Mexico City often stop working altogether when their wives' trading is lucrative. They may help carry crates for their wives, but at other times they simply relax or socialize with other men.[69] Chinese husbands in many agricultural communes enjoy leisure time during their lunch hours that is made possible at the expense of their wives, who must do food preparation and childcare during this time. Their situation is not too different from that of the husband and wife who work in Industry City, USA, and return together, whereupon he sits back with a beer and TV show, eating dinner, then goes out with 'the boys,' while she prepares the dinner, cleans up and puts the kids to bed.

Studies of the total number of hours worked weekly by men and women (that claim to include all of women's domestic work) in Asian and African villages show this discrepancy. In the Philippines women worked 61 hours to men's 41 and Uganda women worked 50 hours to men's 23. In only 2 out of 10 sample villages did women work the same number or less hours than men; and it is doubtful that all of women's childcare and home maintenance work was recorded.[70]

Tables 5 and 6 illustrate the extreme differences in men's and women's participation in the rural and modernizing economy in Africa. Women participate as much or more in every type of work except housebuilding, a job which is done sporadically and infrequently, relative to most of the other work covered by the tables. One might assume from these figures that it is men who are doing the rest of the work that is not done by women. To the contrary, a significant amount of the work is done by girls and women over 55, as the second table illustrates in the case of Zaire, making the female to male ratio of work even more dramatic.

Table 5   Participation by women in the traditional rural and modernizing economy in Africa[71]

Responsibility	Unit of participation*
A *Production/supply/distribution*	
1 Food production	0.70
2 Domestic food storage	0.50
3 Food processing	1.00
4 Animal husbandry	0.50
5 Marketing	0.60
6 Brewing	0.90
7 Water supply	0.90
8 Fuel supply	0.80

Table 5   (continued)

Responsibility	Unit of participation*
B *Household/Community*	
1 *Household:*	
(a) Bearing, rearing, initial education of children	1.00
(b) Cooking for husband, children, elders	1.00
(c) Cleaning, washing, etc.	1.00
(d) Housebuilding	0.30
(e) House repair	0.50
2 *Community:*	
Self-help projects	0.70

* Units of participation indicate the percentage of the work done by women.

Table 6   Division of rural labour in Kivu Province, Zaire[72]

	Unit of Production	Work
Women	1.00	Ploughing, sowing, upkeep of plantation, transport of produce, carrying water, preparation and transport of firewood, marketing, beermaking.
Men (in the rural areas all the time)	0.30	Care of banana trees, clearing land when necessary and help with the cultivation of new fields; certain other jobs.
Children aged 5-9:		
Boys	0.00	No contribution
Girls	0.05	Help with weeding and carrying water.

Table 6   (continued)

	Unit of Production	Work
Children aged 10-14:		
Boys	0.15	Looking after cattle; help with weeding.
Girls	0.55	Help mother with all agricultural work.
People over 55:		
Men	0.05	Very little work; some jobs in banana groves.
Women	0.20	Help with light work in the fields.

As we have seen, in some African societies the presence of polygyny affords husbands not only potential money, but far more leisure time, due to several women's labor. In non-polygynous families, each woman must do field work and all the servicing work for her husband by herself. A village woman in Upper Volta describes what this unequal workload means to her and her husband, in response to the question of who works harder:[73]

> Ha! Women of course. The men have only their field of millet to worry about. We must help the men in their fields and plant our own fields of peanuts, corn and condiments too. It's hard to get everything done, especially in the planting season. And then there are meals to prepare, flour to grind, and the house to clean, not to mention looking after the babies. How often do you see a woman wasting her time drinking in the dolohut (a bar selling millet beer) like the husbands? Why do you think I'm so skinny? I eat plenty, but I have too many worries.

In both rural and urban Greece, the same pattern occurs. Women rise far earlier than men each day to begin their chores, often work through the two to four hour siesta that the men take during the afternoon, and continue working well into the evening while the men are socializing in outdoor taverns. In Greece, Turkey and other Middle-Eastern countries, in the Caribbean, and in many other parts of the world, men's socializing with each other in clubs, lodges and bars, is made possible by women's hard work.[74]

The benefits to men and the costs to women of the unequal enjoyment of time are summed up in Beraët Zeki Ungör's description of the family life of the Turkish population, in rural and recently arrived urban communities:[75]

> The man goes out alone and spends his free time in the cafes in the company of other men; the woman takes care of the household, knits, weaves clothing, and, in the country, works in the fields; or in towns, she works as a dayworker in factories, in mills, or as a maid. In either case, the husband is the one who gets the wages, the money from the crop, or the produce. The woman has no leisure time and no human contacts; she is allowed no social life.

Women's lack of time reflects a frenzied, stressful lifestyle with little reprive. This affects their mental and physical health and seldom permits creative work outside the bounds of their everyday activities. Drudgery and busy-work prevent creative thinking and drain women's energy that could otherwise be channelled into their own interests. The lack of leisure time functions as a form of social control, denying women the time and peace of mind they could use to reflect upon and potentially change their situation. In the Soviet Union, for example, the multiplicity of red tape and long lines prohibits women from having the time to pursue creative or rebellious activities.

The vast and awful loss

> The problem, simply stated, is that one must believe in the existence of the person in order to recognize the authenticity of her suffering. Neither men nor women believe in the existence of women as significant beings. It is impossible to remember as real the suffering of

someone who by definition has no legitimate claim to
dignity or freedom, someone who is in fact viewed as some
thing, an object or an absence. And if a woman, an
individual woman multiplied by billions, does not believe
in her own discrete existence and therefore cannot credit
the authenticity of her own suffering, she is erased,
cancelled out, and the meaning of her life, whatever it is,
whatever it might have been, is lost. This loss cannot be
calculated or comprehended. It is vast and awful, and
nothing will ever make up for it.

Andrea Dworkin,
'The Promise of the Ultra-Right'[76]

Because women the world over do most of the work, control
little of what they produce, and enjoy few of the benefits,
they are in an extremely vulnerable position and their lives
are greatly affected by the conditions of their work. The
plight of many female-headed households highlights women's
position. In the USA in 1975, 26 per cent of white-women-
headed families were below the poverty level, and 49 per cent
of minority-women-headed were. There were 7.5 million
families headed by women in 1976. In the female-headed
household all the forces which exploit women combine,
from lack of social support for child-bearing to inadequate
wages.[77]

Women and hunger

Women often have greater nutritional needs than men because
they are overworked, have little free time and are frequently
exhausted. Long hours of physical labor, menstruation,
pregnancy and lactation all increase women's nutritional
requirements, especially for iron and protein. The average
Zambian woman, for example, works sixteen hours a day
during the planting season, doing agricultural and home
maintenance work, including hauling water, wood and
laundry to and from streams, over long distances.[78] Yet these
women, like women in many countries, are fed less and eat
foods that have lower nutritional value than men's, often
while they are nursing babies.

But rather than recognizing that women, for biological and social reasons, have *greater* nutritional needs than men, and helping to insure that those needs are met, cultures throughout the world continue dietary customs which are harmful to women. Many of these customs originated in the belief that men should receive priority in nutrition because they are the wage earners. A 1974 study done in India showed the extent to which women had internalized the male value system:[79]

Food distribution within the family arises from deliberate self-deprivation by women because they believe that the earning members (and the male members who are potential earning members) are more valuable than those who do domestic work and child-rearing, which they consider devoid of economic value.

Not only do women feed men and male children first in many situations, they may also prepare different meals for men, or abstain from certain foods that are reserved by religion or custom for men. Often these foods are higher in protein and vitamins than those which are permitted for women. Ethiopian women, for example, are required to eat entirely different meals from men, which often contain no meat or other substantial protein. In Northern India it is said that milk is good for boys but not for girls, contributing to a higher female mortality rate.[80] Some Asian cultures forbid fish or other seafood, chicken, duck, eggs or certain vegetables to women.

In Latin America, 10 to 35 per cent of the women suffer from iron deficiency anaemia as compared to 5 to 15 per cent of men, and in Africa, 15 to 50 per cent of women compared to 6 to 17 per cent of men.[81] Even though the knowledge that women need more iron than men exists, neither women's iron deficiency, nor the social conditions exacerbating the problem have been addressed in most countries.

Because of this long term nutritional deprivation, over-work and exhaustion, women have less nutritional reserves and social and economic resources to withstand drought and/

or famine. During the Sahelian drought of the early 1970s, for example, women, especially pregnant women and nursing mothers, were the hardest hit.[82]

In many western societies women also give the best food from each meal to their husbands. This tradition means that women are the most affected by inflation of food prices. Many women also 'diet' or starve themselves in an attempt to meet the cultural standard of female beauty. (Only societies that produce a surplus of food see slenderness as an ideal rather than a sign of undernourishment.) This relatively recent standard for female beauty, originating in the white middle-classes, is so accepted and deeply internalized that increasing numbers of young women literally starve themselves in order to lose weight. This is one of the reasons for the increase in diseases such as *Anorexia nervosa* in young women.

Since men usually control what women produce, some are in a position to use food as a mechanism for controlling women. An Ethiopian woman noted in an interview that 'Many men keep food from their wives to make them behave.'[83] This, added to exhaustion from overwork, has devastating effects on women the world over.

'Protective' legislation

Not only does non-recognition of women's burden negatively affect women's health, but there is little social, economic or institutional reform to equalize the division of labor and rewards. To the contrary, many societies utilize a pretense of concern for women's responsibilities in the home in supporting so-called 'protective' legislation[84] – a concern often motivated by a desire to keep women socially and economically subordinate. Elizabeth Johnstone notes that in many countries:[85]

> it is usually the woman who is accorded what is regarded
> as more favourable treatment, alleged to be justified for
> the sake of her health and welfare in relation to her
> functions of maternity and motherhood. Thus, a great
> many countries place special restrictions on the hours of
> work of women (including overtime), on night work by

women, and on their employment in certain industries
and occupations regarded as particularly dangerous or
unhealthy for them (such as underground work in mining).
. . . . even when women are doing the same work as men,
their earnings tend to be lower because men have greater
opportunities for earning higher bonuses for such things
as overtime, night work, and especially heavy or
dangerous work.

When women demand protection from hazardous working
conditions governments often respond by restricting them
from work situations that would provide them with adequate
income rather than making working conditions safe. In recent
years women in many countries have demanded that protective legislation be extended to men as well in all hazardous
occupations, and eliminated otherwise, to enable everyone
equal access to all job opportunities that are not harmful. Yet
the debate over protective legislation does not address the
underlying burden of women's double workload. Nor does it
address the occupational hazards of housework, which range
from wife-beating to lung cancer, which caused the death of
an American woman who handled and washed her husband's
workclothes which were filled with asbestos fibres.[86] True
concern on the part of governments for women's health
would reorganize society to end women's exploitation, so
that women would not have exclusive responsibility for
childcare and home maintenance.

Women's leisure and creativity

Not many women got to live out the daydream of
women – to have a room, even a section of a room, that
only gets messed up when she messes it up herself. The
book would stay open at the very page she had pressed it
flat with her hand, and no one would complain about the
field not being plowed or the leak in the roof. She would
clean her own bowl and a small, limited area; she would
have one drawer to sort, one bed to make.
    Other women besides me must have this daydream
about a carefree life. I've seen Communist pictures showing

a contented woman sitting on her bunk sewing. Above her head is her one box on a shelf. The words stenciled on the box mean 'Fragile', but literally say, 'Use a little heart.' The woman looks very pleased. The Revolution put an end to prostitution by giving women what they wanted: a job and a room of their own.

Free from families, my mother would live for two years without servitude.

> Maxine Hong Kingston,
> *The Woman Warrior: Memoirs of*
> *a Girlhood Among Ghosts*[87]

In most countries, the double work burden and lack of leisure time has resulted, for women, in tremendous barriers to creative pursuits. Male artists and philosophers the world over – in fact, all men able to pursue any work that is not menial drudgery – have enjoyed the freedom necessary to think and express themselves creatively, thanks to the daily toil of their wives, sisters and mothers which has made that time possible.

Women's work has freed men to pursue religion and governing as well, both commonly male 'professions' from which women have been excluded, though the time made possible by such a specialization of labor was at women's expense.

Throughout Jewish areas in Russia and Eastern Europe, for example, for centuries in some families women not only did all childcare and housework, but also did paid work in a number of professions, to enable their husbands to devote all their time to studying the sacred Torah. As I. Epstein pointed out, 'This was the ideal on which many marriages were founded.'[88]

Women have historically been, and will continue to be, deprived of opportunities for creative expression, until the inequitable distribution of work, money and leisure time is righted. In an article entitled 'The Source of Leisure Time,' Betsy Warrior notes:[89]

In freeing others from the hum-drum necessities of life, women have placed at the disposal of men and children –

leisure time – a wealth of leisure time to be spent with some choice, beyond the hammering necessities of everyday existence.

The amount of time woman has saved for others, to be spent by others, has been paid for at great expense to herself. Historically, women, both as a sex and as individuals, have paid dearly for this time they've lavished so freely on others . . . . While time was used by men and children for personal growth, education, socializing and planning beyond immediate needs, women were chained to the demands of the physical requirements of life.

[Leisure] time is then invested in projects that those who possess the time choose . . . . Time is a birthright we're all given. But women give up much of this birthright to men. In every field, men have profited from this in direct proportion to what women have lost . . . . Though it is woman who creates the time that is used by man as the initial investment, it is man who takes complete credit for the capital gains (in the form of accomplishment) of this investment. Women have paid for these gains with their very lives.

Such is the product of woman's labor.

Each woman's loss of an opportunity to create has done violence both to her and to her society, which has lost the richness that her talent might have contributed.

Women who have had any opportunity to create at all have usually been forced to choose between family and art, since the responsibilities of a family usually preclude the time necessary to develop one's work. Tillie Olson noted that the majority of women writers (an area relatively acceptable for women today) until recently had no children.[90] Women with families have had to do their creative work in bits and snatches between household chores often with children at their feet or on their laps. It took thirty years, for example, for Margaret Walker, a woman with children to write her novel of American Slavery, *Jubilee*.[91] Even women without children who have some time to create have been greatly hindered by lifelong training that told them responsibilities to others are always more important than giving time and discipline to oneself.

The silencing of women has been so extensive that Olsen states:[92]

> We must not speak of women writers in our century (as we cannot speak of women in any area of recognized human achievement) without speaking also of the invisible, the as-innately-capable: the born to the wrong circumstances diminished, excluded, foundered, silenced.

In *A Room of One's Own*, Virginia Woolf wrote:[93]

> When . . . . one reads of a witch being ducked, of a woman possessed by devils, of a wise woman selling herbs, or even of a very remarkable man who had a mother, then I think we are on the track of a lost novelist, a suppressed poet, of some mute and inglorious Jane Austen, some Emily Brontë who dashed her brains out on the moor or mopped and mowed about the highways crazed with the torture that her gift had put her to. Indeed I would venture to guess that Anon, who wrote so many poems without signing them, was often a woman.

Yet there have been women who have made tremendous (and reluctantly acknowledged) contributions to the arts and sciences. Marie Curie and the astronomer Caroline Herschel were brilliant scientists. And from Sappho through the Brontës to Toni Morrison and Buchi Emecheta, women have created brilliant writing, giving us a taste of the richness we have lost.

Indeed, in one culture, women's literary genius far exceeded that of men. Woolf's essay addressed the perennial male question, 'Where is the female Shakespeare?' Her answer was to invent a sister for Shakespeare, equally brilliant and ambitious, and to trace the process of her destruction by a male society as she attempted to follow the course her brother took.

But there is another answer to that question, one that sheds light on what women can do when the culture they live in supports them. The real 'female Shakespeare' was named

Lady Murasaki; she lived in Japan in the eleventh century – five hundred years before Shakespeare was born. The Heien era in Japan was unique in world culture: among the court ladies, women's creativity was not only tolerated, but was part of their job; and it was for *lack* of such creativity that they were penalized.

The rigid class structure, which allowed men little social mobility, did allow women to marry upward in rank. Ambitious fathers cherished the prestige a daughter could bring, and daughters were often more welcomed than sons. Hence these women grew up with a rare sense of self-worth. But they were still considered inferior. In the Emporer's court, both women and men spoke Japanese, while men also spoke, and wrote in, the scholarly Chinese language. Court ladies wrote in the less respected Japanese vernacular. Since the Empress was never permitted to leave the palace, her ladies were expected to write poems for her, describing the wonders of nature (such as the sound of the first cuckoo of spring) which she would never experience.

Women were not permitted to write in Chinese, and those who were even able to understand it risked scorn and possible punishment. There is a beautiful irony to this. The Heien Era is now considered the golden age of Japanese literature, and Lady Murasaki, author of *The Tale of Genji*, occupies the place Homer and Shakespeare hold in the West. Lady Sei Shonagun's *Pillow Book* is only slightly less esteemed. Dozens of women wrote brilliant literature that is still read today, while the men, whose 'superior' Chinese produced a stilted and unnatural literature, are read only for historical information.[94]

The success of women who have been lucky enough to find themselves in privileged positions, or to overcome hardships and still do their work, makes the loss of the majority of women's potential genius and contributions even more tragic.

Woman's worth: subsidizing the world economy

But the salient fact in this discussion is that, whatever
the economic value of the domestic industry of women

is, they do not get it. The women who do the most work
get the least money, and the women who have the most
money do the least work. Their labor is neither given or
taken as a factor in economic change. It is held to be
their duty as women to do this work; and their economic
status bears no relation to their domestic labors, unless
an inverse one.

Charlotte Perkins Gilman,
Women and Economics, 1898[95]

if one would withdraw the work that women do, the
community would topple.

Gloria Scott (of the World Bank)[96]

Women rarely benefit or share in the wealth they have produced. They are chosen by the circumstances of their birth
to be the servants of society. As a biologically defined group,
they are trained from birth to accept the maintenance
functions of society as their lot. By choosing those beings
who will receive no compensation for their work, and then
investing little in these creatures, the patriarchy utilizes its
resources in a very economical, if inhuman, way. Women
perform all the preliminary work and all the final preparation
and the distribution of goods that is essential to the economic and life cycle, at minimal cost, freeing men to be
'more productive' in other areas.

Though women and men may seem to do the same general
kinds of work together (Chinese men and women traditionally work together in the fields), or separately (Peruvian
peasants work in the same fields but perform different tasks),
or do different work within their own spheres (African
women do subsistence agriculture while the men perform
paid labor in the towns), women always have a role that is
'complementary' to that of men. In each case 'complementary' means that men dominate the human ecological niche;
they control the resources available while women share the
left-overs as permitted by the male system.[97]

The work that married women perform in no way relates
to the amount of money they receive from their husbands,
in fringe benefits, standard of living or spending money. A

woman in a richer country often receives more money yet does less work than, for instance, a peasant woman in Ethiopia. The less money a man has, the more work his wife may have to do to keep herself and her children alive. Yet even a rich man's wife has no guarantee that she will be well treated by her husband. She may have no money of her own, and if divorced (unemployed), she might have no way to earn a living. If she does have money of her own before the marriage, or an income from a job, beatings or more subtle pressure may cause her to give up control of it to her husband.

In another example, the favorite or the oldest wife in a polygynous marriage usually has the least to do, while those out of favor work harder and at the same time receive less for themselves and their children.[98]

This relationship between work women do and its benefits is similar to what some economists have characterized as the relationship of factory workers to factory owners, whereby the factory workers produce commodities over which they have no control. The profits from what is sold go to the owners, while the workers are paid the minimal wage – enough to keep them clothed and fed and able to return to the workplace the next day. The profits that the workers produce over and above what they are paid is surplus, which goes to the owners, and makes possible their higher standard of living and greater leisure time.

The same relationship exists between women and men and, on a societal level, holds true for third-world and western countries.[99] But it is less visible because women produce children, potential money and leisure for their husbands, less tangible things than commodities, which are exchanged within the family.

According to some theorists, most industrial labor and economic relationships are in fact an outgrowth of what is considered to be women's work cross-culturally.[100] The responsibilities of women in less technological societies for the production and processing of foods and clothing is replaced in more highly industrialized societies by factory production maintained by the working class. Thus, as production itself becomes more specialized, working-class men and women do for money what women have done free for their own families (yet women are still responsible for the least specialized work of home maintenance).

So the working class, though maintaining society through manual, unspecialized labor just as women do, does not have any more control over what they produce or say in the decision-making that dictates the quality and quantity of their work, than housewives do in the home. And neither have the same access to social resources that those doing more highly specialized work have.

The inequitable division of resources between men and women can be seen within almost every culture around the world, in the ratio that each contributes to the family. In general, men give less to their families in terms of the resources available to them (time and/or money) than women. Middle-class men in the west or men in well-paid, upper-echelon positions in the third world tend to give more money or goods but very little time in the form of childcare or work done around the house. Poor men in the west or the third world are able to give very little money, but sometimes give time, both to children or to maintenance work around the home or compound. Urban working-class men in the west and the third world might give both time and money, but still significantly less than women. The ultimate responsibility for the maintenance of the family almost always falls on women, though in varying degrees.

In the third-world and western cultures we have examined, we have seen how this relationship is borne out – by the leisure time, higher standards of living and potential money that women produce for their husbands and families. If husbands leave their families, or if wives leave their husbands and take the children, men usually participate even less in meeting the family needs through childcare, financial help, or both. In all these situations, it is women who must pick up the slack.

In socialist countries such as China or the USSR, women continue to carry a heavier burden than men. However, frequently women's burden isn't as high as in other third-world and socialist countries because the government is beginning to assume responsibility for some of what has been women's work: providing free services in the form of childcare and sometimes laundry and meals, which decreases women's workload. Still, all the unsocialized work that women do over and above what the men do sustains the male-dominated socialist economies, which continue to exploit women in this way.

In looking at the lives of women and their families around the world, we have felt that across cultures, and within cultures with class and racial variables as we've noted, families within each category of women's power receive about the same percentage of men's resources in time or money, depending on which they have more of.[101] The criteria we have discussed and the status of women in a culture are factors which, as a composite, have a great deal more influence on the proportion of female to male participation in meeting family and societal needs than the class structure of a society (or the class of a woman's husband or father). The class of a woman's husband affects her status and workload only in so far as it affects such criteria. Women as a group, across class, race and national lines, function as a caste within their own communities as well as between communities throughout the world because of all those forces which influence women's lives separately from men's.

The proportion of men's to women's resources, in time and money, that go into sustaining their families changes along the continuum of the woman-centered categories of economies we have described. In cultures where women have minimal power and minimal access to resources, their burden relative to men's is heaviest. In many of these societies women work long hours with no social recognition or independent income. The benefits of their labor, in both time and money, accrue almost entirely to their husbands. In those cultures where women have token power, it varies in form by class (as it does in all categories), but in proportion remains the same – less burdensome than in countries where women have minimal power, but profoundly inequitable just the same. They may have some services such as daycare available, and more paid work opportunities and legal rights, but their workload remains much greater than men's and benefits mostly other people. In most countries where women have negotiating power, they still have the heavier economic and energy burden, but their rewards – in the form of some authority as a group in higher levels of decision-making, some control over what they produce, or more leisure as they grow older – are greater than in other categories.

The total righting of this equation, so that women are not the subsidizers of economies and the leisure time and higher standard of living of men, is not possible within patriarchal countries and institutions. For work and rewards to be equally divided means a profound restructuring of every economy, shaking and transforming patriarchal assumptions and priorities down to their very roots.

6 *The winds of change*

'Womanhood is Awakening'
'Jag Rahi Hai,
Jag Rahi Hai,
Nari Jati Jag Rahi Hai'

Hindu slogan chanted by
Indian women during a
1979 demonstration in
Delhi against molestation
of women on public buses

Had I lived only for myself, I would have gone away. But
my love for my family, that strong Mexican love, was like
a powerful coiled spring pulling me back, pulling me
under. I wanted to advance, but it wouldn't let me.

How I wanted to pack my things and go far away! . . . .
I couldn't be sweet or submissive enough to please the men
here. The *macho* Mexican, in his pride and vanity,
considered women inferior and enjoyed humiliating them.
Only *he* is right and only *his* feelings count. In a discussion,
he is not interested in learning the truth, but only in
out-talking others. If a man in a Nash is overtaken by a
Chrysler, he will speed to pass it, to show that he is
superior, after all. A woman cannot walk alone, without
some virile man asserting his 'rights' over her. All the men
I knew, my father, my brothers, my *novios* [boyfriend]
and my fellow employees, believed it was their place to
give the orders and to be obeyed.

I could never get along with a dominating, imperious

211

man. I didn't like crushing authority, I didn't want to feel
inferior. I even fought my father on that score. A thing
was not right just because he said it! Men were stronger
physically (but not morally), and behind all their
'superiority' was force! I wanted to be independent, to
make my own way, to find the right environment.

I made brave dreams for myself, but when I went to the
Casa Grande and saw the situation there, I faltered. It
would be cowardly to abandon those four motherless
children.

Consuelo Sanchez,
The Children of Sanchez[1]

Historically, women throughout the world have made attempts
in a great variety of ways to take control over their lives,
take back some of the wealth they have produced, and to
end lives of degradation. Sometimes this struggle has taken
the form of individual acts of courage such as leaving marriages or refusing to marry, running away from home, going to
school in spite of heavy familial disapproval, etc. In some
cases the struggle has been a collective one – women in a
village getting together to share work, make demands, go on
strike, or women working outside the home organizing at
their workplaces, or creating childcare cooperatives.

Yet women's socialization has also sometimes led them to
subsume their own interests to the interests of the 'common
good', fighting for the needs or rights of their husbands and
children while denying their own needs and subservience
within the family. If such a characteristic were operating in
a framework of equality, it would serve as an invaluable
mechanism for dealing with conflict and permitting an
alternative, internalized morality rather than authoritarian
social structure. But within the context of exploitation
and oppression it may only strengthen the male system at
women's expense, elevating the existing inequities to a new
level. Women's changed work would then be yet another
form of women serving men for free. If, on the other hand,
women fight to increase their own status and resources
relative to men at the same time that they fight for changes
that will benefit men as well, they are improving collective

life without maintaining the same inequity.

Thus changes in women's lives must be analyzed from the perspective not only of how they affect women, but also of how they affect the imbalance between men's power and women's power, a point emphasized by author Batya Weinbaum.[2] Do they provide women with necessary tools for survival and change yet reinforce women's oppression more subtly by making the male system more viable; do they serve to erode the foundations of male power; do they create qualitatively new forms of social organization and interaction?

A totally new framework for change based on women's lives and perspectives and an independent power base is essential so that women's energy can be directed to their own behalf rather than reinforcing their subservience to patriarchy. The kinds of changes that must take place for such a framework to evolve are profound. Most of the strategies for change that women have used take place within the limits of a patriarchal context.

The particular form of women's struggles to make changes in their lives depends in large part on whether the women live in a culture where they have minimal, token or negotiating power.

In cultures where women have only minimal power, their energies have usually gone into individual survival. They struggle with unwanted marriages, malnutrition, exhaustion, and many work-related diseases. Some women decide that their only option in crisis situations is suicide. Women's efforts in these societies are often directed towards developing networks through which to transform their survival strategies to change, to share work or make demands, or fight for reproductive control, more money for their work, and access to technological aids. Their collective action attempts to consolidate their long hours of work and protect their survival mechanisms. In these countries women are essentially fighting for the tools with which they can gain some control over their lives, which would allow them to make further changes.

Women in token power societies usually have some of the basic rights that women in minimal power societies are fighting for, though such rights are often revoked as the needs of the dominant male culture change. Though their protection of women varies according to whether or not a women's class, race or religious identity gives her minimal or negotiating power as a subgroup, token rights usually are recognized by the dominant culture though often not enforced. This gives individual women more tools to fight with in oppressive situations. With their survival somewhat more secure, they make attempts to consolidate reforms into undeniable rights for women, to move toward establishing a separate power base as women – a lobbying force and power effective enough not only to pressure for changes in women's lives, but to maintain those changes once they have been won.

In these countries women's struggles often focus on the acquisition and maintenance of the right to reproductive freedom, access to resources, and to increased opportunities for women in every area of life so that they are less segregated into the most menial, lowest-paying jobs. In some countries women organize services not provided by the society (such as battered wife shelters and rape crisis centers) to protect and improve the quality of their lives. Other women are demanding that housework be socialized or that men share it. In some countries, women's political caucuses push for the election of officials that are more sensitive to women's issues. These actions are oriented toward increasing the freedom of women and attempting to preserve those rights that have been granted.

In the few cultures where women have negotiating power, they already have a power base and are sometimes using it to make further needed changes in their lives. In cultures where women's power is being usurped, their efforts have gone towards fighting the deterioration of their status. Although these women are united and working together, they still have a long way to go before they achieve either equality with men, or a qualitative transformation of power based on new values grounded in women's experience.

Often social change, which would be extremely progressive in cultures where women hold less power, is viewed as antithetical to necessary change in cultures where women hold more power. A debate at the 1975 International Women's Year Conference in Mexico City for example focused on the question of home industries, arts and crafts. Many women viewed such a direction for women as a reinforcement of their role and position in the home, rather than training them with new skills that they could carry with them into the 'outside world'. Others view this development as a chance for women to form networks and earn some cash which they would otherwise not have access to, while still being able to care for children, animals and fields, within a rural context that they will continue to be a part of for years to come. If the home industries being encouraged in Ceylon, Turkey, Indonesia and the Philippines were encouraged in other cultures where women already have growing social networks and access to a source of independent income, such change might indeed prove to be regressive.

The magnitude of change that is necessary cannot come all at once, it takes generations to build. In most cultures around the world the changes will be small, as women make discoveries and assert their dreams step by step. But if each woman retains her vision of change, and makes sure that the changes she makes bring her closer to that vision, she will help to slowly erode patriarchy's foundations. Gradually, around the world, women can begin to define and create the basis for the new order they envision.

The power of hope: rising expectations

> Our women often don't expect a great deal of men and seem willing to accept the man's irresponsibility as inevitable.
>
> Fatherhood is a learned thing, more than motherhood. In raising our children, we must not regard the more humane virtues as being relevant to the woman only.[3]

This statement, made by a West Indian woman about her culture, touches on several factors crucial to an understanding of how social change comes about. Education and social conditioning play tremendous roles in forming peoples behavior and ideals. However, the most important aspect of change that she refers to is that of expectations. When people feel they have no right to anything from life or from other people, or feel that expectations simply lead to more pain and disappointment, they are not able to act on their own behalf no matter how difficult their life situations might be.

The level of expectation makes the difference between strategies for survival and strategies for change. When women have extremely low expectations of men, of their own lives and the options that will be available to them, much of their energy is directed towards figuring out ways of adapting to their environment. When they internalize the dominant culture's view, they often lack the self-respect necessary to feel they're entitled to more out of life. When their self-respect and expectations rise, so will their sense of outrage at the conditions of their lives, and their energy will increasingly be focused on changes they can make.

Expectations rise when women are exposed to the knowledge that things are different for other women with whom they identify and hence can be for them. A woman might receive such exposure through a friend who's beginning to make changes in her life and tells her about it. She might hear from a neighbor of a project or an incident in which a woman exercised new options. She might hear of such alternatives on the radio or television, or read about them in a newspaper. Or, if she goes to school, she might learn about them there. That's why controlling the sources of information is so important to patriarchy. Men restrict women's access to information, both institutionally through unequal educational opportunities, and interpersonally, as when they beat or browbeat their wives for socializing 'excessively'.

In cultures where women hold minimal power, their opportunities for education and sharing their experiences with other women are the most limited. In Morocco, for example where 97 per cent of rural women are illiterate, they have only the Saint's sanctuaries in which to meet. But as Fatima Mernissi pointed out, the existence of the sanctuaries serves as an escape valve for women's pent-up anger and frustrations. Since women's venting of anger takes place in a context in which they address supernatural powers rather than the male power structure, their energies are channelled away from possibilities for permanent change.[4]

In many cultures women's expectations are so low that they do not even take advantage of the few opportunities that do exist for sharing. For example, there was a very poor response to a conference of Caribbean women planned (and subsequently cancelled) by the government of Trinidad and Tobago, in 1975. Though many people have blamed the lack of visible concern on women themselves (one observer stated, 'women in the Caribbean are their own worst enemies'[5]), this is clearly another instance of blaming the victim. Why would Caribbean women expect that such a conference would be truly relevant to their lives, or that it could offer them real hope?

Excerpts from a 1975 interview with four Caribbean women illustrates the transition process through which women may start to recognize their situation as common and begin to take action:[6]

> The problem seems to be centered about the women moving from the stage of awareness to one of active participation . . . . Actually, the whole concept and struggle, I suspect, is really a movement among the more sophisticated women of our Caribbean society. Most of our grass-root women are just struggling to make ends meet and are struggling to raise their children . . . . As a Caribbean woman, I see Caribbean women not so much in revolution – for many of them are not too conscious of any type of revolution – but as beginning to become conscious of themselves as WOMEN. This concept, unlike the idea of woman as simply a child-bearer or house-cleaner, is a process of evolution . . . . we must proclaim clearly to men and to other women that there is more to womanhood than motherhood.

If women's expectations are too high, raised by the false promises of politicians or religious groups anxious to recruit their support, then their disillusionment can lead to bitterness. This process can only be countered by finding out about and understanding the history of successes and failures and the changes that have been made possible through generations of women's hard work.

Strength in numbers: networking and support

The same ingredients are necessary for change the world over, though the form they take varies from culture to culture. They include rising expectations, self-respect, hope and a sense of new options; validation – the realization that one's situation is not isolated and individual – permitting women to externalize rather than internalize the cause of their pain; and the sharing of strategies for change, mutual support, and the building of networks which use self-help as a model for change rather than dependency on external factors.

When women are able to make small steps in their lives, one at a time, they are able to gradually develop more confidence in their ability to create change. They are then able to form a new vision and, seeing their lives begin to improve, to believe that change will offer them more than the sureness of what they have.

The growing development in many western countries of shelters for women beaten by their husbands has provided this type of support for the women staying there. The self-help philosophy of the shelters encourages women to develop the emotional tools and survival skills to enable them to begin to control their lives. From the first time women share their feelings and experiences with other women in similar situations, the next steps they take in their new lives are designed by their own hands.[7] Sharing their experiences gives them a sense of validation and empowerment. Hearing how other women are changing their lives enables women to see that they are not alone, and to stop feeling powerless in the face of the obstacles before them. This knowledge also helps women to put the responsibility for the crimes committed against them outside themselves, where it belongs, thus allowing hope that there are other ways for them to live. This hope is an essential ingredient of change.

Women are building networks of other services as well, including rape crisis centers, refuges for women in crises and transition (including those for pre- or post-institutionalized women and prostitutes), medical centers, and therapy collectives. These services are controlled by women and represent a base of operations outside the male professions. Though the male economy often attempts to limit the activity of these centers, while they exist they help many women to develop survival and change skills. Women's individual and collective experience of self-determination in these areas also increases their ability to act independently and organize other projects in the future.

Those factors which encourage change can occur in a wide variety of ways and do not necessarily require that women be in the same place at the same time.

Groups of women in the USA, from Puerto Rican women in Boston to women in Appalachia, are teaching themselves to drive cars against the wishes of their husbands and fathers. They wish to increase their mobility, and ability to network, and their opportunity for jobs, and to save time and money for themselves.

In the following excerpts from 'I am not meant to be alone and without you who understand: Letters from Black Feminists', Barbara Smith and Beverly Smith describe the crucial networking that was done among Black Feminists in different cities in the USA from 1972 to 1978:[8]

Having written and received hundreds of letters, we realized that our correspondence was an important part of our Black feminist activity. Letters have always been an important link for embattled groups, perhaps more so in the last century than in this one, before modern means of communication were available. For women, letters have often been life-lines to each other, since traditionally we have had little control over where we live and have had little access to conventional media. Letters have provided an underground communications medium . . . . Most essentially, we write letters because we are apart . . . . The letters have created an emotional support network among the women who shared them. The letters have also brought a network of individual Black feminists together . . . . There is a sense in the letters that the writers are 'family.' One reason for the rich variety of the letters' contents is that we have so few places as Black feminists to send our creations and to share ourselves . . . .

The antidote to isolation is networking, the creation
of community. Networking is also an essential step in
building our movement . . . .

One function the letters have served is to make us
real to ourselves and each other. To write a letter to
another Black woman who understands is to seek and
find validation. The scope of this correspondence among
Black women shows how important we are to each others'
lives. In a system where Black women have primacy to
no one else, we do to each other.

Sharing of information and education as well as networking
help give women hope as well as necessary information to
begin to act on their newly-found dreams. The sharing of
their experiences and dreams with each other provides a
growing sense not only of validation, but of community.
It strengthens and expands women's identities, encouraging
their independent expression, rather than constraining and
reducing their thoughts as traditional socialization does. The
less isolated one feels in one's pain and anger, the more
possible it seems to change the conditions producing it.
This sense of community can be consolidated in a variety
of ways, from the sharing that takes place while working,
to meetings, to a growing culture and art forms that express
the identity, values and dreams of the people creating it.
Historically, there has been a tremendous rebirth of culture
during times of social change, and these new forms of expression both mirror and encourage the rising aspirations of the
people that produce them. In turn, this new culture includes
a process of self-identification that provides a sense of
community, gives form to new visions and encourages their
realization, which is the process of self-identification as a
distinct culture.

Tools of female insurgence

I look around at them [leaving the Kanpur, India,
factories], knowing in my own sore muscles that they
have just finished eight hours of being pounded down

physically and psychologically, seeing them all rush out now to do the next job at home . . . . talking and laughing . . . . young and old . . . . So beautiful and so strong – if only all of them would look around at each other and see that power.[9]

> Woman worker quoted by Raka Sharan,
> 'Factories or Concentration Camps?'

Women have always been active in social change movements and have often played a leadership role, in demanding the meeting of theirs and their families' immediate needs and greater access to resources.

Striking is a common strategy of women across cultures to use their leverage as underlying producers to their advantage in winning back some of the money and enjoying some of the time they have produced. Women have often played leading roles in strikes at their workplaces, as in the case of a 48-year-old Guyanan woman, Haliman, who had lived and worked on a sugar plantation from the age of thirteen. While raising eight children she worked in the Task Weeding Gang from before sun-up to after sun-down, rising at 3 a.m. to begin her day. For this she was paid $10.00 to $12.00 a week. In the mid-1970s she played a leading role in a strike and sit-in at the plantation where she worked, which was part of a country-wide strike for higher wages and better working conditions. Because of her actions she received a severe beating from three police officers, ironically, on International Women's Day. One of twenty-five women involved in the strike, she was imprisoned for two nights and charged with assaulting police officers. In spite of this Haliman has remained firm in her resolve to continue fighting for what she believes in.[10]

During the 1980 demonstrations in Zimbabwe, during the transition to majority rule, women were far more active and militant than the men, saying that their families couldn't wait for reforms to eat. They also encouraged men's shutting down of mines, plants, and farms in wildcat strikes.[11]

Sometimes women's participation in national liberation efforts have also brought about changes in their status as women, since their energies are greatly needed.

After the founding of the Palestine Liberation Organization in 1964, many women began to agitate for their own rights as women. In 1965 the General Union of Palestinian Women was founded to organize Palestinian women to work with the Palestinian liberation efforts, and by 1967 men were largely forced to accept women's new role in the movement. Though men's views and support of women's independence might change, women are learning skills and developing networks that will not easily be crushed.[12]

The kinds of changes that are necessary in the lives of women the world over are so fundamental that it's impossible to speak of them only in the limited terms of legislative action, new committees, studies and their recommendations. This kind of reform is common to liberal societies which tend to be extremely skilled in the fine art of absorption of reforms, in making women struggle tirelessly for years for the smallest changes, by which time they are either too tired and cynical to continue, or they have convinced themselves that the changes won are indeed significant and that there's no further need of continuing. Those fighting the most vociferously are often offered positions within the male power structure, where resistance, sexism and bureaucracy impede their making changes. Those who accept such employment sometimes come to identify with the power structure and lose their commitment to broad-based transformations.

Even so, both the process of fighting and the end results provide many women with significant relief and sometimes more power. Even when change is initiated by church or political groups, the networking, exchange of ideas and validation that women experience are crucial ingredients of social change. These have allowed some women to gain confidence to take more control over their lives. Some initiate their own changes on a grass-roots level, entirely independent of external institutions and often even opposed to them. Although such changes can be seen as reforms that merely strengthen the male system, women have so little power in many cultures that the process itself of fighting for change gives them new organizing tools that are essential to a breaking down of male power. When women start with almost nothing, any changes that give them self-respect and tools with which to fight, though perhaps temporarily reinforcing the existing power structure, pave the way for more fundamental change. Education, progressive legislation, a higher standard of living, more access to wealth, property and relief from violence – the ingredients of women's rising status – give many women some time, money and hope that can be used to fight for deeper changes, *as long as a radical vision of change and long-term goals is maintained.*

Education: from self-respect to social change

> Attaining a degree of self-respect is by no means the least reward from the most humble education.
>
> Ina Beasley,
'Education is the Key for Women'[13]

Self-respect is perhaps the most primary of tools women need in order to fight for further changes in their lives. Although training and educational programs, when initiated by governments, are often tools of assimilation, acculturation or suppression, the ability to read and write open for women new and crucial channels of communication, access to information and greater options in employment.

For example, during the 1960s, literacy programs in Ghana, centers of practical animal husbandry for Kenyan women sustaining village economies, and Women's Institutes in Ceylon specializing in health and cooperative food-production,[14] all provided women with specific skills that could raise their standard of living and income, as well as their self-respect and ability to form networks.

In West Indian countries during the 1970s, community agencies such as the YWCA developed School-Leaver's Institutes to provide secretarial training for unskilled women in Guyana, Jamaica and Belize, and classes in food production and preservation in St Vincent and Grenada.[15] Such programs are clearly graded towards reinforcing women's traditional role as mother/servant/secretary. Yet in many of those countries women are isolated and poverty-stricken, and the chance to get together with other women while learning skills enabling them to increase their income also gives them validation, enables them to develop some economic independence, self-respect and expectations about their lives. In minimal power societies, this is no mean feat. For these reasons, education is usually viewed as a primary goal for women in many minimal power societies, and in that context, is often an extremely radical concept. The following description of the program of the Antillean Women's Liberation Movement in Curaçao, Netherland Antilles, would probably sound very mild to many women in token power societies, yet in that country represents an extremely radical concept in sexual politics:[16]

> [The program] includes considering that women's liberation means (1) self-recognition, and (2) recognition by men. Self-recognition is the non-acceptance of herself as inferior in any sense of the word. Being recognized by men means that she must be valued as a person and as equal partner . . . . We will achieve our goal by the organization of forums, lectures and debating clubs in all districts of Curaçao; by obtaining time on radio and television in order to communicate with the female population, by forming a library.

Fighting from within: legislation and participation in male institutions

Legislation has been used, both as a reaction to progress made by women, in a backlash to take away the rights they've won, and as a mechanism by women to legislate greater equality.

Few governments or international agencies have contributed to broad-based changes in the lives of women independent of pressure placed on them by women at the grass-roots level. Those few governments whose visions of progress include vast transformations in women's lives have still fallen short of full economic and social equality of the sexes. For these reasons the fundamental transformations that are necessary will not take place without massive efforts by women, within each society and across cultural boundaries.

Government-sponsored strategies for change are significant in so far as they help individual women to survive, increase women's access to resources, or represent a response to demands made by women which facilitate the building of networks that can be used as a power base. But these advantages are usually temporary.

When new laws are made in almost any culture, they represent a response to broad-based demands for change, or an attempt to inhibit it. Even the laws which are viewed as progressive are usually an attempt to maintain the status quo. Laws do not determine the values, behavior and institutions of a culture, but reflect and maintain them. They are made by people in power to maintain their power. In every culture where men have more power than women and make the laws that govern people's lives, their laws are a mechanism to maintain that power.

This is most obvious in societies which prohibit women from education and certain forms of work, and render them powerless in the family and unable to obtain divorces, birth control or abortions. It was also very clear in countries such as Franco's Spain, where there were laws forbidding more than twenty people to meet without permission from the authorities, where people were jailed, exiled or lost jobs for signing petitions, and where police investigated any formally declared group, which resulted in such fear and lack of experience in organizing that the women's movement consisted of only about fifty or sixty activists.[17] However, progressive legislation is also simply a more subtle way for men to maintain their power and sometimes involves a trade-off in privileges: For example, when women obtained the vote in the USA many men expected to benefit by family and class affiliated votes.

If women do not hold equal power in the decision-making process, or are locked into a male-defined power structure, the same men who voted for change can at any time revoke the laws they implemented only a short time before.

In Argentina, when the women's suffrage bills were supported and eventually passed, it was only because men perceived it to be in *their* best interest to do so. In 1929 the Radical Party opposed suffrage for women because it was seen as a way to strengthen the power of political parties. In 1945 men opposed to the new military regime began to support women's suffrage because it was seen to be connected with the denial of men's political rights. When the government began to support revision of the Civil Code, (a nineteenth century code severely limiting women by defining their existence only in relation to their husbands) it was because the courts were overwhelmed with cases of women staggering under the responsibilities of their husbands' debts, (for which they were responsible under the Code). The crowded courts, not the unjust burden on women, were the impetus to change.[18]

The value of reform-oriented legislation should not be underestimated, however, only understood in its proper context. When it makes survival easier for women, increases women's access to resources, or gives women more tools to fight with, more self-respect, or opportunities to get together and build networks, it is an extremely important step forward. The recently amended Personal Status Code in Iraq permits a divorced woman to retain custody of her children until they are fifteen years old (an improvement from the previous nine for girls and seven for boys). Tunisia's Personal Status Code abolished polygyny and forbade the repudiation of wives and set a minimum age for marriage. And the 1978 Civil Code in Portugal permits women to pursue their own careers and allows both husband and wife to sue for divorce after two years of marriage. All these laws, in permitting women more rights in marriage also allow them greater personal and economic independence from their husbands, and render them less dependent on persons who hold arbitrary authority over them. The long struggle in Italy for the law permitting state-subsidized abortions on demand gives women a great deal more control over their reproductivity, and thus over their economic and social lives.[19]

Legislation can – if it is enforced – also serve to protect women from male abuse. Women in the Jewish ghettoes of Eastern Europe during the Middle Ages were given an incredible amount of enforced legal protection in comparison with that afforded (or not afforded) the women of the dominant Gentile culture. I. Epstein attributes this to the fact that the economic contribution of the women was considered essential to men's ability to study the Talmud and thus keep the religious tradition alive in the midst of a hostile culture.[20] In the twelfth century the rabbis decreed that 'no husband should be allowed to leave his wife without the sanction of the community, a sanction which was to be granted only for the purpose of work and study, and to be limited to eighteen months.' Further, wife-beating was prohibited. 'In an age when wife beating was fashionable, and when a husband was allowed, according to rule, to strike his wife on the face or back for daring to contradict him, the Jewish wife was protected against violence and abuse; and the Jewish wife-beater was compelled to provide his wife with separate maintenance.'[21] In the eleventh century Rabbi Gershom 'abolished the long-standing right of the husband to forcibly set aside his wife .... No longer was the wife placed at the mercy of her husband for fear that she might incur his displeasure and suffer divorcement ....' Later, the rule was extended: 'no court was allowed to draft a bill of divorcement unless the husband had first obtained written sanction from three communities.'[22]

In the seventh century, Mohammed granted to Arab women many new rights and condemned female infanticide. Muslim women were given the right to possess property, a right French women did not have until the late 1950s.[23]

The problem has been that such rights were systematically violated over the years. Not only is the legal protection and status of women world-wide dependent on benign male rule for its creation, it is also dependent on men for enforcement, which helps explain why laws are not necessarily always a woman's best friend.

In some societies women are given legal power or token representation in male institutions, but face such hostilitiy once they arrive in powerful positions that they prefer to leave altogether. When extra effort is not put into further recruitment of qualified women, the positions often mysteriously vanish and men point to this process as further proof of women's inability to function equally in the male world.

An example was cited in *The Role of Women in Caribbean*

Development concerning:[24]

> the severe reduction in the involvement of women in
> missionary societies when their specifically women's
> organizations were merged with the general, male-led
> bodies working in the same areas . . . . where special
> concern is not given to the recruitment, training, and
> appointment of women, their representation is
> increasingly neglected, and their numbers dwindle.

Though government or agency-sponsored efforts on
behalf of women are an institutional response to demands
militantly presented by large numbers of women, the recognition and the jobs created by the passage of a new law or the
creation of a new agency relating to women often do not get
to women who pushed to make such changes. Because men
so firmly control these areas, the resulting decision-making
power usually does not rest with the majority of women who
fought for change, but rather with a few isolated individuals
who are accountable neither to those women, nor to the
women whose lives it will most dramatically affect.

This process takes place not only in capitalist and third-
world countries, but in socialist countries as well. The kinds
of changes are different, but the process by which change is
allowed to take place often remains the same. Here it is
'the Party' as opposed to the prime minister, congress or
corporations, that determines what change will be allowed. It
is seldom women, because they are rarely part of those male
institutions. If women's demands for change are heeded, they
are considered and acted upon by the 'Party', usually in a
more watered-down form. It is still not the masses of women
who directly determine the form the change will take. Nor
do women decide who will make the decisions, as the upper-
echelon decision-makers are usually male and appointed by
the Party.

Because change or development is thus controlled by men
or by men in combination with a few token women who
aren't in touch with the majority of women's needs, women
will sometimes resist it, even if on the surface it looks to be
in their best interest. In China, for example, many women

were resistant to the revolutionary government's changes in the marriage law. Although it provided for a far more egalitarian relationship between husband and wife, it also took away the only sources of security and personal control women had known, before alternative sources were well established in the society at large. Women were understandably reluctant to give up their survival strategies before being assured that alternatives existed.[25]

The same under-representation of women holds true within the United Nations and in the non-accountable representation during the 'United Nations Decade for Women' (1976-85). Many of the women who attended the International Women's Year conference in Mexico City were members of wealthy or political families who were not elected or appointed by other women in their countries, and who simply voiced their governments' policies. Rarely are 'representatives' at international conferences truly representative of the aspirations of the majority of women in their countries.

Improving working conditions: the standard of living

In many parts of the world women's first change efforts independent of outside initiative are geared towards raising their own or their families' standard of living. This is probably because so much of women's work is based in the home and an improvement in living conditions often means a lightening of their workload.

Women in a mountain town of Peru discussed a water-powered generator for electricity as a measure which would improve all of their lives. In Italy women are the backbone of the community movements to reduce prices, and in one case in Turin 600 families moved into empty apartment complexes because of the housing shortage and high rents. In some buildings they organized collective daycare. In some Italian cities they are refusing to pay consumer rates for electricity, and pay the lower industrial rates instead. Demonstrations against illegal food price increases have taken over stores and sold goods at half price for a day.[26]

In some countries women's collective efforts have resulted in projects that save them time and allow them to eventually raise their standard of living. For example, in Kenya, village women have formed roofing collectives. These women are responsible for the maintenance of the thatch roofs in their compounds, a time-consuming and difficult job. None of the women could afford to replace their thatch roofs with a tin one alone, but together they can pool their savings and buy one roof at a time.[27]

Rural women's groups throughout the world are forming to effect change in the lives of their families and villages, in their own behalf, and to help women in other countries. Over 150 groups (such as the All-India Women's Conference, Gruppi Donne Rurale in Italy and the Norges Husmorforbund in Norway) from 45 countries belong to a group called the Associated Countrywomen of the World, whose two major goals are to raise the standard of living for rural women and act as a voice for them in international affairs. Ina Beasley describes a project in which one of the member groups was involved:[28]

> In Ceylon, for example, one of the major national problems was also a global one, namely, the wastage of seasonal crops. Lanka Mahili Samiti – with a membership of 150,000 women – established a Rural Bottling Project with the help of the Cooperative for American Relief Everywhere (CARE). Within the first year, over 1,000 students from 1,700 local units all over Ceylon had registered at ten centers to study food preservation; each of these women went back to teach others in their village. Starting from this one pilot project, thousands of tons of food were preserved which would otherwise have been wasted; production was increased as people realized they could profitably add to their plantings, and many small bottling industries, truckers, and distributors were given extensive additional business.

Alison Raymond Lanier described other projects:[29]

> Projects supported wholly or in part by rural women range from literacy classes to vocational training. Often they are aimed at helping women to augment family

incomes – rug-weaving in Turkey; handcrafts in Indonesia
and the Philippines; tailoring, sewing, or soap-making in
India; food-preservation in Jamaica. Others contribute to
primary schools or raise scholarships to send girls to
universities.

Aside from the short-term help that such projects could
supply to many villages, they also establish the basis for
women to build networks through which they could work to
create more broad-based and long-term changes in their lives.

Love's labor lost

There are a variety of ways that women have tried to get
their unpaid work in the home recognized, which have
addressed the issues of loss of time and lack of pay. In many
countries community education about women's role in the
home has been a priority. In Norway, for example, women's
groups are doing public education about family law as it
pertains to women.

A group of women in Quebec have written and produced
a play called *Mom Doesn't Work, She Has Too Much Work
To Do*. The play describes several women who go on strike
for wages for their housework. The judge eventually grants
them an increase in their family allowances of five dollars
a month. The women change through the process of arguing
their case. They begin to expect help from their families in
running the house, and run a small used-goods store together
to make money for further projects.[30] The play illustrates
the processes of change, and lively discussions afterwards let
women share their experiences as houseworkers.

Discussion among Cuban women on a grass-roots level
about the Family Code reflects their increasing unwillingness
to shoulder the national development effort through their
unpaid work in the home. The statement of a Cuban woman
that 'If they're going to incorporate us into the workforce
they're going to have to incorporate themselves into the
home, and that's all there is to it!' shows the growing mili-
tancy of Cuban women against their double workload.[31]
With this kind of attitude the new Family Code, which can

only benefit women to the degree that it is enforced, is likely to be much more effective.

Aside from a few court settlements, however, the only actual cash benefits for work in the home that may come in the near future are social security benefits for women working in the home, for which women in the United States and West Germany are fighting, and increases in the family allowances, as in Britain. Women in West Germany are also demanding changes in divorce laws that take into account the years of labor that women put into housework. In Norway, women's groups are fighting for pensions and holidays for women working in the home, and to increase options for part-time paid work outside the home.

Yet none of these strategies address the underlying organization of women's work in the home. Over the years, these token power governments may grant more benefits such as these to stave off more widespread discussion of the underlying inequities. Giving women in the home their own social security and training them in the event of the loss of their husbands in no way addresses women's underlying role in the home, yet the benefits some women receive will increase their economic viability and thus their independence and self-respect.

In many of these same countries the underlying issues of women's lack of choice other than slave labor to men and children is being addressed by lesbian groups who are fighting to change laws concerning homosexuality. While in a few big cities women with sources of income independent of dominant male institutions are able to be open about their sexual preference, the vast majority still remains 'in the closet' for fear of losing their jobs or custody of their children. The violence of the backlash (ranging from loss of lesbian custody suits, to the beatings of women leaving gay bars) attests to the importance placed on women's continued coercion into their unpaid work in the home.

In minimal power societies efforts have gone into lightening women's workload in the home and providing a source of income, which has also facilitated network-building in rural areas. In Japan, for instance, women are organizing for more and better daycare facilities, so they may work where and when they want, without worrying about their children's safety. The Ministry of Agriculture has employed 1,000 women to visit homes and help districts to develop health centers and cooperative day nurseries, laundries and cooking centers.[32]

In other countries, similar projects run by predominantly female community groups also help women to develop skills that they will eventually be able to exercise on a grass-roots level, independent of outside initiatives.

This process of helping women to build networks and work collectively to make changes in their lives is evident in a West Indian women's handicraft cooperative, 'Madonna House,' which helps women through courses in developing and organizing cooperatives, community building, etc.[33]

All such projects give women important skills that can be used to develop strategies geared in the future towards changing their role, taking back some of their lost wealth and reclaiming time of their own.

Control of women's bodies

All over the world women are fighting for better health care and to protect themselves from violence committed against them by individual men and male institutions.

In several countries women are focusing directly on the protection of their lives and health, through demands for abortion and improved health care.

These actions bring women's lives more under their own control. They now have some opportunity to use their time for themselves, that would otherwise have been claimed by illness and more child raising.

The most important aspect of these strategies is that they have been developed by women to meet their own needs, not the needs of their 'society.' Japanese women, for example, are working to have more of women's work-related illnesses accepted as occupational hazards. Workplaces there are being held increasingly responsible for the neck and back pain called 'inflammation of the tendon sheath and cervical syndrome' that women develop from typing, keypunching, and doing childcare jobs. Employers may then be held responsible for the woman's health care, job security during treatment, and improved working conditions.[34]

HATT, the Housewives' Association of Trinidad and Tobago, ran a media campaign encouraging women to breast-feed their infants rather than use expensive and potentially dangerous infant formulas. The double-edged campaign also represented an attempt to address women's negative feelings about their sexuality as exemplified in their reluctance to breastfeed.[35]

Women are organizing against violence against women in a variety of ways besides providing the kinds of services we discussed earlier. In India women have begun campaigning against the dowry murders. Demonstrations are held outside the homes of families who have killed their daughters-in-law. Demonstrators in front of the home of a family in New Delhi accused of fatally burning their new daughter-in-law chanted, 'Women are not for burning.'

In the United States women formed groups and coalitions to mobilize their communities against the rapes and murders of women, such as the murders of black women in Boston in the winter of 1978-9.[36] Marches and street theatre focusing on issues of violence, as well as legislation to provide greater legal protection for women in crisis are also common. Increasingly, women are filing suits in rape and battering cases, and winning large settlements.[37]

Women are also fighting pornography and female sexual slavery. In Stockholm lesbian women's groups are campaigning against the 'Live Sex Shows' that abound there.[38] In Korea as well as Vietnam and Thailand, where the withdrawal marriage tours which provide prostitutes for travelling businessmen, for which young women are recruited from Korea as well as Vietnem and Thailand, where the withdrawal of the American military left a vast surplus of prostitutes.[39]

7 The economy of the world of women

A Woman's Intuition has often proved truer than man's arrogant assumption of superior knowledge.

Mahatma Gandhi

Women have no need to prove their manhood.

Wilma Scott Heide

Once made equal to man, woman becomes his superior.

Socrates

Across all cultures women share some basic experiences that separate their lives from those of men. Though specific surroundings vary from formica kitchens to hand-plowed fields, and jobs that are men's work in one society are women's work a few miles away, women share responsibility for much of the maintenance of society. Many of the similarities in women's low status cross-culturally are based on the inequitable divisions of labor by sex.

Until now, we have attempted in this book to document some of the inequalities in work and rewards. In this section we will be asking questions and posing theories which are hard to back up with the scarcity of data currently available. In fact, we are plunging here, not only into the *content* of the question of a matriarchal economy and culture, but into a female-value-based way of discussing such a question. By this we mean that many women think what they think based on their own experience, regardless of statistics and 'hard facts' presented to them. If something doesn't 'ring true', no amount of 'hard facts' will make it seem any truer. Whether this section rings true to the reader or not, we hope it will provoke further thoughts on the questions involved.

Of sugar and spice, snakes and snails

> Because of the eternal vanity, the *pendejo machismo*
> of the Mexican, I couldn't humiliate myself by going
> back to Graciela . . . .
> Mexicans, and I think everyone in the world, admires the
> person 'with balls' as we say. The character who throws
> punches and kicks, without stopping to think, is the one
> who comes out on top .
> If any so-and-so comes to me and says, 'Fuck your
> mother,' I answer, 'Fuck your mother a thousand times.'
> And if he gives one step forward and I take one step back,
> I lose prestige. But if I go forward too, and pile on and
> make a fool out of him, then the others will treat me
> with respect. In a fight, I would never give up or say,
> 'Enough,' even though the other was killing me. I would
> try to go to my death, smiling. That is what we mean by
> being 'macho,' by being manly.
>
> Manuel Sanchez,
The Children of Sanchez[1]

> Thus, to my sorrow, was my first, bitter encounter with
> that infamous, cursed Mexican *machismo*. I, like an
> infinite number of other Mexican women, was part of that
> cruel game, in which the domineering male wins. 'Shall I
> knock you down or let you free?' There is nothing
> generous, noble or worthy in it, for there is a price to
> being let free. It is a barbarous act of egotism and
> advantage, adorned with persuasive words.
>
> Consuelo Sanchez,
The Children of Sanchez[2]

Because women the world over share a similar relationship to the male-dominated economies in which they live, they have been socialized in similar ways to do similar work. Women have also developed common personality traits to help them adapt to the conditions of their lives, and common survival strategies which have in turn affected their personalities and world-views.

Certain common themes emerge when we look at the literature, the myths, the expressions and proverbs of different cultures concerning women, their role and the culture's expectation of them. If we examine them more closely, it becomes clearer that many of these themes can be traced to the exigencies of women's work, including women's role in the past and the demands made on them in the present.

A feminist anthropologist, Michelle Zimbalist Rosaldo, has pointed out that 'Women . . . . lead relatively comparable lives, both within a culture and from one culture to the next.' Because women's lives are seen and understood in most cultures only in relation to the lives of the men in their families, and 'because cultures provide no fine social classification for kinds of women and their interests, women are seen and come to see themselves as idiosyncratic and irrational.'[3] Rosaldo also quotes the anthropologist Landes on the sex roles of the native American Ojibwa people: 'Only the male half of the population and its activities fall under the traditional regulations, while the female half is left to spontaneous and confused behavior.' Women's lives, Rosaldo points out, are repeatedly seen as unstructured and spontaneous because they don't fall into male-defined categories of behavior. Most male scientists simply do not see or understand the rationales motivating women's behavior, and so they do not examine them as women's responses to sexism, or as survival strategies in a male-dominated world, where others define the game and make the rules. They make no effort to separate stereotypes from actual commonalities in women's lives based on common experience.

The dominant (male) culture sees women as:
breeders
better with children
closer to the earth
big talkers, gossipers
passive, devious, indirect
without a sense of self-preservation or of how to get ahead
preoccupied with details, the 'petty', home-oriented
emotional, irrational, emotive

silly, 'not serious', more child-like
'Good women' are those who keep quiet, don't argue, do their work diligently, and have no needs or demands independent of their families'.

These lists we all know well. We've only mentioned the most obvious stereotypes here. What is more interesting is the way in which the previous lists differ from a new list we might make, of how women who have rejected the male definitions of their behavior perceive themselves, for it is often radically different from how individual men or the dominant male culture sees women.

The difference between how men perceive women and how women perceive themselves can usually be explained by the fact that men see women as they would have them be in order to meet male needs and expectations, or as women respond to those expectations. The extent to which women accept men's estimation and expectations of them is the extent to which they remain powerless and unable to act in their own behalf. Women who do not identify with men's uninformed view of them have an opinion of themselves and each other which is far more respectful and reality-based. Individual women often have a clear view of experiences they are familiar with while accepting other stereotypes that have not been challenged by their experience.

When women are grounded in a firm sense of themselves, are strongly identified with women rather than men, and have respect for who they are, they usually can and want to effect change in their own behalf.

In the following list, the same traits are interpreted positively from a female perspective:

creators of life
nurturing and caring
down-to-earth, having common sense, reality-based
value communications, sharing information and
    discussing it
clever at making something out of nothing, getting what
    they need in a hostile environment, getting around
    barriers erected to keep them back
cooperative, sharing, placing other's needs above their own
diligent, hard-working, dependable

sensitive, intuitive
   in touch with spontaneous self, and preferring harmonious
      to threatening behavior.

Both women and men see women primarily in their role as bearers of children and workers in the home. But men have little or no respect for women's work, except when it is directly beneficial to them and when they can put it on a pedestal. They see all other aspects of that work as stereo-typical female behavior.

Some women, aware of the difficulty of the conditions of their work, see their behavior for what it is: survival strategies, a need for an alternative communications system which meets their needs, the necessity of coming across as 'not serious' so as not to scare and anger men, of being indirect in getting what they need to maintain men's perception that men are always in control, etc. Men see only women's powerlessness since they have such an investment in maintaining their own control in each interaction with women, and so do not see women's behavior in the total context of women's lives.

Though the categories of women's work are the same worldwide, they are manifested differently in different cultures. Nurturing, for example, might mean providing food for her children to a poor woman from southern Italy; teaching her daughter skills in trading for a West African woman; or providing verbal emotional support to her children for a middle-class western woman. While mothering means different things to different women (disciplining v. spoiling their children), in all cultures it is viewed primarily as the means by which children are reared and survive. Because survival necessitates differing strategies depending on the economic and social context, so too does mothering behavior. Thus in poor and working class urban black communities in the United States, streetfighting can be a part of the female value system because it is required for survival.[4] But it would be a foreign skill, perhaps viewed only as a part of the male role, by white middle-class women in the same country.

Kris Rosenthal, a feminist sociologist, explains the origin of many of the stereotypes of women by describing them as characteristics of a 'guest' culture, as viewed by the dominant culture:[5]

> You can get a lot of understanding about men's and
> women's interactions by simply understanding how
> two different cultures with some different codes interact
> . . . . the female culture has been defined for us by men
> . . . . and when you look at women and how they are
> described, they are described as strangers in another
> culture. So for example, women are described as modest.
> Of course you're modest, because you're in front of
> strangers. And that modesty is not an inherent quality of
> women, but a condition of someone who's a guest in
> somebody else's house. A lot of the manners between men
> and women exemplify the fact that women are visitors.
> When a man holds open a door for her or pulls out a chair
> for her, it really means, 'you're in my house, you're a
> guest, you're visiting, and this is the chair you sit in. And
> I will hold your coat and light your cigarette, and if I
> don't want you here, I'll usher you out.' It is an expression
> of who owns the space and who's visiting. What it means
> to go into exile, [is that] things that have a meaning in
> your own culture acquire a different meaning and that
> meaning becomes derogatory. The sense of the word
> 'demeaning' is to make insignificant, but really means to
> take the meaning away from it.
>   [For example,] the other culture doesn't respect
> [women's] products . . . . You clean a floor and they come
> in with muddy shoes. Women are put down as shrill and
> stupid because they don't let people walk on the floor
> they just cleaned. But they're desperately trying to get
> people to appreciate their products.

In exploring the notion of a woman's culture, we will be referring to the characteristics attributed to women and positively interpreted as 'female values'. Those which women and men attribute to men we will call stereotyped 'male values'. Men who comprise the dominant culture have defined themselves, and so we are only using one list of stereotypical male values. It is interesting to note, however, that while both sexes define male traits similarly, men tend to assign a positive value to them. Whereas women, who are more alienated from the dominant culture's value system, often view male traits with disdain, pity, or great reserve.

This list is also familiar:

aggressive, competitive
strong, invulnerable
unemotive, stoical
territorial, domineering, in control
individualistic
noncommunicative concerning feelings and interpersonal motives
emotionally distanced from those close to them, etc.

When referring to a 'female' or 'matriarchal' value system, culture, economy, etc., we will be alluding to a system based upon values and characteristics commonly attributed to women by self-identified women such as the second list of women's characteristics we gave. Similarly, a 'male' or 'patriarchal' system is based on such stereotypical male values and traits as we just listed. Not all women share female or matriarchal values, nor do all men live patriarchal life-styles. The use of these terms refers to the ways in which men and women are socialized as groups, and to this understanding of the meaning of 'male' and 'female' values. Though we are not precluding the many exceptions to these general definitions, all present societies reflect patriarchal values to a much greater extent than matriarchal values.

The world of woman

> Freud said once that woman is not well acculturated;
> she is, he stressed, retarded as a civilized person. I think
> what he mistook for her lack of civilization is woman's
> lack of *loyalty* to civilization.
>
> Lillian Smith[6]

Do women, by virtue of their common work and common characteristics, share what could be considered a common culture? If so, is this culture a result of a shared history, shared role in society, shared biology, or some combination of these and other factors?

For the purposes of this discussion, we are defining culture as a set of beliefs, values and behaviors that characterizes a certain group whose identity has evolved out of a particular historical experience.

Separate culture theories

There are many theories as to whether social minority groups have distinctly separate cultures from the dominant culture, 'shadow' cultures, or no common cultural features at all.

Eliot Liebow, in describing what he refers to as a 'lower-class shadow culture', believes that these values are 'derivative' of the dominant culture, based in adaptive behavior rather than 'real' values, as a result of distortions in the 'lower-class' environment.[7] This view of 'lower-class' culture is questionable because it sees the dominant cultures as the norm and compares the less powerful culture to it, finding the latter 'less weighty' and 'subsidiary in nature.' It ignores distinct cultural values belonging to different racial, ethnic and gender groups.

The debate as to whether socially oppressed groups have distinct cultures has been affected by the fact that often social scientists justify discriminatory treatment towards non-dominant groups by seeing them as culturally distinct. Just as many politicians, businessmen, government officials and others have used their interpretation of a distinct 'lower-class' culture as a justification for impeding much needed economic reforms, so have many men referred to women's supposed biological destiny to keep women powerless. The middle-class assumption that people on welfare in the United States don't want to work excuses the use of them as a reserve labor force, meaning that their presence as a large number of unemployed people helps to keep wages down while maintaining high profits.

This myth is suspiciously similar to the common male assumption that women love the home, feel safe and protected by its isolation, and couldn't cope well in the 'male' world. Adages like the familiar 'a woman's place is in the home,' with thousands of multi-cultural variations, have been used to link women's biology with their slave status in the home.

Some theorists who criticize separate culture theories because they are used to justify discrimination believe that oppressed people react to the facts of their position and relative isolation rather than according to separate cultural values. Their emphasis has been on pushing to change the 'background conditions .... rather than [focusing] on presumably different class or cultural values', as another anthropologist states.[8]

Yet the fact that in the past the dominant culture has defined social minorities as subcultures for its own purposes does not mean that there is no value in such a group *defining itself* as culturally distinct. Recognition by less powerful individuals of their common experiences and of real differences from the dominant culture has been a tremendous source of self-knowledge and thus self-respect. To be grounded in a strong sense of self, and to be self-identified rather than looking to others or a more powerful culture for definition have served as a solid base from which to act in one's own behalf and have also helped to perpetuate a variety of cultures.[9]

Kris Rosenthal describes the importance of self-identification as saying to women: 'You're not an ugly duckling in the duckling family. You're really a swan and this is what the swan experiences.' Rosenthal adds that even though it 'is underground, confused, seems like a mark of oppression and many women are very ambivalent towards it .... the coherent presentation of [female] culture would provide a lot of insights for people. It gives them some strength.'[10]

Historical base of women's culture

Theories about ancient matriarchies are among the wide variety of arguments that have been developed to explain the basis for women's culture today. Such arguments have drawn from biology, history, and women's relationship to patriarchal economies.

One theory is that a continuing and separate women's

culture is a carry-over from ancient woman-controlled, woman-centered matriarchal societies. There is clear evidence that these societies once existed, though what they were actually like is open to much speculation.[11] Some historians attribute to them a range of female-based values. In her article 'Matriarchy: A Vision of Power' Paula Webster summarized this view[12] as saying that women's

> reproductive abilities and consequent attachment to life over death, creation over destruction, and harmony over conflict make women innately different from, and superior to, men . . . . The matriarchy . . . . was not a mirror image of the patriarchy that followed it, for the society . . . . was harmonious and spiritual.

While there also exists some evidence of a few woman-controlled societies where women actually have had the upper hand, the most widespread evidence is that of 'egalitarian' societies where there was little or no class stratification and the only major division of labor was by sex.[13] Theories about these cultures are reconstructed from historical accounts of travelers, archeological data, oral histories and contemporary analyses of how foreign influence altered them. Unfortunately, it is hard to determine the male and female perceptions of their roles and power, the true division in *volume* of work, and the social value placed on it. Thus it is hard to tell whether women actually held equal power within a sexually egalitarian or matriarchal context, or whether they held negotiating power within a patriarchal context. What is clear, however, is the relationship between female power and the degree to which female values are incorporated into the culture, for in most of these cultures there are far fewer social and economic hierarchies, and less competition, than are found in cultures where women hold less power.

This historical perspective might help to explain the origin of women's relatively high status in some pre-colonial African societies. The rulers of Egypt until roughly 2,000 BC are believed by some to have been primarily women – high priestesses who came to the throne after forty years of training in the sciences, mathematics, medicine and astronomy. It was women who were believed to have travelled from ancient Egypt to all corners of the globe, establishing astronomical observatories where they took readings of the stars to predict eclipses. These voyages help to account for the prevalence in other cultures of religious symbols used in ancient Egypt, and common names given to constellations, statues and idols sculpted in similar styles throughout the world. The downfall of this culture appears to have brought about an accompanying change in the role of women, as Arab and Muslim influences overtook northern Africa, and Mecca was established at the site of an ancient priestesses' worship temple.[14] Many of the people of ancient Egypt are believed to have travelled to the south and west, across the Sahara, to ancient Mali, and then along the Niger River to what is now Nigeria, settling there and further west along the coast of western Africa. These coastal Akan-language cultures are among those West African societies where there were Amazon warriors (as in the kingdom of Dahomey) and where women are still supported by such institutions as female priestesses, divinities and queen mothers, economic independence, and some variety in the marriage structures.[15]

Historical arguments have also been used to address the common male view that women are so different from (i.e. inferior to) men that they are incapable of participating equally in the world. Such arguments point to women's equal participation and power in earlier societies. Examples such as the Amazon warriors in ancient Dahomey and the recently discovered graves of female warriors in Germany who fought, were lauded, and died next to male soldiers two thousand years ago, are used to prove that women's biology does not determine their destiny.[16]

But for many, the value of the matriarchy theories lies in the future, not the past,[17]

in its rejection of power in the hands of men, regardless
of the form of social organization. It pushes women (and
men) to imagine a society that is not patriarchal, one in
which women might for the first time have power over
their lives. Women have been powerless, and have had their

reality defined for them, for so long that imagining such
a society is politically important.

Some women writers have tried to fulfill the need for
mind-opening new visions and to express their own values
with realistic novels, science fiction, or feminist fantasies.
Charlotte Perkins Gilman published *Herland* as a serial in her
feminist magazine, *The Forerunner*, in 1915, along with
theoretical analyses and news. Her description of a matriarchal society shows her personal view of a women's value
system. It explores how a culture might look where the
female values inherent in the mothering role had become a
social ethic – cooperation, sharing, creativity and independence – guiding everyone's life and aspirations.[18] More recently
authors such as Marge Piercy, Suzi McKee Charnas, Joanna
Russ, and Sally Gearhart have also created mythical societies
with female values.[19]

Biological base of women's culture

Some feminists have seen women's culture as being grounded
in their biological make-up and have affirmed the biologically-
based characteristics.

One theory is that the culture itself derives from the
biological fact that the fetus's needs are put above those of
the mother. If, for example, the mother doesn't have enough
calcium in her body, the fetus will take it, often at the
woman's expense. Once the nine month investment in the
baby's life is made, its needs continue to come before those
of the mother because it is completely helpless. Rosenthal
says this is the real meaning of investment:

> Your product is something that you own but don't own,
> that you use all your power to take care of . . . . and that
> eventually takes its place beside you in some equal or
> better fashion. That colors women's attitudes towards
> their products in general . . . . they have a different kind of
> respect for them.

Thus women's role as nurturers is biologically based but passed on through socialization to reinforce it, so that women inherit the culture whether or not they have children.[20]

That women create and maintain life sensitizes them to its value and makes them more invested in not seeing it destroyed. That women are bound into monthly cycles and pregnancies grounds them in a respect for and knowledge of nature's power, the antithesis of the arrogant, patriarchal notion that nature can be controlled and other lives destroyed at will.

Some theorists believe that women are inherently superior and should therefore have more power than men so as to create a more human culture and prevent men from exercising their violent tendencies. (This argument usually refers to the aggression associated with testosterone and the male Y chromosome, or women's natural reproductive abilities and stamina.)[21] Other arguments state that men must be eliminated entirely or geographically separated at least temporarily, from women [except a few for reproduction] since they are innately destructive and non-creative.[22] Others, who are concerned with how some 'biology is destiny' theories have been used against women, argue that women are basically the same as men, and all functions which have been considered women's biological destiny should in the future be de-sexualised through the use of test-tube babies, so that men and women can share all responsibilities and become the social equals they have the potential to be.[23]

Economic base of women's culture

The very fact that women talk in a different way when they are among themselves, without men, proves that there is a whole capital of specifically feminine values which has not yet been exploited. These values are clandestine and they are submerged in the history of mankind, which, as the word suggests, has always been the history of men.

'Feminitude', for me, means the responses created by oppression and these can become the leaven of our struggle, a dynamic force enabling women to change themselves.

Gisele Halimi,
'Feminine Values – A Capital to be Developed'[24]

The economic determinants of women's values and characteristics are often overlooked. Many of the ways women think,
act and react are really requirements of their job: women's
collective responsibility for bearing, raising and nurturing the
next generation and for maintaining the home in which their
families live. This responsibility, this unpaid 'employment'
that women inherit from birth, necessitates certain behavior
both to be able to do it and to be able to survive doing it.

To begin with, women's work in many societies, whether
negotiating, token or minimal power societies, takes place in
a realm which is divorced from the male world to varying
degrees. An early English traveler noted of Iroquois life:[25]

> Indian habits and modes of life divided the people
> socially into two great classes, male and female. The
> male sought the conversation and society of the male,
> and they went forth together for amusement, or for the
> severer duties of life. In the same manner the female
> sought the companionship of her own sex. Between the
> sexes there was but little sociality.

The same is true of market women whose social networks
are shaped during the long days at the marketplace, of women
in purdah who work alone in their homes or with female
relatives or friends, of middle-class American and European
women whose work in the home is totally divorced from that
of their husbands, and of mothers whose emotional and
financial sharing among their peers is often what keeps their
families going.

In the Carib culture (before colonization of the Caribbean),
women had a separate and radically different history, culture
and language from men, which was based in their economic
role. Many of them were originally captured Arawak Indians
who retained their own language, which they used only in
speaking with each other, but which the men understood yet
did not deign to speak. The women also knew the men's
language and used it when addressing men, but not with each
other. Men who had been to war, especially older men,
spoke a third language, which only they understood.[26]

The Arawak people were described as 'simple, quiet,

serviceable and hospitable to strangers' by travelers in the region who also noted that the Caribs regarded the Arawak women 'as a subject race and . . . . compelled them to retain the simple and gentle characteristics of their former nation.'[27] Thus it is clear that women's separate value system served an extremely useful function to the men they were serving. Yet it is also possible that the women *chose* to retain these traits for purposes of their own.

As the servant class, the women sustained the economy.[28] Their work was not accompanied by corresponding power and the women were regarded with contempt. 'They were despised when not needed for some utilitarian purpose.'[29] The women bore from 10 to 15 children each, but the girls were neglected after their tenth year, and the men and boys ate first, the women and girls eating what remained.[30]

The women's unaggressiveness, combined with the men's violence toward them, is probably what prevented them from revolting in large numbers. One priest noted that:[31]

> Their women are taught the strictest obedience from their tenderest youth, but it is obvious that they feel this harsh yoke although they are always gentle and quiet . . . . the only people who are obliged to obey are the women and the men are their absolute masters.

Their obedience was often enforced with extreme violence.[32]

Yet women's distinct value system must have been a tremendous source of bonding and support. Although women's networks were not recorded by the male authors, they did make some passing references, noting, for example, the women 'working together so amicably and quietly, that I never heard a cross word spoken.'[33]

Thus women's separate value system was retained by the women both because it was permitted and encouraged by the men, and also because it served as a tremendous source of support for the women.

Women's responsibility to sustain their families often necessitates their developing systems of reciprocity – to share scant and irregular surplus, with the knowledge that it will be returned when the recipient has surplus and the sharer is in need. Carol Stack's study of women's networks in a low-income urban black community shows how it is precisely this choice to give away and share surplus that insures the community's survival. The sharing (of work, meals, money, clothing, or housing) within their peer groups, rather than competing and accumulating, is a value fundamentally opposed to the patriarchal territorial and acquisitive impulse, yet it survives alongside the dominant male culture and its value system. It's women's job to take care of others, whether or not the 'others' are willing or able to express what they need. Men, on the other hand, are taught they don't have to be sensitive to the needs of others, that they will be tended to by women. Though in some cultures men are allowed to be sensitive on a superficial level, they do not have the underlying commitment to put others' well being before their own, and their 'sensitivity' is in fact often a more subtle mechanism for getting what they want.

Men's lives generally have so little to do with the realm of emotional and service work, that they can far more easily make distinctions between their work and personal relationships. Such a distinction is part of the process of generalized social stratification which encourages extreme specialization to increase material productivity. This stratification is generally equated with women's decreasing social and economic autonomy and power since women are usually relegated to low-status, low-paying service occupations which are seen as an extension of the servicing skills acquired in the home.

This stratification necessitates an increasing schism in the talents, interests and abilities of each individual, which is a fundamentally dehumanizing process. The fact that women's work is relatively unspecialized and calls upon a variety of emotions and skills to perform is probably partly responsible for women's greater integration of feelings, intuitive skills and intelligence, relative to men who often divorce their feelings and intuitive abilities from their work lives. This separation often results in flagrant abuses of power by men in decision-making roles.

It is not always possible to separate and understand the many historical, economic, and biological strands which comprise women's culture. At what point, for example, does a value socialized into women for economic purposes become an independently chosen trait?

It is clear that women share a great deal more than biology, though the factors which have influenced them across cultures are varied and complex. There are objective biological, historical and economic ties that bind women together and create tremendous similarities in women's culture across racial, class and national boundaries.

A statement written by women from many different cultures participating in a seminar on 'Women and World Disarmament' in Vienna in 1978 echoes the female values inherent in many women's peace groups around the world:[34]

> The statement called for general and complete disarmament and it said that the women wanted the one billion dollars now spent daily on arms to be used to eliminate unemployment, disease, hunger and illiteracy, and to improve the existing conditions of the millions living in want and economic underdevelopment.
>
> In a background paper prepared for the seminar, Ms. Sipila said . . . . that peace is not just the absence of war, but rather the creation of conditions in which peace could be maintained and that women must start action against the wasteful use of national wealth.

Whether women were once powerful and created matriarchal cultures grounded in female values is a question which will be open to debate for years to come. Whether some of women's values are derivative of ancient matriarchies, or adaptation strategies for coping in a male-dominated world is also a question for debate. What's more important, at this point, than where these values originated is the fact that women have claimed and held onto them because they were desirable, useful and a source of strength. They have been of value as survival tools to help them live in a hostile, male-dominated world and in trying to improve the conditions of their lives. If it can be said that many of these traits are biologically and perhaps historically based, they therefore exist separately from the dominant male culture. Though economic-based characteristics could be seen as deriving only from the dominant culture, as work requirements or adaptation and survival strategies, even these characteristics are not 'shadow values.' Women, even in their reactions to the dominant culture, usually do *not* share the general values of the dominant culture, nor are their values 'derivative' or 'insubstantial'[35] To the contrary, women's values and behavior which respond to their economic exploitation are radically different from what is promoted by dominant male ideology. This is because those women's values which are a response to economic exploitation are closely linked with those aspects of women's culture which are biologically or historically based.

A woman's culture across cultures?

To say that women share a common culture, similar values and responses to their environment, is *not* to say that all women in all cultures identify with each other, or that their shared culture is experienced or manifested in the same way. The point is not that all women think, act and respond to the dominant culture in the same way, but that their biology, their relationship to the economies in which they live and perhaps even their history, structures their experience in similar ways. Women can only know and understand this underlying structure of similarities in their lives if they explore the differences in these experiences. Though the same values are manifested differently in different cultural contexts, they still share characteristics different from those of the men in women's lives and have the potential to become bonds between women's lives across cultures.

The value in exploring the concept of a women's culture lies in shedding some light on the many forms by which patriarchal cultures exploit women, and the many mechanisms which women have devised, both to survive their hostile worlds and to begin to change them.

To understand other women's experiences is to strengthen each woman's potential for change – to give her new tools and new understandings of what has worked for women in other situations and the myriad of ways patriarchal cultures have found to maintain women's subservience. Ultimately it will be through the joining of women of diverse, rather than similar, experience, with diverse priorities and strategies, that a powerful movement with the capacity for truly broad-based change can be built. Difference can only be divisive when it is feared and not understood.

The same social and economic forces have not affected each woman identically. The characteristics of the dominant male culture make a great difference, as do the class, racial, ethnic and religious background of each woman within each culture. These other social forces are so strong that often women do not identify with each other across these (male-defined and male-maintained) boundaries. Many Latina, native American, Asian-American, black or white women married to working-class men in the United States, for example, are hard put to identify with white women married to upper-middle and upper-class men. Michele Russell, in an article entitled 'Sexism and Racism: The American Reality,' says:[36]

A fourteen year old girl assembling transistors in a Hong Kong factory, a German waitress in a hotel, a typing instructor in Mexico, and a senior accountant commuting from Westport, Conn., all women, all also work for the same company . . . . [This represents] an economic range in the market value of women's labor from 30c an hour for 14 hours of work a day to $30,000 or more a year plus fringe benefits and no time clock at all. It also indicates that, MS magazine notwithstanding, Sisterhood is an ideology that just isn't powerful enough to bridge that range.

Sisterhood, or a shared culture, does not mean that every woman in every culture necessarily identifies more closely with women from other cultures and experiences than with the men in her own world. It means, rather, that each woman encountering sexual, racial or class exploitation in her work-life shares the same relationship to the male economy as her female peers, both at her paid work place and in her home. It means that each woman could benefit most by discussing her problems and experiences with women in similar situations, at the same worksite, for example. With these other women she shares a common experience, culture and perspective, forming one of the variants of women's culture. And with these other women she can unite to begin to create changes in their lives. Women working for change with other women of similar experiences then might unite in coalition with women from differing experiences, to push for bottom-line changes that affect them all.

The commonality in women's shared cross-cultural experience can best be seen when the circumstances of their lives as women carry them through similar events. The bond which is created can be shared in the maternity ward, the hospital emergency room tending a sick child, recovering from a rape, at a shelter for battered women, taking refuge from an abusive husband, at the welfare office when their husbands have 'fired' or left them. The dynamics of all these women's daily lives may be very different, but their experiences, within their cultures, as women, forge bonds between them that are shared by women within each culture and during woman-centered experiences or crises, across cultures.

The element of conscious identification with other women is not a primary factor in considering the question of a woman's culture. Many women are not aware of identifying with other women. They experience their lives as focused around their families and the men in their lives, yet share their feelings about these lives, and look for solace and support with each other. Whether women consciously identify more closely with each other or with the men in their lives is simply a determinant of women's ability to make changes in their lives. Carol Oliver, in her article, 'On Black Feminism and Culture,' expands on the importance of one's culture in forming one's world view:[37]

> Cultural resistance is the fight for autonomy – self-determined survival and growth. Assimilation is the expected passive reaction . . . . that requires some level of adaptation . . . .
> These two ways of defining the self and viewing the world have evolved from the fundamental need for survival in a completely hostile, antagonistic, dehumanizing foreign

environment.

When women look to men's culture for definition and identify more closely with the men in their lives, they are less able to act in their own behalf. When women internalize their adaptation strategies and live for male approval, their culture begins to approach a 'shadow culture' rather than an independent source of support, respect and growth. The extent to which women are conscious of and grounded in their own (women's) culture, and feel the gap between their lives and the view of the dominant male culture, is the extent to which they are able to become independent, and to use their women's space, not for letting off steam, but for growth and change.

Women's culture as a survival strategy

One focus of [Australian aboriginal] women's solidarity and autonomy, in the past as now, is the single women's camp, the *jilimi*. Here live widows who have chosen not to remarry, the estranged wives of violent husbands, women who are ill or visiting from another country, and all their dependent children. In fact, any woman who wishes to live free of the conflicts of heterosexual society may seek refuge in the *jilimi*. Married women who are living with their husbands congregate in the *jilimi* during the day to talk and plan visits, family affairs, and ritual matters. The *jilimi* is taboo to all men, who often must travel long, circuitous routes to avoid passing nearby.

Diane Bell,
'Desert Politics'[38]

Most women experience their lives and values as separate from men's even if they do not consciously see this as a difference in culture. These distinct values are useful in that they offer women a source of support in a hostile environment, and make possible various strategies for their physical and emotional survival. Men have also tolerated women's culture because they also benefit from women's continuing to produce for them. While women's quality of placing the needs of others before their own makes their networks extremely supportive, the networks exist within a patriarchal framework that is largely sustained by this same characteristic. Unless women's cultural values can be used to generate change through the development of a female power base, women's culture will continue to function largely as a survival mechanism for women, and a source of free labor for men.

Much of women's behavior can be understood as a combination of separate, preferred values which comprise female culture and of adaptive values and behavior that women have adopted to help them survive in the male world. While women's collective survival strategies have tended to reinforce their separate culture, women's *individual* survival strategies have often represented adaptations of isolated women to the male culture in which they are living. Thus, female behavior that might not seem in keeping with the matriarchal values we discussed earlier can often be understood as methods women have devised for coping in a hostile male world.

Many elements of women's cultures, from the use of their networks, values and even, in some cases, distinct language as methods of communication and support, to the creation of a women's space to share problems, strategies and sometimes to break out of their constraining lives can be seen as collective survival strategies. These networks or cultural spaces provide a basis for women's bonding.

For women living in minimal power societies, the simple creation of women's networks as sources of support is of tremendous importance to their survival, emotionally and even physically. The use of these networks for change usually does not even fall within their frame of reference. In token power societies, networks and women's spaces are an obvious emotional necessity for US, Soviet, Cuban and Swedish housewives. Within negotiating power societies, the shared work lives of Ewé and Chinese women create the same kinds of bonding that the Iroquois women received from each other. A white woman who was adopted into the life of the Seneca people (part of the Iroquois) described the sharing involved in their work:[39]

In the summer season, we planted, tended, and
harvested our corn, and generally had all of our
children with us; but had no master to oversee or drive
us, so that we could work as leisurely as we pleased . . . .
We pursued our farming business according to the
general custom of Indian women, which is as follows:
In order to expedite their business, and at the same time
enjoy each other's company, they all work together in
one field, or at whatever job they may have on hand.

In minimal power societies, and to a certain extent in
token societies, women's networks also serve the additional
function of insuring women's physical survival, as in instances
of friends helping and sheltering a woman threatened by
her husband.

In discussing the values concerning marriage in a low-
income black community in the US, Liebow unwittingly
illustrates the cultural difference between men's and women's
expectations and values in marriage, and their differing
survival strategies in response to a hostile, racist and economically unstable environment:[40]

Few married men, however, do in fact support their
families over sustained periods of time. Money is
chronically in short supply and chronically a source of
dissension in the home. Financial support for herself and
her children remains one of the principal unmet
expectations of the wife. Moreover, although providing
such support would be so far as the husband is concerned,
necessary and sufficient, the wife – who seldom gets even
this much – wants more, much more . . . .
It is not enough that he simply gives money for her
and the children's support, then steps away until the next
time he shares his pay day with them. She wants him to
join them as a full-time member of the family, to
participate in their affairs, to take an active interest in her
and the children, in their activities, in their development as
individuals . . . . She wants the family to present a united
front to the outside world.
Alas, she ends up standing alone or, worse perhaps,

having to hold him up as well . . . .

Thus, marriage is an occasion of failure. To stay married is to live with your failure, to be confronted by it day in and day out. It is to live in a world whose standards of manliness are forever beyond one's reach, where one is continually tested and challenged and found wanting. In self-defense, the husband retreats to the streetcorner. Here, where the measure of man is considerably smaller, and where weaknesses are somehow turned upside down and almost magically transformed into strengths, he can be, once again, a man among men.

Although the view of black men as failures is surely grounded in the racism of many white social scientists, men's lack of responsibility within the home (which is common to many cultures) has also been described by black male social scientists such as Robert Staples, who notes:[41]

There is a curious rage festering inside black men because, like it or not, they have not been allowed to fulfill the roles (i.e. breadwinner, protector) society ascribed to them . . . . That black men are not staying with their families is due to a confluence of certain factors, not the least among them is the fact that some women do make the decisions and desertion is his form of masculine protest . . . . Desertion, moreover, is the lower-class male's style of exercising his masculine perquisite.

Here we see a situation where women and men share the same economic reality and racial discrimination, yet their responses to it are diametrically opposed. The standards and expectations that women have of marriage are entirely different from men's, yet not terribly different from those of women of other classes or races. Men's retreat to the street-corner is, again, not terribly different from the retreat of men of other races and class backgrounds, to bar-rooms, pool halls, or men's exclusive clubs. Here, women's response to economic deprivation is to pull together as a unit, while men's response is to pull away from them, and retreat to a non-demanding, low expectation, male environment. Women carry the cost of the separate culture system, both in their disproportionate share of work in sustaining their families, and in the degrading stereotyping of their role as demanding and castrating matriarchs.

A cross-cultural example of the survival value of female characteristics is that told by Charles Nordhoff and James Norman Hall in *Pitcairn's Island*, derived from the true story of a group of British men and Tahitian men and women beginning a new life on a South Pacific island. Within a few years, some of the British men tried to make the Tahitian men subservient, the Tahitian men resisted and revolted and most of the men killed each other. When the remaining men's lives grew increasingly degenerate, the women moved to the other side of the island with their children, built a stockade for protection and raised their children in peace and quiet. They eventually moved back when the remaining two men came to their senses and adopted what might be considered female values.[42]

In some cases a survival strategy which is effective within one cultural context does not work against men from a different culture. For example, Igbo women fought the British in 1928 during the period of colonization of Nigeria. The British attempted to impose a system of taxation which would severely affect women's economic viability, and also tried to take away women's traditional right to extra-marital sexual relations. The Igbo women had strong organizations which they used in making laws for women, negotiating legal cases involving women and regulating the markets. When the British intervened, the women got together and tried to negotiate with the British interests. With the men's refusal to negotiate, the women began to demonstrate, and their efforts became increasingly volatile as they were continually ignored. During the next year women engaged in the 'women's war' (as they called it, while colonial males described it as 'the Aba riots') and began to burn the homes of the British and their Nigerian representatives who collected taxes. The British soldiers then intervened, but the Igbo women held their ground. They strongly believed that the 'spirit of womanhood' was protecting them, and that they were invulnerable to male bullets. Unfortunately the huge cultural differences and male military superiority meant that the women's strategy failed. The soldiers opened fire on the women, killing fifty-three, while the British doctor ran over another woman with his car and killed her.[43] Within Igbo society, however, the strength of women's networks would have protected them and been an effective way to deal with conflicts with men.

Women's space

Societal discrimination and hostility towards women and their responsibilities in the home places them in a world apart, a separate 'space,' that can be transformed by women into an opportunity for developing networks, support and a sense of self-worth. Because so much of women's lives takes place away from men, women's separate culture is allowed to survive and sometimes even flourish. Michelle Zimbalist Rosaldo points out that:[44]

> When men live apart from women, they in fact cannot
> control them, and unwittingly they may provide them
> with the symbols and social resources on which to build
> a society of their own. Such women's groups, ranging from
> convents and brothels to informal neighborhood friend-
> ships in China . . . . or African political organizations and
> cults . . . . are available to women in men's absence, and
> they add social and moral value to an otherwise domestic
> role.

No matter how small and vulnerable, a 'woman's space' allows them to share feelings and survival strategies. These spaces can also be seen as adaptations to women's economic situations. They provide shared moments that usually take place in the context of women's work-lives. Whether it's at the village well, the market, or the laundromat, women use these occasions to share both their work and their feelings about their work. (This is why many contemporary develop-ment programs, which are designed by men totally oblivious to the composite of women's needs, often destroy networks in the process of technologization and westernization. They take away women's primary mechanisms for socializing with each other, and the programs often fail due to the women's lack of interest.) The survey of Bombay prostitutes mentioned in Chapter 4 also showed that 'their closest relationships are with each other. They live as a community and care for all the children together. The children are equally fussed over and adored by all the women.'[45]

Much of women's sharing in these situations takes the form of discussing problems and tensions which are usually perceived of as 'personal' rather than collective or social, even though the problems are usually job-related. Topics may range from fights with the boss or husband and beatings, to not enough money for the children's needs. Although some of the anger is also directed toward other women, it is significant that it is usually shared with women (not men), and that the comments and judgments of such peer groups usually fall within a more or less articulated morality defined by the women themselves, as in the Saints' Sanctuaries, one of the examples which follows.

Sometimes the women's space is created in a religious context, especially when their work-lives do not often bring them together. Rural women in Ethiopia, for example, who are totally isolated from each other in every aspect of their lives, are able to meet and talk at church. Consequently religion takes on an extra importance in their lives.[46] The non-holiday-related, ongoing work and prayer services of the churches in the Caribbean often create an entirely female space. The women share and reinforce their morality while their husbands drink together or 'pick up' other women in areas where tourism is prevalent. Men often feel that their wives are 'no fun' and a burden, that for some 'inexplicable' reasons, the women prefer to go to church and take care of the home rather than have a good time. The women know they must stay at home and watch the children or no one else will. They enthusiastically seek the support and reinforcement they give each other in church, for the difficult, demanding and otherwise unsupported lives they lead. (There is also a history, in legend and mythology, of women using religion to make a space for themselves. One legend tells of

Ursula, the daughter of the King of Cornwall, who took a journey to the Holy Land in the fifth century. Many of her friends wanted to accompany her, and eventually 11,000 other young women, none of whom were anxious to get married, did so. However, men could not permit such adventures to go unheeded. The women were attacked and killed by Huns on the way home.[47]

Women in Morocco often frequent the Saints' sanctuaries. Though the sanctuaries are not formal places of worship, they none the less receive the kind of social sanction accompanying religious activity in other cultures. Although men are permitted into the sanctuaries, they are far fewer in number than women, and often end their visits early due to the large numbers of women present. Women take their troubles – from health problems to fights with their husbands – to the saints, and receive support from each other, a crucial alternative to the impersonal powerless treatment they receive elsewhere. Women use the sanctuaries as sources of precious solitude, and for support from each other which is seldom available anywhere else.[48] A twenty-year-old maid from Salé, Morocco, explains why the sanctuary is so important to her:[49]

When one has a family as desperate as mine, the shrine is a haven of peace and quiet . . . . the sound of the fountain is the silence. An enormous silence where the sound of water is as fragile as thread. Mostly it's women who cry without speaking, each in her own world . . . . When you are separated from someone or when you have a very bad fight, the saint helps you overcome your problems. When I go I listen to the women. You see them tell everything to the tomb and mimicking all that took place . . . . They cry, they scream. Then they get hold of themselves and come back, join us, and sit in silence.

As Fatima Mernissi put it:[50]

This insistence on going to saints' tombs exemplifies the North African woman's traditional claim that she is active, can decide her needs for herself and do something about them, a claim that the Muslim patriarchal system denies her. Visits to and involvement with saints and sanctuaries are two of the rare options left to women to *be*, to shape their world and their lives. And this attempt at self-determination takes the form of an exclusively female collective endeavor . . . . Undeniably therapeutic, the sanctuary stimulates the energies of women against their discontent and allows them to bathe in an intrinsically female community of soothers, supporters, and advisors . . . . It is primarily as an informal women's association that the sanctuary must be viewed.

In many countries women often visit spiritualists, psychics or healers for consultation on personal problems and life questions. This has a long history dating back over centuries and continents, from the priestesses of ancient Egypt to the witches of Europe in the middle ages, to the present. Whether seeking tea-leaf readings from gypsies, divine consultation through the medium of a West African religious initiate or a woman who is 'touched by the spirit' in fundamentalist Christian church services, herbal remedies from sorceresses or 'the old lady down the block,' or predictions from the community clairvoyant, women the world over have gathered in groups of twos or tens to share information, help and support in a soothing personal and spiritual environment.

These and other women's spaces are often characterized by a reinforcing of belief in female values and female-value-based morality which serves as a guide to behavior outside this space. This shared morality, which is infused with a religious or spiritual faith or foundation, is integrated with material life and reinforces women's networks. It also provides standards for human life which, when not met, can compel women to efforts for social change more compatible with their values.

Individual strategies

Though women do not complain of the power of husbands, each complains of her own husband, or of the husbands of her friends. It is the same in all cases of servitude; at least in the commencement of the emancipatory

movement. The serfs did not at first complain of the
power of the lords, but only of their tyranny.

> John Stuart Mill,
> The Subjection of Women, 1869.

I wish I were like other women, like my aunt and my
stepmothers, who took their sufferings with resignation.
They never complained of their lot or thought of throwing
themselves into a life of perdition. But some of us are not
prepared to bear up under great trouble, and we act crazy.
Like me, for example. I took my children and up and left,
without knowing what would happen to us. Not until we
were on the bus, did I think, 'And now what? Where am
I going? What shall I do? I haven't any money.'

> Marta Sanchez,
> *The Children of Sanchez*[51]

When women don't have access to networks they are often
forced to resort to individual strategies for survival. Their
behavior often reflects their adaptive rather than their
preferred values, ranging from taking the path of least resistance and conforming (at least temporarily) to their expected
roles, to breaking out of such roles through escape (physical
or mental, i.e., madness) or violence against their abusers.
Though such strategies are common in all cultures, they
abound in those where women hold minimal or token power.
These are especially noticeable in cultures where women are
socially isolated.

The behavior of women can be compared to that of the
colonized: some try to 'pass' to get into positions of power
as tokens; some have internalized the dominant culture's
view of them as inferior but nevertheless try to be acceptable
and 'make it' within that system; and some prefer their own
culture and don't try to assimilate, but direct their energies
to their own survival as a sub-culture.

Usually these strategies involve the giving and taking of
the few things women have that men want. Called 'manipulation' by some, it is a response to a concrete lack of alternatives and resources. Women may influence the decisions of
men by various strategies, from withholding their services to

flattery or to playing off men against each other.

Rosenthal refers to the behavior that society sees as manipulative, as simply a mechanism used by women to get what they need:[52] 'the model of socializing a child with some rewards and punishments is more a woman's way of doing things .... Basically they get their way by bartering for affiliation.'

Women will do what they have to to seek advantage from each situation that lies in a basic context of unequal power. From culture to culture, and varying by factors such as race and class, the loopholes women find and use in the power structure vary. So while it might be to one woman's advantage to play the game and demurely comply because her loophole lies in subtle manipulation, it will be to another woman's advantage to argue and confront, since the objective realities of her life leave no room for manipulation, and the confrontation might bring some result by the simple wearing down of her opponent's defenses. Thus one component of women's culture is this ability to perceive and use loopholes or situations to women's advantage, though the form it takes varies greatly in minimal, token and negotiating power societies. The results are not often 'pretty', though they may be effective.

Margery Wolf, feminist anthropologist, quotes a missionary writing in 1899 about covert strategies used by Chinese women before the revolution:[53]

To defend herself against the fearful odds which are often pitted against her, a Chinese wife has but two resources. One of them is her mother's family, which, as we have seen has no real power . . . .

The other means of defense which a Chinese wife has at her command is – herself. If she is gifted with a fluent tongue, especially if it is backed by some of the hard common sense which so many Chinese exhibit, it must be a very peculiar household in which she does not hold her own . . . . If a Chinese wife has a violent temper, if she is able at a moment's notice to raise a tornado about next to nothing, and to keep it for an indefinite period blowing at the rate of a hundred miles an hour, the position of such a woman is almost certainly secure . . . .

But if such an endowment has been denied her, the next best resource is to pursue a course exactly the opposite, in all circumstances and under all provocations *holding her tongue*.

Women throughout the world have also used spiritual and interpersonal powers as survival strategies. In many cultures where women's sexuality or biology is feared (i.e., menstrual blood, the 'powers' of a pregnant woman, etc.), women have used the threat of exposing men to these powers as a way to affect their behavior. Women have also used their sexuality or the threat of the withdrawal of their sexuality to affect behavior on an individual level. The Greek play *Lysistrata* provides an example of the level of male fear of women collectively withdrawing their sexual services to affect male policy.

Many women across cultures have also resorted to running away from their husbands as a last hope for a better life for themselves and their children, when none of these strategies have been feasible. Urmila Bannerjee cites an Indian woman's story in the journal *Manushi*:[54]

I was married through a marriage bureau . . . . Why does a girl get married? For some protection, some security . . . . But they only wanted a slave to do the housework . . . . Within a week of my marriage, my husband said to me, 'Your body? I can buy better than that in the bazaar, much better.' . . . . I am not going to be beaten every day. He even took a knife and attacked me . . . . And when I had shouted and screamed, my husband's brother had also come to beat me, because what would neighbors say? . . . . Four times I went to my family. But my brothers and sisters say that I am a hindrance to them. My father says, if I am unhappy, why don't I commit suicide . . . . I live in a hostel now. I told them I was an orphan . . . . You see I have to remain hidden because I do not want my husband to find me. Otherwise I'll be in danger.

Through coping resourcefully with the dominant male

culture, many women have developed the necessary skills to deal effectively with other foreign cultures as well. A Turkish sociologist, Deniz Kandiyoti, discusses the study of Turkish migrant 'guest workers' mentioned in Chapter 4:[55]

> The women who migrate to Germany seem to adjust better to the new situation than the men; it may be that their socialization as in-marrying brides trained them for entering a potentially hostile environment. This situation demonstrates women's potential for flexibility and rapid adaptation to change.

Since there are many other situations that are difficult in a male-dominated society, this skill and flexibility is probably also acquired by many women from diverse cultures. It is interesting to note that Kandiyoti, a woman sociologist, perceives women's behavior as open to change, as opposed to the traditional male stereotype of women as conservative. What men interpret as conservatism is actually often women's resistance to male-controlled change forced upon them, which often threatens to erode the few areas in which women do exert control over their lives.

Women's behavior (such as the manipulation discussed earlier) sometimes appears to be contradictory to female values (like the valuing of communications and sharing of information). It often makes sense if it is seen as an adaptation to the complex imperatives of surviving within the dominant male-value system. The systems of female values and adaptive strategies coexist, so that the degree to which a woman's behavior is adaptive has to do with the amount of control she has over her life and the desperation she feels in the fight to survive emotionally or physically. For example, a woman involved in a relationship in which she feels exploited and powerless might steal or lie in her attempts to gain some control in the relationship, actions she would not resort to if she felt respected and equally powerful.

Women living with the double sexual standard, institutionalized in some societies in the form of polygyny, may be forced to carry out their extra-marital sexual affairs secretly and dishonestly. They would not have to make that choice in a society which permitted them the same freedom it allows their husbands. Some women who become pregnant through rape, or otherwise, are forced to get abortions they don't want simply because they do not have the necessary resources to raise a child. Some women who want to work are forced to accept welfare because of the unavailability of adequate childcare facilities. A woman with a few children on welfare may be forced to hide a second job or steal when the welfare payments can't support her family above a starvation level.

Rarely, however, will a woman resort to the degree of violent behavior which is associated with the extremes in male conditioning and the dominant male culture. For example, women who are the victims of sexual double standards and have few outlets for their sexual needs almost never commit the sexual crimes that men commit towards strangers as well as members of their own families.

Women are laid off because they are the last hired and first fired, and work in the home, attempting to make ends meet during times of inflation, recession and depression, but almost never beat their husbands. Though women everywhere are more frustrated by a lack of money and power than their male counterparts, their lack of power is rarely expressed in physical violence toward men.[56] The few times that women strike at or kill their husbands are almost always in self-defence, in desperation after years of physical abuse and humiliation, and then their violence rarely compares to the severity of the ongoing torture they have been subjected to.[57] Women who are severely beaten up by their husbands often opt for killing themselves or letting themselves be killed, rather than hurt or kill their tormentors. When women are driven to beat their children through desperation, that behavior remains socially unacceptable, while male battering of women is accepted.

Some women who embody what we think of as male behavior such as aggression, violence, non-cooperation and insensitivity, like the Indira Gandhi's of the world, are women who have decided that their best chances for making it in a man's world lie in trying to play the game on male terms. In order to survive in the male role they attempt to be as ruthless as the worst of men. As one West Indian woman put it:[58]

> Those women who do make it to the top (usually through
> the professions) are either so exhausted from their upward
> struggle to 'arrive' or so insecure once having made it that
> such a position is jealously guarded and protected.

Or, as a Ghanaian woman judge said:[59]

> But let us look dispassionately at the facts. Almost all
> these women have fought their way to the top in the
> face of great masculine resentment and hostility. They
> have heard it said, 'She is a woman, she can't cope, she is
> out of her depth, she is too weak or sentimental, she
> hasn't got what it takes.' For these women to get to the
> top, they had to be better than the best, and they strained
> every nerve to achieve their objective. Somehow during
> this process, they did violence to their true nature as
> women. Compassion to them became a sign of feminine
> weakness and so they unhappily and unknown to
> themselves became almost as hard as nails. These women
> are casualties in the process of emancipation of
> women . . . .
>   In playing her part in society a woman has to be true to
> her nature. Doing what is wrongly called a man's job does
> not require a woman to turn herself into the caricature of
> a man.

Indeed, the simple fact of being accepted into positions
of power normally held by men may require a woman to
have already given up her women-centered perspective and
accepted male priorities. Adrienne Rich describes this process
and the need to maintain a woman-centered perspective
very clearly:[60]

> There's a false power which masculine society offers to
> a few women who 'think like men' on condition that they
> use it to maintain things as they are. This is the meaning
> of female tokenism: that power withheld from the vast
> majority of women is offered to a few, so that it may

appear that any truly qualified woman can gain access to leadership, recognition, and reward; hence, that justice based on merit actually prevails . . . .

Tokenism essentially demands that the token deny her identification with women as a group, especially with women less privileged than she . . . .

I would like to believe that any profession would be better for having more women practicing it . . . . but it will not happen *even* if 50 per cent of the members of these professions are women, unless those women refuse to be made into token insiders, unless they zealously preserve the outsider's view and the outsider's consciousness.

For no woman is really an insider in the institutions fathered by masculine consciousness. When we allow ourselves to believe we are, we lose touch with parts of ourselves defined as unacceptable by that consciousness.

As token women identify less with other women, their competitiveness and hostility towards other women grows, an example of a successful divide-and-conquer strategy by the power structure. Toni Morrisson addressed this problem in a commencement address at Barnard College in 1979.[61]

I am alarmed by the violence that women do to each other: professional violence, competitive violence, emotional violence. I am alarmed by the willingness of women to enslave other women. I am alarmed by a growing absence of decency on the killing floor of professional women's worlds . . . .

I am suggesting that we pay as much attention to our nurturing sensibilities as to our ambition . . . . Let your might and your power emanate from that place in you that is nurturing and caring.

The final choice that many women make, whether on a temporary or permanent basis, is to comply with male domination. When the odds are overwhelming, when the only options seem to be suicide or running away to an uncertain fate, women often choose to try to wait it out. Sometimes the woman allows herself to be owned on the outside but holds onto her sense of self internally. This conflict may result in angry outbursts or depression. Others with no perspective on the context of their lives, no hope of alternatives, and a sense of self that is shaped by their powerlessness, do not try to escape or change their lives. They understand their lives to be the norm, and look to whatever form of recognition or approval that will make their lives more comfortable. Satisfaction usually comes from living the prescribed option completely, getting as much recognition as possible for the role they are playing, and gleaning pride from playing it well. Whether a woman prides herself in being the 'Total Woman', the 'best whore on the block',[62] or the best of a husband's four wives, it all amounts to pride in their total and well-played subservience, because on many complex social and psychological levels, they feel there is no alternative.

In her article 'Safety, Shelter, Rules, Form, Love: The Promise of the Ultra-Right,' Andrea Dworkin describes the protection some women hope to derive by conforming to men's expectations of them:[63]

> [Some of women's deepest fears] originate in the
> perception that male violence against women is
> uncontrollable and unpredictable. The Right promises
> to put enforceable restraints on male aggression, thus
> simplifying survival for women – to make the world
> slightly more habitable, in other words – by offering
> [form, shelter, safety, rules, love] . . . . a woman
> acquiesces to male authority in order to gain some
> protection from male violence . . . . Sometimes it is a
> lethargic conformity, in which case male demands slowly
> close in on her . . . . Sometimes it is a militant conformity.
> She will save herself by proving that she is loyal, obedient,
> useful, even fanatic in the service of the men around
> her . . . . So the woman hangs on, not with the delicacy
> of a clinging vine, but with a tenacity incredible in its
> intensity, to the very persons, institutions, and values that
> demean her, degrade her, glorify her powerlessness, insist
> upon constraining and paralyzing the most honest
> expressions of her will and being . . . . This singularly
> self-hating loyalty to those committed to her own

destruction is the very essence of womanhood as men of all ideological persuasions define it.

Many women the world over make this choice, while others who rebel in the myriad of individual, everyday forms available to them, are labelled the 'bad women'.

The dominant culture then blames the 'bad women' for having developed survival strategies. These women are using new tactics – instead of quiet compliance, they are making some noise. They let people know the extent to which they are abused, and the extent to which the abuse is hidden. Rape victims and battered women who are speaking out, are thus blamed for their victimization. If the problem is no longer invisible, then it's the 'bad women' who are surfacing to air it. Some women are fighting back at the time of the abuse and sometimes killing their assailants, but it's these women, rather than the assailants themselves, who end up in prison.

Other women are often in prison as punishment for exercising 'undesirable' survival strategies, from the poverty-stricken woman who steals to feed her family, to the prostitute trying to earn a living. One out of five women arrested are charged with prostitution or commercialized vice in the USA. The president's Commission on Law Enforcement and the Administration of Justice found that over half of girls in court are there for general non-criminal behavior problems (such as running away), while only one-fifth of boys are there for non-criminal behavior, but the girls are committed to institutions with proportionately the same frequency as boys. They also serve longer sentences.[64] Those in prison are being punished for attempting survival strategies that don't conform to men's idealized notion of how women should behave.

In this context, the 'madness' of angry women can also be seen as a form of survival – of clinging desperately to a reality independent of the patriarchal norm.

Adrienne Rich wrote of:[65]

The freedom of the wholly mad
to smear & play with her madness

write with her fingers dipped in it
the length of a room

which is not, of course, the freedom
you have, walking on Broadway
to stop & turn back or go on
10 blocks; 20 blocks

but feels enviable maybe
to the compromised

curled in the placenta of the real
which was to feed & which is strangling her.

Thus, women and their culture have survived in many ways, ranging from mechanisms that sustain and respect their own culture to those which furiously deny it. But only when women are grounded in their culture and support each other's efforts to survive, will such individual and collective survival strategies create the basis for efforts towards change.

When proving manhood becomes economic policy

Male culture, like women's culture, is rooted in a combination of biological, social and economic factors. These all have profound implications concerning the ways in which men have structured their cultural institutions.

Biological base of male culture

The whole (Moslem) system is based on the assumption that the woman is a powerful and dangerous being. All sexual institutions (polygamy, repudiation, sexual segregation, etc.) can be perceived as a strategy for containing her power.

Fatima Mernissi[66]

There are a number of possible biological explanations for various aspects of male culture and behavior. It is clear that women's ability to produce children, and their longer relative sexual capacity, are a tremendous source of problems for men. Since men cannot be sure who has fathered a newborn child, they must construct elaborate mechanisms to possess women and therefore the means of reproduction, and to control women's sexual behavior, thus insuring knowledge of their own heirs when inheritance is passed through the male line.[67]

One explanation of men's more promiscuous sexual activity is that of an unconscious cultural need to spread semen to assure paternity.[68]

Karen Horney, in *The Feminine Psychology of Women*, states that the theory of 'penis envy' is actually a projection of male womb envy.[69]   In many cultures, social and religious rituals reflect both fear and envy of women, and in some, the processes of menstruation and child-birth 'are imitated by men: men seeking to cause their own purification by blood or fathers "giving birth" to the young.'[70] In their mythology men have given themselves women's power of birthing: Eve is born out of Adam's rib, Athena out of Jove's ear. In the Middle Ages, semen was believed to contain the homunculus, a tiny, complete human being transferred to the woman's womb. Anthropologist Ashley Montagu theorizes that 'Man's drive to achievement can, at least in part, be interpreted as an unconsciously motivated attempt to compensate for the lack of biological creativity.'[71] As Phyllis Chesler put it 'To create without killing, to make something out of "nothing" the way women seem to make new life out of nothing . . . . male science, male alchemy, is partially rooted in male uterus-envy, in the desire to create something miraculous.'[72]

While penis envy, which exists only as a desire on the part of the female for an equal share in the social power enjoyed by men, is correctable through social change, womb envy is not yet socially correctable. Thus men must be in charge of the social system to control what women produce, because once the social inequalities were corrected, the real biological inequality would be revealed.[73]

The belief of some men and of male religions in women as inherently evil, 'carnal creatures with insatiable lust,' may stem from biologically based fear.

Andrea Dworkin states:[74]

> we are dealing with an existential terror of women, of the
> 'mouth of the womb,' stemming from a primal anxiety
> about male potency, tied to a desire for self (phallic)
> control; men have deep-rooted castration fears which are
> expressed as a horror of the womb . . . . These terrors form
> a substrata of a myth of feminine evil which in turn
> justified several centuries of gynocide . . . . men enter the
> vagina hard, erect; men emerge drained of vitality . . . .
> The loss of semen, and the feeling of weakness which is its
> biological conjunct, has extraordinary significance to men.

Many carriers of the ancient fear and envy of women have
transmitted it to each new generation; mythology has been
shaped into law, religion, psychiatry and psychology, and the
media.[75] So women are veiled so they are as invisible as
possible, and degraded in their sexuality through pornography. They are made the victims of their ability to reproduce and deprived of control over that ability. They are also
kept apart, for if individual women and their powers are to
be feared, what might happen if men were faced with women
as a collective whole?

Adrienne Rich has pointed out that it is highly likely that
men's greatest fear is that they 'could be allowed sexual and
emotional – therefore economic – access to women *only* on
women's terms.'[76] They therefore attempt to control women's
sexuality and reproductivity to insure continued access to
women and their products – male instead of female ownership of the means of reproduction.

Social and economic base of male culture

> The Miri in Bengal do not permit their women to eat the
> flesh of the tiger, lest they become too strong. The
> Watawela of East Africa keep the art of making fire a
> secret from their women, lest women become their rulers.
>   Karen Horney[77]

Many aspects of male behavior, their values and institutions are rooted in the division of labor by sex.

Sociologist Nancy Chodorow's cross-cultural theory of the effects of mothering by women helps to explain much of men's behavior toward women and the home. She points out that most young girls throughout the world grow up around their mothers and sisters who are also their sex-role models, and learn from them an over-all picture of what their lives will be like and the skills they need to know. This experience:[78]

> is in contrast to the experience of boys who must *learn*
> to be men. Adult male activities, whether hunting, politics,
> or farming, are rarely visible or available to young children,
> and fathers are often away from the home. At some point
> the boy must break away from his mother and establish
> his maleness as a thing apart. Therefore, when his sister is
> learning 'to be a mother,' he is apt to be restless and
> assertive and to seek out . . . . ties with male peers . . . . to
> establish himself, to 'be a man,' the boy is often required
> to dissociate himself, ritually or in fact, from the home . . . .
> 'becoming a man' is a feat . . . . [a young girl] develops a
> 'feminine' psychology. Boys, in contrast, are apt to know
> manhood as an abstract set of rights and duties, to learn
> that status brings formal authority, and to act in terms of
> formal roles. Their success or failure is judged in terms of
> male hierarchies.

Rosaldo agrees that because the male world and its standards evolve outside the home, the process of growing up, for a man, is thought of as an achievement. Male social groups set up a variety of hierarchies and tests through which a boy must pass to become a man, and through which men must continue to pass to maintain their status. In this way, men actually create a social hierarchy for themselves, in which they must constantly compete. Most social scientists, and the public at large, think of this hierarchy of men as *the* social hierarchy or definition of that society. Rosaldo points out these male rituals further separate them from female values:[79]

> [The rituals] enforce the distance between men and their
> families; for the individual, they provide a barrier to

becoming embedded in an intimate, demanding world. Distance permits men to manipulate their social environment, to stand apart from intimate interaction, and, accordingly, to control it as they wish . . . . by avoiding certain sorts of intimacy and unmediated involvement, they can develop an image and mantle of integrity and worth.

Although most of the examples we have given in this discussion have been of non-industrialized societies, the same mechanisms are used by men in highly stratified societies. Anthropoligist Felicia Ifeoma Ekejiuba points out that this process is formalized in industrialized societies through the economy:[80]

which transforms male superiority and power from the symbolic and fragile to real domination by . . . . making the knowledge, skills, professions, and products of these processes first available to men. In consequence, men are placed in a position where they define these as scarce and prestigious commodities and discriminate legally and informally, through male-created myths of female inferiority, against women's participation in these processes.

The more women are left out of the distribution of resources the more they fall behind in the power relationship with men, which further strengthens the differences between the sexes. When social and economic hierarchies are more developed, people's lives are more at the mercy of those in power.

Rosaldo has pointed out that many of the more egalitarian societies have the least differentiation between men's and women's worlds. Men are more involved in the home, and the relationships between men and women are highly valued:[81]

When a man is involved in domestic labor, in child care and cooking, he cannot establish an aura of authority and distance. And when public decisions are made in the household, women may have a legitimate public role.

Rosaldo points to several cultures, including the Arapesh of New Guinea, in which both women and men are said to 'give birth to' and 'grow' their children and share equally in domestic life. She also discussed the Ilongot people of the Philippines, where 'women have the right, and the confidence, to speak their minds .... in the home we find relatively egalitarian relations between the sexes, cooperation rather than competition, and a true closeness of husband and wife.'[82]

She also notes that among the Ilongot people, 'Because boys' earliest experiences are shaped by the intimacy of fathers as well as mothers, they are relatively unconcerned with a need to "achieve," or to denigrate women; men involved in domestic tasks demand no submission from their wives.'[83]

In general men have responded to women in one of two ways depending on the power that women have in their society. In token and minimal power societies, most men have feared and therefore denied the female values, behavior and biology that they could not understand or control. They are the most divorced from female-value-based behavior. In cultures where women have held negotiating power, men have dealt with their fear and awe of women by ritualizing it.

Rosaldo notes that in cultures where men have ritualized their feelings toward women, women enjoy a higher status. One male anthropologist, in speaking of some African cultures, (which we consider negotiating) said that 'African men ritualize rather than deny their basic dependence on women' and further states that 'the innermost secret of every religious club barred to women is the male's ultimate dependence on women.'[84] This ritualization might help to explain the existence of the queen mother in a culture such as the Ghanaian which currently denies to women an ongoing role in politics. Yet in such negotiating power societies, because men are not socialized within a female culture, they still maintain their need for control, and women's power, though recognized in male ritual, is clearly secondary.

Men have invented the myth of male intellectual, physical and spiritual superiority and projected their feelings of inferiority onto women. They have structured minimal and token power societies to deny and denigrate women's capacities and glorify and institutionalize their own. Their aura of superiority is maintained by minimizing their contact with women, and the differences between men and women are exaggerated and institutionalized, while female traits and capacities are devalued. Men use force and institutions to insure this social order and their control over women's labor and production of children. Having made the possession of male values a prerequisite for inclusion into male-dominated power structures, they deny the validity of female behavior in themselves and prohibit the creation of female-value-based social structures.

Patriarchal institutions around the world are really social constructs developed by men to deal with their biologically and economically based insecurities. Most men's need to prove their masculinity has left them and their culture arrested at an adolescent stage of human development. With few exceptions, their behavior is that of spoiled little boys who are convinced of their rights over women and become angry and violent when they don't get their way.

For men to grow up, they must learn female-value-based behavior, which is not simply the performing of jobs hitherto considered female or the expression of emotions. (Men in most cultures only exercise the veneer of female behavior when they perceive it to be in their best interest.) Men must put a genuine concern for the needs of others, and a concept of power that is based on cooperation and creativity rather than control, before their egos, competitiveness, vanity and need to prove themselves. They could probably develop this capacity in a matriarchal culture, but will not be moved to do so of their own volition with their present power.

Patriarchal economics

> To have a whole human creature consecrated to
> his direct personal service, to pleasing and satisfying
> him in every way possible, – this has kept man selfish
> beyond the degree incidental to our stage of social
> growth . . . . Pride, cruelty, and selfishness are the
> vices of the master, and these have been kept strong
> in the bosom of the family through the false position

of women.
        Charlotte Perkins Gilman,
        Women and Economics, 1898[85]

As we have seen, there are a variety of theories that could help to explain the similarity in male characteristics across cultures, from male aggression and domination over women to a tendency to hierarchical social organization.

In fact, male culture is so similar across the world that most people have come to mistake male culture for human culture, male values and behavior for human values and behavior.

In the same way, patriarchal beliefs underlying the economies men have constructed are so taken for granted that the very notion of economy and economics has little objective meaning, but reflects the patriarchal values of which it is a part. Most of us consider it to be so divorced from our lives that we are bored even by the thought of it. The 'economic implications' of female values which we have begun to explore are so vastly different from those of patriarchal values, that they would be considered by most people to be 'uneconomical'. Patriarchal economic concepts are rooted in cost-benefit analysis which does not quantify human costs or human benefits.

Once patriarchal institutions are no longer taken as the ideal, it is possible to question all the economic structures that have developed from patriarchal values: women's slavery, class stratification and social and economic hierarchies, ways of dealing with conflict and the underlying morality that governs human behavior.

In denying their dependence on women to create life, men distance themselves from women, life-sustaining processes and from other men. Thus they do not hold themselves accountable to each other or to women. In their drive to deny and to prove, they attempt to control women and their sexuality as well as nature itself. Their only recognition of the value of the female is in her service to them. Men in most cultures have institutionalized so profound a disrespect for women's reproductivity and life sustenance that they have isolated themselves from the creation and nurturing of life itself (except in the role of 'experts' like Dr Spock who exert control over women). Having lost the wonder of its creation, they can far more easily tolerate its destruction and comprehend the loss of life as a necessary sacrifice, a means to whatever end they deem most worthy. Men's striving for the acquisition of land and property could be seen as a desire to be more a part of the creation of life, except that many men who take others' land are not farmers. Perhaps their acquisitional impulses can be understood as their assertion of their 'manhood', the control over land and life since they cannot give birth to it, as well as the desire for profits and territory. Viewing their territory as a measure of their worth, they strive to control what they perceive of as theirs. As recipients of women's slave labor they believe they are entitled to the labor and property of other people as well.

On the most fundamental level, men have structured their economies on the foundation of women's slavery. They have categorically defined certain work as belonging to one group of people, socialized and trained them from birth to do this work and to be unprepared for other options (which are, at the same time, made unavailable), and then not paid for it, leaving it outside the money economy. For women's slavery to be eliminated would require the total restructuring of every patriarchal economy.

Most male cultures manifest their values in other forms of stratification as well. Men's hierarchies are based on and maintain divisions of power understood as control rather than skills. Achievement facilitates the climbing of the hierarchies. Thus, men often become rigidly identified with their roles and with what they themselves produce. Knowledge is viewed as a means to prove worth, and its sharing is controlled, the withholding of information a mechanism for obtaining and maintaining power. Those with the most specialized information and skills have a higher status in the hierarchy. Thus as men's work-lives are increasingly divorced from their emotional/intuitive selves, social stratification and job specialization progressively involves abuses of power.

Technology, as most people understand it, has been developed only within the framework of the male status hierarchy, which is separated from people's daily needs. As skills and knowledge are separated from the rest of human life, people's thinking becomes increasingly separated and linear. Ideas and information are considered the most useful and important when backed up with scientifically acquired, specialized data. People look increasingly to the hierarchy to get what they need, which usually comes in relation to their power and connections within this framework. Money is no longer viewed as a means of exchange but as an end in itself, a way to prove worth.

In many cultures, the notion of cost efficiency has come to mean producing the most profits at the least financial cost, with the human costs – feeding, clothing and housing the most people – a secondary consideration. The notion of investment involves return, bigger is thought to be better, and growth at all costs is the ultimate ideal. This growth model of development, which was discussed in the introduction to Chapter 2, has necessitated a constantly expanding demand to fill the requirements of constant growth in production. This need for, and belief in, ever-expanding territories is also reflected in the myopic assumption of ever-expanding resources.

Of course such behavior inevitably results in much conflict. The ways that conflict are dealt with on an interpersonal as well as national policy level in most countries are consistently patriarchal. Most fighting, social change and male history is centered around struggles for control of territory or property, as assertions of ego-identified concepts of self. Difference is seen as a cause of conflict and results in discrimination or assertions of power and control. Conflict is dealt with by forced confrontation, or withdrawal and avoidance without constructive dialogue. Peace is envisioned as a state to be won through war, and thus arms and defense become priorities over daily human needs.

All this distrust and competition results in a view of human nature as instinctively bad and in need of being controlled. Morality is enforced externally which necessitates increasingly authoritarian forms of social control. This control is exercized by time-consuming bureaucracies (to prevent the potentially rebellious use of free time) and legal systems, criminal justice systems, police, the military and prisons.

Although not all these social forms exist in all cultures, their seeds are sown wherever the patriarchy is in power. Even though some socialist societies espouse feminine life sustaining and non-authoritarian values of cooperation, equitable distribution of resources and decision-making and the primacy of human needs, no socialist society to date has fundamentally redistributed power and work between men and women. None have dealt with sex-role politics and values to the degree of permitting freedom of choice, whether of one's occupation, or the gender and number of one's sexual partners. Power and decision-making have not been decentralized. To the contrary, some have highly centralized them in the hands of a few select males. And most socialist societies openly condemn homosexuality.

Thus, although some socialist men may not be as well trained in the competitive and acquisitional role as men in capitalist cultures, they are nevertheless raised with the assumption that life maintenance is not their 'natural' responsibility. Those tasks properly belong to another set of people – women – over whom they maintain varying degrees of control. They come to believe from an early age that it is their birthright to have life-long servants – mothers, then wives. This fundamental sense of prerogative is the breeding ground for the conviction of entitlement and of territorial values. If a group of people truly believes that they have rights over one set of people, then it is a logical next step for them to feel that they can justly impose their wills on anyone or anything. With this basic assumption of male prerogative, economic and social policies can never be equitable.

Understanding women's position as a colony within the dominant patriarchal economy makes the connection between territoriality and male domination clear. Men across cultures seek to own and control women so as to insure that they reap the benefits of what women produce: children, in the form of their heirs; and the actual and potential money, leisure time and higher standard of living we discussed earlier. Militarily dominant nations making colonies of other nations to 'own' their resources and benefit from their cheap or free labor are reproducing men's colonization of women.

As long as women as a colony are not freed, men will have a sense of entitlement to the land and products of other colonies or territories. Viewing such behavior as patriarchal helps to explain imperialism in societies which ostensibly embrace more female-based economic values. The Soviet invasion of Afghanistan, the continuing wars between China and Vietnam, and the decimation of Cambodia are less confusing in this context.

For example, though post-revolutionary China developed economic policies of full employment and a more equitable division of resources, it did so without abandoning the underlying patriarchal values. China continued policies which were antithetical to the new values they attempted to bring to their model of development. The new China still supported an age-old foreign policy involving hostilities and border wars with the Soviet Union and Vietnam.[86] In addition, China did not fundamentally question the division of life maintenance and life decision-making work between men and women. Though women are slowly being integrated into some decision-making positions on a political level, their role as raisers of children, whether in the home or collectively in daycare centers, has not been changed. Rigid sex roles are still enforced, resulting in repression of homosexual people. People (men) who are not in touch with basic life maintenance tasks are in decision-making positions. Coupled with the assumption that men have some kind of *right* not to do this life maintenance work, this helps to explain China's often aggressive foreign policy as well as the reservation of childcare and life maintenance work for women.

China is still, in the truest sense, a male-run country, operated by men in what they perceive as the best interest of all the people. At the time of the revolution the best interest was perceived to involve the mobilization of everyone, women included, to help expand the process of development. Now, the national interest is perceived to lie along a more western model of development, including a regression in the status of women.

Patriarchal cultures have dominated over female-value-based cultures because of the values behind them. Cultures rooted in more female values than today's societies have been destroyed precisely because they did not think in terms of acquisition and did not develop a sophisticated enough system of defense to prevent being slaughtered by outside forces. This has happened to many native American, African and Asian peoples.

Today's world is being run predominantly by men who are totally immersed in male culture and values and who have grown up with a profound sense of male entitlement. For any one group of people to live their lives with the conviction of their natural right to women's subservience and of their own isolation from the sphere of nurturance, sensitivity, and daily maintenance of life work, is appalling. If the world seems to be on a suicidal course, it is because it is being run by people socialized into patriarchal values – insecure, irrational, aggressive, competitive, self-serving, and acquisitive people. How could these people be expected to structure their own lives, and the lives of those over whom they have power, in ways that are equitable and mutually beneficial, when they have no comprehension of what the maintenance of life requires?

In examining the layers of assumptions and values that have been shaped by patriarchal culture throughout the world it is not too difficult to see why it has been so hard for women to shed the patriarchal world-view and assert their own. At the same time, however, the importance of doing so becomes clearer. When we consider who these people are who are running our world, the imperative to change sexual politics looms large.

Towards an economy of female values

In exploring the concept of a matriarchal economy, a culture based on female values, we will be extrapolating and imagining the kinds of social institutions that might result from such a cultural framework. The specific components of such institutions, in transition from different male cultures, would vary a great deal and depend on the needs and priorities of the women living in those cultures. It would not only be inappropriate but impossible for us to describe the forms that such changes would take. They must evolve organically from each culture's unique history. All that we can do here is attempt to identify some of the values and assumptions that would underlie matriarchal economies and explore some of the ways that women are fighting for just such changes. If this combination of matriarchal values and institutions sounds Utopian and totally impossible, we have to try to overcome the scepticism which reflects the degree to which we are all steeped in patriarchal assumptions and values, limiting our imagination and our faith.

Female values and power

Mira, used to the egotistic male world with its endless 'I' being in fact part of it herself, was astonished by the selflessness of these women. She had always enjoyed asserting *her* intellect, *her* opinions, *her* knowledge, but as she listened to what a month ago she would have called stupid conversation, she heard what the women were really saying and it shamed her. It was: yes, I am like you. I worry about the same things as you – the everyday, the trivial, the petty economies, and small repairs. And I, like you, know that these mundane events somehow mean more than the large sweeping things, the corporation mergers, invasions, depressions, and decisions of the President's Cabinet. Not that the things I am concerned with are important. Heavens, no, they're just little things, but they matter, you know, they matter most to a life . . . . those are the times I am happy. When I feel useful, when there is harmony in my world.

She listened and she heard their acceptance, their love, their selflessness, and for the first time in her life, she thought that women were great. Their greatness made all the exploits of warriors and rulers look like pompous self-aggrandizement, made even the poets and painters look like egotistical children jumping up and down shouting, 'Look at me, Ma!'

Marilyn French, *The Women's Room*[87]

Women who are more a part of the female culture have a different concept of power than men. Most women have been socialized into the role of mother, which makes them well trained to responsibly look after the needs of others. They have also learned tactfulness and resourcefulness from having survived in a male world, and they share economic and biological bonds which can potentially serve as the basis for understanding each other across male-defined boundaries.

In this sense, women and their values can be seen to be civilizing influences and have a potential to be far more so. This is true on a variety of levels, ranging from the order women create in households left chaotic by men's lack of interest, to the fact that one woman in a group of men can inhibit aggression towards other women, to the civilizing effect female values could have on a war-torn world.

A matriarchal concept of power has more to do with creativity and cooperation, the power to change that comes from the caring for others, than with coercion or control. It also involves a respect for nature, the tendency to place the needs of others first and a commitment to life over death, creation over destruction and harmony over conflict. Because this concept of power does not imply coercion, it is supportive of the independence of the individual, with a sense of collective responsibility that also calls for account-ability. To put such a matriarchal concept of power into form requires decentralization, with collective decision-making. Information is shared rather than controlled. Respect for the individual involves respect for individual needs, independence and creativity, rather than the stifling and controlling of creative impulses.

A matriarchal society would also integrate feelings and intelligence into work just as mothers are currently required to do in the home. Such an egalitarian social structure would mean no differentiation in people's power on the basis of biology, and the integration of the public and private spheres. Public decisions would evolve from, be grounded in, and accountable to the community. Home and country would not be conceived of as territories to control or conquer, but rather places to be respected and from which to share, inviting guests to 'feel at home.' People's intuition would be integrated with their feelings and thinking, grounded in an understanding of experiences as a whole. In a well-established matriarchal society, morality would be internalized without the desire to coerce and dominate, people's sense of right and wrong would evolve spontaneously from a respect for individual and collective life, and would not have to be enforced with military or legal force.

Female values and economics

What we have to figure out is how to have a society that doesn't punish people for being members of the female culture . . . . Part of that culture is you do things free for people you love, you barter instead of sell . . . . it's a very reciprocal culture. And you produce necessities . . . .

Women are products of a culture that values cooperation . . . . and a real inability to coerce others . . . . Understanding that, you have to redefine the concept of power. Because in this society the concept of power very much implies coercion.

Kris Rosenthal[88]

The economics of female values are implicit in the mothering role, where products such as cleanliness, standards of living and time are produced which improve the quality of life, where investment in these products is in their eventual independence (as with children) or sharing, rather than control and profit. These concepts of cooperation, sharing, nurturing and pulling together as survival mechanisms, are very powerful when conceived of on a social and economic scale. The values underlying matriarchal economies would probably take the form of a non-growth model where surplus would be shared, where everyone's material needs would take priority over other potential expenditures, and decision-making as well as wealth would be collectivized.

Women and other socially disenfranchised groups have consistently done the least specialized work, and this division of labor has both reflected and created other forms of exploitation. Thus, in a matriarchal economy, the least specialized work would have to be mechanized or shared among all persons, so that everyone would have equal responsibility and power. (In a country or world economy with little economic surplus, work might remain unspecialized until the collective standard of living was raised. In an economy with surplus, the shared unspecialized work would only have to be done for a relatively short period, by each person.)

Divisions of labor would be made on the basis of skill, and preference in a societal context that encouraged each person to identify and develop their skills. Such a division of labor would be structured horizontally, collectively, rather than with a vertical or hierarchical division of power. Decision-making, access to resources and remuneration would be shared equally, rather than distributed on the basis of an unequal power and wealth evolving from an unequal access to resources.

The spheres of home and life maintenance and of commodity production would also be integrated. Whatever form this took the wealth of all that was collectively produced, and the decision-making concerning the organization and distribution of work and its rewards, would be collectivized as well.

With the current organization of technology, 'efficiency' is seen as the over-all goal, and this efficiency is chosen as an organizational priority – everywhere but in the home. No one would ever think of organizing industrial labor as housework is organized, with the same work being duplicated for units of one to ten persons the world over. One could then ask 'why not socialize housework?' Yet an equally valid question is 'Why not decentralize industry?' This way the work would be less alienating, more controllable by the people served, and more related to people's lives.

What is actually needed is a synthesis of the two in our social and economic institutions: a more rational organization of housework, and a more human decentralization of industrial production. Similarly, that work which is considered the responsibility of women (servicing and home-related labor) needs to be integrated with that which is considered men's domain (the 'outer' world, of social institutions and government). And all people's responsibilities in both worlds also need to be integrated into a balanced whole.

It has often been noted that a decline in women's status has usually accompanied technologization.[89] Yet most technology has been developed with similar assumptions: i.e., the primacy of 'efficiency', growth, and a higher standard of living for some, even if that compromises social and economic equality. Of our examples, only the Chinese attempted a differing model of technological development, which was ultimately compromised in the interest of greater 'efficiency', output and a higher standard of living. Yet their earlier choice in economic policy (during the same period that women experienced their greatest gains in China), opens the vision for an organization of industrialization based on female values, the meeting of human needs, and the possibility of social equality. Many of the current world crises – ranging from irresponsible medicine to dangerous military development – are in fact logical outcomes of a technology developed by and for a patriarchal social framework. Yet the problem lies not in technology itself, but in its improper use and organization, and a broad range of social alternatives exists.

The concept of 'appropriate technology' refers to a lifestyle that many women have always lived.[90] The constant recycling of scarce resources, of garbage saved for gardens and cloth scraps used for quilts, has been an ongoing part of most women's lives. Whether because they have had little access to other resources, or because they are more respectful of the need to give back to nature what they have taken, women have more consistently seen resources as non-renewable. Only recently has the influence of multi-national corporations and their promotion of the quick-consume-throw-away culture that insures their high profits begun to reduce some women's economy. It has offered women ostensible 'liberation' from the drudgery of housework at the expense of the environment, without changing the economy that keeps women slaves to the home in the first place.

Women's non-exploitive attitude towards the environment has also had an effect on many women's non-acceptance of the use of nuclear energy and nuclear weapons. In contrast to the patriarchal view of infinitely expandable resources (one manifestation of assumptions governing territorial acquisition) and the value of science and creation for its own sake (rather than to meet specific needs), many women have strongly objected to the use of nuclear power. Aware of the dreadful power which wrongly unleashed has the potential to destroy on such a magnitude, many women have been in the forefront of organizing against nuclear energy and nuclear weapons.[91]

With an alternative, decentralized organization of technology, many economically-based transactions that are currently highly impersonal in over-developed economies would become personalized. In some cultures bargaining in the market place is viewed not as a ruthless profit-motivated exercise, but as an art form whereby two or more parties with differing interests come together and work out a compromise. In the process, a personal relationship is established, networks are expanded, and the transaction reaffirms a commitment to compromise, harmony and collective endeavor.

This model for meeting one's needs incorporates many of the female values we have discussed. Since female-based economics are similarly-based in trading and bargaining rather than in control and coercion, and needs are more often aligned with survival than with profit, a matriarchal society might well not use money as a means of exchange, but barter or trade. It is under patriarchy that the spheres of home and community are separate, that women are relegated to the private sphere, and that their work is excluded from the male economy where money is used as a means of exchange only between households and communities. If these spheres were integrated and commodities were produced and distributed on the basis of need rather than profit, in decentralized home- and community-based industries, neither money nor the related bureaucracies would be necessary. A tremendous amount of social energy goes into the non-productive work of keeping track of people and money, from banking and taxation to advertising. One way of institutionalizing the matriarchal value that people should have the free time to develop creative pursuits of their choice would be to organize society without money, and other patriarchal necessities (such as the military), so that social production existed only for the meeting of human needs at the level of an equalized socially defined minimum standard of living.

The possibilities are vast and far-ranging, limited only by all our patriarchal assumptions so internalized that they present blinders to Utopian vision.

Yet if women have managed to sustain their volume of responsibilities and their culture, in the face of repressive patriarchal cultures and internalized patriarchal judgments, the possibilities are tremendous if they were to create and sustain a new vision, and direct their energies towards that vision instead of towards the maintenance of a patriarchal world order. Women have the commitment and organizational skills – they need only to believe that a new order is possible to begin to build it.

From expropriation to liberation: female culture and change

Having learned from her tenderest years that hers is a domain 'inside', inside a family, inside a house, inside a body, it is not surprising that a woman should come to see herself as a 'vessel' . . . . it is not surprising that one's relationship with her ideology would be viewed in terms of 'service', rather than 'recruitment' . . . . The principal themes of . . . . [the] male revolutionary/prophetic type is authority, objectivity, domination, and ultimately hierarchical institutionalized authority. The female radical experience . . . . is one of mutual aid, of compassionate identification and nurturance in the path of revolutionary development . . . . In politics, the identification of self with one's beliefs is intellectually compatible only with an ideology that affirms the unity of means with ends . . . . Many activist women's action has been oriented toward moving with – 'flowing with' – the most positive and far-reaching elements of the revolutionary tide, rather than . . . . to stem, direct, or in any way manipulate this tide.

Marian Leighton,
'Anarcho-Feminism and Louise Michel'[92]

Across time and cultures, women have fought for lives grounded in female values, especially female economic values. Women have been in the forefront of social change organizing that has been related to their children, food, housing and medical care – such as childcare organizing in Japan, consumer organizing in Italy, and health care organizing in the USA. These are all issues for women dealing with poverty, daycare and food prices, the effects of which it is their job to absorb. This can be seen and understood in the general context of fighting for the realization and implementation of female values. In contrast, much of the impetus behind male-dominated social movements has been territorial or power-oriented, from major wars to political campaigns.

Women's culture also provides them with skills and tactics that are unique to their experience. Female-value-based methods to break down male power have ranged from refusal to support the male system on an individual and collective level, to utilizing peer pressure to 're-socialize' men and make them afraid *not* to change, to creating an independent power base from which to build new institutions to supplant the old. These aspects of women's culture that provide positive bases from which to push for change often transcend those elements of women's culture that can make it difficult for them to work for change in their own behalf (such as putting their own needs second, or internalizing anger and pain). The importance of women's friendships to each other and the intimacy of their shared experiences, has provided a bond. Their sensitivity and tact, their instinct to pull together in adversity and fight for collective survival, are crucial elements to the organization and survival of change-oriented groups.

Skills women have developed for dealing with conflict and surviving within a patriarchal framework are invaluable in fighting for change as well, including developing creative alternatives to both antagonistic confrontation and passive acceptance. Their flexibility from living in the foreign male culture and their resourcefulness are needed to develop effective change strategies.

For example, some women in pre-revolutionary China helped meet their own and their families' survival needs as soul-raisers, communication mediaries between the soul of a deceased family member and the living relatives. This occupation required a deft combination of psychic, spiritual, interpersonal and sociological skills which enabled many women to become effective activists at the time of the Revolution.[93]

Women's daily lives also suggest various perspectives on change: thinking based in material and personal reality instead of theory; getting what's needed through perseverence, dialogue, and positive reinforcement rather than coercion; and withdrawing from men's destructive and non-productive activities to create an ongoing, life-sustaining culture.

Implicit in women's culture is the idea that the foundation of peace is a model which provides for people's basic needs and for effective nonviolent means of resolving conflict.

Female non-compliance

We can then begin to study women's struggle against powerlessness, women's radical rebellion, not just in male-defined 'concrete revolutionary situations' but in all the situations male ideologies have not perceived as revolutionary: e.g. the refusal of some women to produce children, aided at great risk by other women; the refusal to produce a higher standard of living and leisure for men . . . . that female anti-phallic sexuality which, defined as 'frigidity' and 'puritanism,' has actually been a form of subversion of male power . . . .

The fact is that women in every culture and throughout history *have* attempted the task of independent, non-heterosexual, woman-connected existence, to the extent made possible by their context often in the belief that they were the 'only ones' ever to have done so; even though few women have been in an economic position to resist marriage altogether; and though attacks against unmarried women have ranged from aspersion and mockery to deliberate gynocide, including the burning and torturing of millions of widows and spinsters during the witch persecutions of the 15th, 16th and 17th centuries in Europe, and the practice of suttee on widows in India.

Adrienne Rich
'Compulsory Heterosexuality and Lesbian Existence'[94]

Female non-compliance has generally not been understood as rebellion because the total context of women's responses to their enslavement under patriarchy has not been comprehended, even though the implications of such acts of rebellion often generate a tremendous hysteria.

Individual women's non-compliance has taken many forms. Betsy Hartmann has observed that women in Bangladesh participate individually and collectively in small rebellious acts which help them to retain their sense of self-worth and make their lives more bearable, though they lack the economic resources to make broader changes. They rarely feel that they are 'giving in'. One woman runs and sings through the village without the veil, and goes fishing on the sly. An older woman influences village affairs as her thoughts and proposals pass from house to house through women's networks. While men are at the market, the mosque, or in the fields, the women get together in each other's kitchens, working as they talk, offering support in times of crisis. Sometimes they try to protect friends from brutal beatings, as on the occasion when the husband of a woman named Roshana beat her with an iron pipe, and the neighborhood women surrounded the house, successfully demanding that he open the door.[95]

Other individual forms of resistance by some African women have included their refusal to help their husbands with cash-cropping because they wanted to grow their own food crops, and their refusal to do household chores or help with cash crops unless their husbands paid them a wage.[96]

The demand for wages for housework has also been posed by some women's groups in the United States, Canada, Britain, Germany and Italy, addressing the governments who are functioning because of this slave labor. Court cases in some of those countries demanding compensation for women's work in the home on the basis of hourly minimum wage rates have also been a mechanism for posing the same demand.

Refusal to comply with male domination on a broader,

more collective scale, has been much more problematical for women, especially when work stoppages in the human services would cause suffering. This also is true because many working women have children dependent on them alone and can't lose a paycheck.

But women have begun to use strikes to demand recognition for their role as paid and unpaid houseworkers, at local levels around particular issues.

In Sweden in the 1970s there was a national strike of women cleaners. These women were traditionally isolated from one another, ignored by the unions and by job legislation, and paid very poorly for their 'women's work'.[97] Their success had to come from building networks among themselves and acting on their experience, outside of male definitions of work organizations.

Today in West Africa, in areas where women have been active in trading (such as in Ewé society) there are associations of market women who have come together to lobby for their own interests, and periodically they organize strikes in the town and village markets, sometimes initiated with the help of the queen mother.

Once in recorded history women have struck an entire nation, refusing to do *all* their unpaid work as well as paid work, for twenty-four hours. In Iceland 90 per cent of women in the capital and 99 per cent of women in the villages went on strike on 24 October 1975, and attended public meetings to discuss the status of women. Their display of unity successfully stopped the country's economy for the day, demonstrating the economy's inability to function without their work. Male bank administrators were forced to work as tellers, often with their children tugging at their coat-tails. Male restaurant owners waited tables with their children at their feet. If women had continued their strike much longer, the society would have completely collapsed.

Women organized and attended this demonstration because of the lack of wages for their work in the home and their lack of power in institutions affecting them. If their demands for higher pay, equal employment, representation in the Farmers' Union and Trade Union Congress, daycare and financial recognition of their work in the home are not met all the women of Iceland will be aware of it.[98]

The fact that women, throughout the world, sustain the economies in which they live, holds the potential for the most radical and far-reaching social change imaginable. It is precisely because women have such potential power that their development of that power is so thoroughly prohibited in social institutions throughout the world.

The male dominated world could not function a single day without them, as the Iceland strike so beautifully showed. But an international women's strike, or even the concept of women across cultures 'unionizing' around their unpaid labor, organizing into alliances on the basis of common work, common concerns or goals, points to the question of how the needs of the dependent will be met if women strike. Women have been put in the position of sustaining their societies and at the same time of being concerned about those they are caring for. This has been the double bind: women have feared that to use their ultimate power in their own behalf would jeopardize the survival of those most important to them – their families, children, the sick, the aged. Women have historically been too close to the needs of others to take actions which would make those others suffer. And the suffering of others has always been less tolerable to women than their own.

One response to this problem has been to bring children to demonstrations. The presence of children during welfare-rights demonstrations, or sit-ins or occupations of buildings used by government officials has served to dramatically illustrate women's demands as well as to enable women to participate. Another response was evident in the reasoning of nurses who struck at a Boston-area hospital in the United States in 1980. The nurses hesitated to stop providing services, especially when it would result in the physical suffering of innocent patients. Yet the women ultimately struck because they realized that in the long run, *more* people would suffer by their *not* striking and thus perpetuating their inability to provide quality services. In the long run, the needs of the patients and the needs of the nurses were the same – hospital conditions and services would improve if the nurses' demands, which would improve their own working conditions as well, were met.

Situations are similar for women the world over. Women everywhere are exhausted, harried, overworked and unpaid or underpaid, which drastically affects their ability to work inside and outside the home as they, ideally, would like. If women's status and working conditions changed they would be in a better position to provide the kinds of care they would ideally like to provide, dictated by love and not by lack of options. If society took the responsibility that belongs to it – of adequately and humanely providing the services that women currently perform for free – instead of disguising women's slavery as women's responsibility, women would not be in the position of feeling that working in their own self-interest to meet their own needs would jeopardize society.

In the long run, women's self-interest is the interest of society. For women to see through the lie that they are responsible for the unhealthy, uncreative environment of patriarchy, is to perceive the possibility and the necessity for change.

Women and violence

When women individually or collectively refuse to comply with their subordination, they are frequently forced to deal with male violence in response. From threats against women planning to participate in national conferences or to work with multi-racial women's groups, to the beating and raping of wives or women known to be political activists, male violence has historically been and will continue to be a counter-force women have to deal with as they begin to make concrete changes in their lives.

Violence has historically been more abhorrent to women, perhaps because women nurse the sick and wounded, and have to put everything back together after wars have torn it apart. Women have resisted wars, spearheading peace movements, working behind the lines to attempt to persuade husbands and sons not to contribute. Women have been the victims of rapes, beatings, mutilations and mass-murders, but almost never the perpetrators.

Women have a long history of organizing collectively against male violence, and their efforts are intensifying in the wake of the nuclear weapon build-up. Their organizing strategies have reflected specifically female-value-based ways of dealing with conflict, which stem from an understanding of peace that is radically different from the patriarchal interpretation. Ann Patterson Ligon, in a study entitled, 'Are These the Peacemakers?' notes that the dictionary defines peace as 'the absence of war.' She defines it as 'the pro-active, ongoing peaceful resolution of conflict.' She notes that cooperative action is the key to female-value-based change 'since it is power which does not subjugate nor elevate but resolves by bringing resolution *out* of conflict.'[99]

One United States' feminist group, Feminist Women for Peace: SOS (Sisters Organized for Survival) states clearly that peace is only possible by the creation of conditions which permit it:[100]

> The use of violence is an acknowledgement of impotence, and war (organized violence) is collective impotence disguised as strength. Militarism is not human nature but habit patterns inherent in patriarchy which intrinsically results in dominant and subordinant groupings. The male 'leaders' now have the technology and the obscene irreverence for life to risk and plan total destruction in the name of 'national interest.' Feminists know there are dynamic, life-affirming alternatives . . . . Femininism denies that a war economy is healthy, that militarism creates security, and that peace is possible without justice.

Another US women's group, Wo-men For Survival, is also using explicitly female tactics in fighting nuclear arms. They are taking pies to the offices of congressmen to let them know in a supportive way that they disagree with their policies. If and when they are not listened to, they plan to occupy the offices with their children. Uniting with other women around the world, such groups are developing international strategies to fight nuclear arms and other patriarchal atrocities.[101] For women to choose violence goes very much against the grain. But this represents a tremendous problem, given that men frequently respond to gains in women's power, with violence against women, on an individual and/or group level. They have, for the most part, used violence only in self-defense, for their individual or group survival, from defending themselves against violent husbands, to participating in liberation movements fighting violent and oppressive regimes.[102]

When women have used violent tactics, their violence has far more often been directed against property than people. Women's respect for life tremendously inhibits their ability to destroy it, and the fact that most property is owned by men clearly diminishes women's respect for it. In most of the demonstrations we've discussed, women's most violent acts have been to occupy or destroy property but never to maim, abuse or kill people as men do in their wars.

For example, in 1959, in the Kon region of Eastern Nigeria, traditional women's organizations initiated massive demonstrations against the deterioration of their role as farmers, fuelled by a fear that the government would sell their land to male farmers. Two thousand women marched to a nearby town and occupied and set fire to the market. Among their resolutions were demands for the elimination of all foreign institutions and the expulsion of all foreigners. This demonstration sparked further demonstrations by women in other nearby regions.[103]

Some of the mechanisms women have used to deal with male violence on an individual level may also provide models for dealing with men collectively. Women have used the principles of peer pressure and accountability to make men afraid *not* to change. In Texas women printed the names of known rapists in the local newspaper. In other states, women have gone to the employers of known but unconvicted rapists to inform them of their employees' extra-curricular activities, which has sometimes resulted in loss of jobs or at the least, articulated disapproval and some ostracization from fellow employees. Similar models have been proposed for dealing with batterers, such as picketing in front of their homes, churches or work-places (once their wives are safely elsewhere) to direct peer pressure against their behavior. Female university students are publicizing sexual harassment from professors which has resulted in the suspension of some of the harassers.

Of course, these tactics must be accompanied by widespread educational campaigns designed to change public opinion so that male peer pressure will work against violence rather than supporting it.

Women's collective responses to violent male collective and institutional behavior have sometimes used these same models, asking what men are most afraid of in each culture and how women can use that fear to their advantage. In some African cultures, taboos concerning women's sexuality have meant that a woman's disrobing in front of a man in a public place carries tremendous mystical and spiritual ramifications and usually compels him to change his behavior without further dialogue. (But this tactic only works in the appropriate cultural context.)[104] Making men and their institutions accountable for their actions on a collective level, as women have done to violent men individually, is a strategy that needs to be explored. If every time individual men or institutions exploited women their actions came back to them in some form, they would eventually become afraid to continue.

Transitional strategies

The transition from patriarchal to matriarchal social and economic institutions necessitates transforming or eliminating patriarchal institutions while at the same time building matriarchal ones. Yet in both instances, the change must come about by explicitly female-value-based *means*, so as not to recreate patriarchal power dynamics in different forms. The building of a separate matriarchal power base from which to fight for change must involve a transformed comprehension of power – not to simply switch the place of what social groups have control over others, but to ensure every individual's control over their own, and only their own, life. To use patriarchal means – such as centralized, hierarchical social organization, or violence – in either fighting patriarchal institutions or building matriarchal ones, is a contradiction in terms. A new society based on new values and concepts of power cannot be built by using change strategies that feed into and strengthen existing values and behavior. There would then never be the point at which the 'new society' was realized, because attitudes, behavior and institutions shaped during the transition would be but new forms of the old. Yet to develop and use explicitly female strategies is extremely difficult and involves enormous amounts of work: to be self-aware enough to ensure that the new is really new; to think of new ways of dealing with some new, but a lot of very old dilemmas, to fight the backlash and repression that will continue to respond to women's efforts towards change.

Women's change strategies need to evolve both from this understanding and from the knowledge that for women to have true equality, they must have freedom and equal economic power. And as we have seen, the higher the status of women in any given culture, the more equitable the distribution of wealth and decision-making in general. Thus the concepts of equal female economic power and matriarchal social organization go hand in hand and underly all of women's movements towards change.

Some economic changes will come about through women's resistance and non-compliance. For example, Ester Boserup has noted that as women increasingly resist doing the menial back-breaking agricultural work in many countries (which are unable to afford the wide-scale capital investments that would enable them to take advantage of technological improvements) and opt for other economic alternatives, many countries may be forced to narrow the gap in the wage differentials for men's and women's agricultural work.[105]

Other economic changes are made possible through women's building of independent power bases on a local level. For example, in the Indian city of Ahmedabad, a social worker helped to organize 6,000 female street vendors, mostly from extremely poor and migrant families, into an economically viable group. Each woman put 5 rupees into a fund which was deposited in a bank. With this fund behind them, the women were able to get loans from the government bank instead of moneylenders charging interest rates of 200 or 300 per cent. Their new economic power resulted in tremendous changes in their status within their families and undoubtedly in the community as well. The women said, 'My husband doesn't beat me any more and he can't leave

me, because I'm the one who brings the loan from the bank.'
Devaki Jain, a lecturer in economics at Delhi University,
feels that this kind of change is much more effective than
organizing large campaigns, with politicians saying, 'Women,
you must rise, you must not allow your husbands to domi-
nate you':[106]

> We have to approach the problem through the back door,
> and, to me, the back door is association. If you associate
> women according to their trade – women who sell
> vegetables, fisherwomen and so on – you build up their
> self-confidence.
>   Women are much more relaxed with women, especially
> in traditional societies; they are not used to sitting with
> men and taking decisions. But the very fact that they
> belong to an institution which provides economic support
> gives them confidence. And once they have that they can
> fight the world!

In addition to locally-initiated change, some possible
transitional strategies on the level of economic policy are
necessary to increase all women's access to economic options.
These range from development planning which decentralizes
industrial development in small-scale village industries, to
various mechanisms for reimbursing women some of the
wealth they have produced.[107] These alternatives take various
forms according to the present position of women in different
cultures and the particular mode of patriarchal economic
organization. In affluent western economies with large
accumulations of capital, this capital, the private resources,
could be 'nationalized' and distributed to pay women for
their work in the home.[108] In countries which are poor
because their profits are going to multi-national corporations
which are foreign-based, these corporations could be nationalized and their resources, again, distributed to women as
partial payment for their double and triple workloads. In
countries with a work point system, all of women's services
could be recognized and allotted work points. These can all
be seen as intermediary alternatives, to working towards the
balancing of male and female responsibilities and rewards.

Since socialism often increases women's access to resources, it can help to raise women's status, and in this context the struggles of many women to transform oppressive economic forces to socialist structures in their countries, is also a fight for an increase in their status as women. Yet as we have seen, no socialist society has yet redistributed work and wealth between men and women on the most fundamental level in the home or in society in general. Even the most libertarian socialism is thus only a partial solution, unless women and female values are in the forefront of building a new economic model involving total redistribution of society's resources. This new model, in addressing male entitlement, must of necessity address entitlement by race and class in the process. Socialist societies have not even been able to create equality on the basis of race and income because they have not recognized male entitlement and its ramifications.

Transitional strategies are needed for transforming social institutions which are grounded in women's slavery. Changing the division of labor in the home is an obvious first step if accompanied by women's increased access to resources and strong networks. Kris Rosenthal has pointed out that in a female culture, mothering skills would be a source of respect and high status for those who possessed them. If men worked in the home, their values would change because they would be influenced by the presence of children and need to develop mothering skills to care for them. 'In bringing men back to [the home], you are bringing them back to the experiences that will alter their world, and therefore alter their culture.[109] If much of male aggression and competitiveness is also caused by boys' lack of male role models in the home, male culture would be directly improved by men's full presence in the home. Yet in a patriarchal context, men who have grown up with male values and have not spent enough time in the home to fully adopt female values, would not necessarily provide alternative role models for their male children and is some cases could do more harm than good. As we have seen in the case of Sweden, such 'role' changes taking place without concurrent changes in women's resources and power base, do not fundamentally alter women's unequal power.

A diversity of change strategies used by women, from fighting the old to building the new, are crucial in bringing about broad-based change in all women's lives, and are often most effective when addressing the same issue from both perspectives.

In religious life, for example, women are both protesting at the structure and policies of traditional patriarchal religions and creating new forms of female-based spiritual worship. From research concerning ancient religions worshipping goddesses and the earliest form of Christianity (the Gnostic religion, which was quickly suppressed because of its worship of female as well as male principles), to the contemporary creation of a feminist spirituality practiced by women in feminist communities, in token power societies, women are searching for new forms of spirituality that are less oppressive to women.[110] Women worshipping within traditional patriarchal religions are fighting to change their structures from within as well. This is evidenced by the boycott by members of the Boston Archdiocesan Sisters' Senate of the mass led by Pope John Paul II during his 1979 visit to Boston, in response to the Vatican decision to bar women from distributing Communion during the visit and the exclusion of women from the planning process for the visit.[111]

In order to build matriarchal alternatives, another transitional strategy suggested by Rosenthal is to address the weak points of the male culture with the strengths of the female culture, rather than trying to develop all the strengths men have and beat them at their own games. There are already a number of men and alternative male institutions, in token and negotiating power societies, which have recognized these weak points and are evolving in a more cooperative direction, precisely because of all the problems generated by patriarchal thinking, values and institutions. Yet these 'alternatives' still often ignore or don't change some facets of male-value-based thinking, behavior and organizational structures. Because of this, it is crucial that women with clear visions of matriarchal goals are in the forefront of change. If they aren't, it will simply become 'another permutation of the male culture.'[112]

The form that all such tactics take – from peer pressure

and accountability to building independent power bases – varies tremendously and evolves out of particular cultural contexts. But the underlying principles are common and effective for women across cultures. To plot such actions necessitates well-developed organization to prepare for the reaction by the male culture as well as requirements of the new social structures. The basic skills, nevertheless, are ones possessed by all women.

Their experience in dealing with the fall-out from male institutions that aren't working properly can be used in dealing with any of the repercussions from the effects of their own actions.

No part of this process will be easy. Women must create an independent power base from which to fight for such change, to provide a positive direction with a clear goal for women's change-oriented energies, and to ensure that positive and creative alternatives exist to replace the patriarchal structures as they deteriorate. But it can ultimately be done.

Individual men's mechanisms for prevention and punishment of change, collective backlash against gains made by women, and government policies designed to contain, diffuse or prevent change, all represent enormous counter-forces women must deal with. From battering and rape, to threats against women involved in network-building, to the closing down or defunding of battered women's shelters and state and local government commissions on the status of women, the power of male resistance is not to be underestimated.[113]

Just as the status of women in different societies exists along a continuum, so do the changes and male responses to such changes that women make in their lives. If women with negotiating power lose their independent sources of power and supportive institutions due to male resistance, or colonization, their status will devolve closer to that of women with token power. In turn, male backlash where women have token power can destroy women's independent power bases, income, and the bits of control over their lives that they may hold, pushing women back into a situation with minimal power.

One of the tactics of repressive governments and right-wing movements in disrupting the work of the feminist movement and other social change movements has been that of divide and conquer. Through a variety of mechanisms they aim to get social movements to focus on their own differences and invest more energy in fighting each other than the power structure, thus drastically weakening the power and support of these movements. This is a typical tactic in token power societies that indirectly attempts to prohibit widespread change.

In countries where women hold minimal power, their repression is usually far more overt, and in countries where women hold negotiating power, their networks are usually given. But where women hold token power, less is 'given' and everything is more easily disrupted and taken away. As a consequence, it is crucial that women in these countries maintain a clear radical vision of change, and do not allow their demands to be diverted or watered down, a process that is subtle as it is insidious. The illusion that it's possible for women to be equally integrated into the male power structure is very seductive, and it often leads women to work harder in building associations with male power than working with other women.

In addition to individual women identifying with and forming alliances with male power, women's groups are also often influenced by patriarchal values. Some large national organizations are hierarchically structured, and not accountable enough to all their members. Other groups use male tactics in fighting for their 'piece of the pie' and become as corrupted by their own power and divorced from the needs of women on the grass-roots level as men in power. Still others let artificially created male boundaries blind them to their common experiences with women from diverse male cultures, and their groups are not inclusive enough of the needs and priorities of different women.

Yet with a radical vision of both new means and ends, and a sincere commitment to the integration of the two and the freedom of all women, such obstacles can eventually be overcome.

Standing the world on its head: international strategies and a matriarchal power base

At the Dawn of Freedom, we have no Freedom.
Iranian feminist chant during
March 1979 demonstrations for
women's rights in the Islamic
Revolution

The mechanisms by which women begin to take back the time, money and resources that have been appropriated by men and patriarchal institutions have varied and will contine to vary a great deal cross-culturally. There is no one strategy or goal that is appropriate for all women across cultures, and all strategies that are most effective for women are grounded in each woman's needs and modelled upon her own priorities.

Yet invariably, for women to be able to consolidate their gains as well as to continue making new ones, they must have independent sources of power from which to fight. A recent encouraging development has been the growing formation of links, communications, and dialogue between women from different countries and cultures, which has begun to create an international women's power base. Since some women have gained more access to resources and begun to struggle against racism in their own countries, they are now more able to effectively forge links with women in other countries. To a certain extent, these links have occurred on an individual level, as third-world and western women travel, live, and study in each others' countries and as black, Latina, Asian-American and white feminists in the USA work together. Women have also pulled together collectively to learn about each others' experiences and develop support networks and communication links between countries.

A women's university in the USA, Wellesley College, sponsored a 'Women in Development' conference in 1976, which a great many women from throughout the world attended. However, the conference was dominated by white North American academic women in form, structure, process and content, precluding the possibility for real interchange.

As three third-world participants noted:[114]

> The notion of united power is based on the false belief that
> the mere fact of being women is a binding enough
> characteristic to create instantaneous international sisterhood
> above and beyond political differences and unequal power
> distribution . . . . we were invited to attend a conference
> where mostly American 'scholars' were interpreting for us
> our condition, our cultures, our religions and our
> experiences. The absence of papers on American women
> restored for us the hardly-healed colonial experience wherein
> the detached outsiders define your world to you . . . . The
> organizers did not understand why the Third World women
> were uncomfortable with their powerlessness to participate
> in the design of the panels, or to contribute in any way to
> the rigidly structured conference. They acted just like the
> men who organize meetings involving women's issues,
> without getting the women involved in the planning and
> policy decision-making. For them, power was not the issue
> because they *had* it.

Because some of the third-world women who were at the
conference aired their grievances and their own issues, the
conference began to deal with the issues of ethnocentrism,
race and class that so often divide women. This experience
highlights the need for western women to confront their own
racial and cultural biases to make the dream of international
feminism a more viable option.

On a grass-roots level, a number of international feminist
campaigns have been waged, totally independent of and often
opposed to governmental or institutional support.

International feminist support was rallied in 1972 for three
Portuguese women who wrote *The Three Marias*, and who
were arrested on charges of outrage to public decency. Their
book explored, through events in their own lives and those of
other Portuguese women, the realities of being a woman
under strongly patriarchal conditions. It was banned because
they included sexuality. The international support greatly
affected their case, which ended in 1974 when all charges
were dropped.[115]

In March 1976, women held an International Tribunal on Crimes Against Women, in Brussels, sharing information and experiences for days, and publishing a volume to document the history.[116] Out of this conference grew the International Feminist Network, which women around the world can use to gather international support and share information. This network is being coordinated by an international resource and documentation center, ISIS, which also produces a quarterly bulletin.[117] Another International quarterly journal, Women's International News, has been published since 1975 and contains 80 pages of news from all over the world, focusing special attention on violence against women.[118]

A strong and radical women's movement is emerging in India, as evidenced by the publication *Manushi*, which serves as a communication link for women of all classes and castes in India, also speaks to women around the world, with a consciousness of the need for women to form links between countries. *Manushi* has reported demonstrations such as the one in 1979 in which 800 women marched to protest molestation of women on buses. The demonstration received wide press coverage resulting in a debate in Parliament, and caused buses to put up signs saying, 'Eve-teasing is an offence; offenders will be taken to the police station and may be arrested. Passengers are requested to cooperate.' Large rallies have taken place on International Women's Day, and conferences have been organized to promote discussion of everything from the problems of industrial and agricultural workers, to educational discrimination and violence against women. Conference demands included daycare for children of working mothers, drinking water for rural and urban poor, social recognitions of women's work in the home and more hostels for working women and students.[119]

In addition to communication between countries, the influence of advances for women in one country, on the status of women in others, is very important. For example, the fact that women in North America and Western Europe had a higher status than in Argentina, helped to influence popular opinion towards reform of the oppressive Argentinian Civil Code, since those cultures were admired and emulated. Similarly, Argentina was encouraged to grant suffrage to women when Spain did so in 1931, since Argentina was so closely linked, culturally, to Spain.[120]

Pressure by feminists, in countries with token and negotiating power, on the policies of governments where women hold less power can also be effective. In 1979 there were many demonstrations of women throughout the world in support of the resistance by Iranian women to the severe repression and loss of status they were experiencing at the hands of the Khomeini government. On 8 March 1979, 5,000 Iranian women demonstrated, and their numbers swelled each day, despite stabbings of some women and stones thrown at them by men who arrived in government buses to harass them, until on 11 March 1979, 15,000 women took over the Palace of Justice.

Their eight demands included equal civil rights with men; no discrimination in political, social and economic rights; a guarantee of full security for women's legal rights and liberties; and freedom for women to choose their most appropriate attire.[121] Twenty thousand women demonstrated on 12 March. Women then marched on the radio and television stations after news of the demonstrations was suppressed. The fact that Kate Millett, an American feminist, was invited to give an International Women's Day speech, that women in dozens of countries demonstrated in support of Iranian women, and that an international group of feminists met with officials of the Khomeini government in an attempt to put pressure on the government to change its policies concerning women, all points to the growth and potential strength of an international feminist movement.

For women the world over to unite and present demands in behalf of women in a particular area, presents the vision of an international advocacy force for women (just as the Canadian Feminist Party does for Canadian women), with the power to press for women's political rights and articulate moral and ethical stances that are explicitly feminist, independent of governmental or institutional cooptation, and grounded in the needs of women of all national, racial, class and religious identities.[122]

The number of international feminist projects has raised just such a possibility of an international power base of women, with an explicitly feminist ideology that at once transcends all patriarchal cultural differences and addresses the varying forms of women's oppression in a consciously female-value-centered way.

This sort of advocacy force might be likened to the support networks that women in token power societies are able to develop and wield as a tool for change or the traditionally strong networks of women with negotiating power. On an international level, the resources of these women with token and negotiating power can be used to help build tools and networks for women with less access to such resources. And once these networks are developed throughout the world, women can begin to build an independent power base, with the potential not only to function as an advocate for women, but to begin to transform the structure and distribution of male power, to break it down, according to female-centered values, and to replace it with viable alternatives based on the institutionalizing of female values.

However women create such change, whether it's done within isolated communities, or as a part of a unified whole, or both, this is the direction the world must go in to survive. We have too many people, too finite resources, to allow patriarchal cultures to continue plundering the earth. But women must take a leadership role in order to bring about the change from patriarchal to matriarchal cultures, with an equality of all people, and the development of cultures in female-value-centered directions.

Since so many social divisions are modelled and built upon the underlying division by sex, the shifting of that division would of necessity involve the reshifting of all others as well. For a society to so profoundly question and restructure its social priorities and institutions as to equally reward women for *all* their work, it would have to be fundamentally non-exploitative in its world view and all social stratification and inequities would be addressed in the process. Every woman's economic independence and equality would necessitate the breaking down of all other social barriers as well. A new social order, based on equal structuring of work, rewards and power, would be ushered in.

For true equality to exist between women and men in any

culture, the very basis of domination and exploitation will have to be eradicated, including all the patriarchal norms and assumptions which are sustained by women's oppression. Patriarchy must be completely transformed from its very roots, including the extent to which women have internalized male values and assumptions. The creation of matriarchal economies and cultures throughout the world will mean just such a transformation – not a reversal of power, but a whole new way of comprehending and structuring power.[123]

This is crucial in the face of the magnitude of the lies which have distorted and veiled female experience, the depth of the suffering and destruction. To begin to see women's experience for the slavery that it is will fundamentally transform the thinking and the history of the world.

Women create the wealth that men use to build nations. They create the time that men use to create art, science and government. They create the standard of living that men use for recreation and all the enjoyments of material 'civilization.' And they create the future of the human world: children.

In return, women have been enslaved, exploited, empoverished, starved, brutalized, maimed and killed. They share in little of what they have produced – it is in fact used to perpetrate their servitude.

Yet the world could not continue a single day without them and will not survive long if the patriarchy continues its wanton destruction. The unity of women must grow strong enough to refuse to comply, as a whole, to redirect their energies in their own behalf towards a fundamentally transformed, matriarchal world.

Notes

*Unless otherwise stated, all addresses are in the United States

Introduction

1 Ewé – pronounced 'Eh-vay'.
2 Charlotte Perkins Gilman, *Women and Economics* (1989), Harper & Row, New York, 1966, p. 4.
3 Batya Weinbaum has developed a unique approach in the last chapter of *The Curious Courtship of Marxism and Feminism*, South End Press, Boston, 1979.
4 Elizabeth Fisher, *Woman's Creation: Sexual Evolution and the Shaping of Society*, Anchor Press, Doubleday, New York, 1979, pp. 47-8. See also Elaine Morgan, *The Descent of Woman*, Stein & Day, Briarcliff Manor, New York, 1972. Sally Slocum, 'Woman the Gatherer: Male Bias Anthropology,' *Toward an Anthropology of Women*, ed. Rayna Reiter, Monthly Review Press, New York, 1975.
5 Frederick Engels, *The Origin of the Family, Private Property and the State*, International Publishers, New York, 1975, p. 125.
6 These talks became the international speakers series, sponsored by the Women in the Economy project of Goddard-Cambridge, 1976-7.

1 Sexual economics explored

1 Jules Henry, 'The Economics of Pilaga Food Distribution,' *American Anthropologist*, vol. 53, April-June 1951. Carol Stack, *All Our Kin*, Harper & Row, New York, 1974.
2 'Ongka's Big Moka,' presented as part of the television anthropology film series, *Odyssey*, based on Andrew Strathern's research. Transcript available from: Ongka-Odyssey Series, Public Broadcasting Association, Box 1000, Boston, Mass. 02118.
3 Lisa Leghorn and Mary Roodkowsky, *Who Really Starves? Women*

314

And World Hunger, Friendship Press, New York, 1977, p. 22.
4   United Nations Commission on the Status of Women, Newsletter, no. 3, 1980. UN Decade for Women Conference, Copenhagen, 1980.
5   Ester Boserup, *Woman's Role in Economic Development*, St Martin's Press, New York, 1970, p. 74.
6   Magda Cordell and John McHale, *Women in World Terms*, State University of New York at Binghamton, 1975, p. 39. 'Women Workers Today,' US Department of Labor, Employment Standards Administration, Women's Bureau, 1976, p. 8.
7   Elizabeth Johnstone, 'Women in Economic Life: Rights and Opportunities,' *Annals of the American Academy of Political and Social Science: Women Around the World*, January 1968, Philadelphia, p. 103.
8   We are indebted to Adrienne Rich for her analysis of compulsory heterosexuality. See 'Compulsory Heterosexuality and Lesbian Existence,' *Signs: Journal of Women in Culture and Society*, University of Chicago Press, Summer 1980.
9   Gabriel Kolko, *Wealth and Power in America*, Frederick Praeger, New York, 1962, pp. 46, 51.
10   'The Earnings Gap Between Women and Men,' US Department of Labor, Employment Standards Administration, Women's Bureau, 1976, p. 12.
11   'Minority Women Workers: A Statistical Overview,' US Department of Labor, Employment Standards Administration, Women's Bureau, 1977 (Revised), p. 13.
12   Adrienne Rich, 'Taking Women Students Seriously,' *On Lies, Secrets and Silence*, W.W. Norton, New York, 1979, p. 241.
13   John Lombardi, 'A Structural Hypothesis on Social Mobility in the United States,' unpublished paper available from Lombardi, Dept. of Chemistry, City College, City University of New York, Convent Ave. at 138th St, New York, N.Y., 10031.
14   Lozi Pounding Song, *New World Outlook*, New Series, vol. 31, no. 8, April 1971, p. 59.
15   See, for example, Paula Webster, 'Matriarchy: A Vision of Power,' *Toward an Anthropology of Women*, Monthly Review Press, New York, 1975; Emily Culpepper, 'Female History/Mythmaking,' *The Second Wave*, vol. 4, no. 1, Cambridge, 1975.
16   See Boserup's description of the Tutsi and Hutu people of Burundi, op. cit., p. 67.
17   Ann Stoler, 'Class Structure and Female Autonomy in Rural Java,' *Signs*, vol. 3, no. 1, Autumn 1977, pp. 74-89. Barry Newman, 'Mixed Blessing: Do Multinationals Really Create Jobs in the Third World?' *Wall Street Journal*, New York, 25 September 1979.
18   Newman, op. cit.
19   Lourdes Arizpe, 'Women in the Informal Labor Sector: The Case of Mexico City,' *Signs*, vol. 3, no. 1, Autumn 1977, p. 28.

20   Fatima Mernissi, 'Veiled Sisters,' *New World Outlook*, vol. 31, no. 8, p. 36.
21   Yolanda T. Moses, 'Female Status, the Family, and Male Dominance in a West Indian Community,' *Signs*, vol. 3, no. 1, Autumn 1977, p. 142-53.
22   Marion Martinez, 'Cultural Diversity in Shelters,' *Aegis, Magazine on Ending Violence Against Women*, March-April 1979, Box 21033, Washington, D.C. 20009, pp. 40-41.
23   A.B. Meskiani, 'An Interview with Josephine Buanga,' *New World Outlook*, vol. 31, no. 8, April 1971, p. 34.
24   Margery Wolf, 'Chinese Women: Old Skills in a New Context,' *Woman, Culture and Society*, ed. Rosaldo and Lamphere, Stanford University Press, 1974, p. 162.

2   Shouldering the high cost of development

1   Ann Cornelisen, *Women of the Shadows: The Wives and Mothers of Southern Italy*, Vintage Books, New York, pp. 2-3.
2   G. Carl Wiegand, *Economics: Its Nature and Importance*, Barron's Educational Series, Inc., Woodbury, N.Y., 1976, pp. 110-11.
3   For the effects of this on women's health, see Lisa Leghorn and Mary Roodkowsky, *Who Really Starves? Women And World Hunger*, Friendship Press, New York, 1977.
4   Robert Cuthbert, 'The Church in Caribbean Development,' *The Role of Women in Caribbean Development*, Report on Ecumenical Consultation, 19-23 July 1971, Caribbean Conference of Churches, Barbados, 1975, p. 6.
5   Fatima Mernissi, 'Veiled Sisters,' *New World Outlook*, vol. 31, no. 8, April 1971, p. 36.
6   Barry Newman, 'Mixed Blessing: Do Multinationals Really Create Jobs in the Third World?' *Wall Street Journal*, New York, 25 September 1979.
7   Earl Grant, Ancient Egypt Lecture Series, October 1975-April 1976, Tufts University, African American Cultural Center, Medford, Mass.
8   Weka-Yawo Aladji, Personal Communication with the Togolese journalist, Paris, France, February 1974.
9   Grant, op. cit.
10   Josephine Trinidad, 'The Emancipation of the Antillean Woman,' *Caribbean Women in the Struggle*, sponsored by Caribbean Church Women of the Caribbean Conference of Churches, September 1975, p. 44. See also Leghorn and Roodkowsky, op. cit., p. 13.
11   Cuthbert, op. cit., p. 9.
12   John Hood, 'Can I Talk With a Woman?' *The Role of Women in Caribbean Development*, p. 54.
13   Newman, op. cit.

14 Ibid.
15 Ibid.
16 Leghorn and Roodkowsky, op. cit., p. 28.
17 Ibid., p. 28.
18 Michael Kennedy, Peace Corps, Togo, Personal Communication to Lisa Leghorn, August 1975.
19 Newman, op. cit.
20 Frances Moore Lappé and Joseph D. Collins, *Food First!*, Houghton-Mifflin Co., Boston, 1977.
21 Editors of *The Ecologist, Blueprint for Survival*, Houghton-Mifflin Co., Boston, 1972, p. 6.
22 Cuthbert, op. cit., p. 6.
23 Barbara Gamarekian, 'World Bank Noting Women's Influence,' *New York Times*, 23 December 1979, p. 7.
24 Dorothy Vellenga, 'Ghana: Liberation,' *New World Outlook*, vol. 31, no. 8, April 1971, p. 26.
25 Annie Jiagge, 'Politics: A Woman's Job,' *New World Outlook*, vol. 31, no. 8, April 1971, p. 13.
26 Stephanie Urdang, *A Revolution Within a Revolution: Women in Guinea-Bissau*, New England Free Press, Somerville, Mass., p. 2.
27 Achola Pala and Ann Seidman, 'A Model of the Status of Women in Africa.' Paper presented at the Women and Development Conference, Wellesley College, June 1976. For further information contact Pala, c/o IDS, University of Nairobi, Kenya, or Seidman, c/o International Development and Social Change Dept., Clark University, Worcester, Mass., USA.
28 Elise Boulding, *Women, Bread and Babies: Directing Aid to Fifth World Farmers*, IWY Bulletin no. 4, United Nations, 1975, p. 4.
29 Ester Boserup, Preface to *Signs: Journal of Women in Culture and Society*, vol. 3, no. 1, Autumn 1977, p. xii.
30 Ester Boserup, *Woman's Role in Economic Development*, St Martin's Press, New York, 1970, pp. 80-81.
31 Ibid., p. 58.
32 See, for example, Pala and Seidman, op. cit.
33 Claire Robertson, 'Twentieth Century Changes in the Organization of the Fish Trade in Accra.' Paper presented at the Wellesley Women and Development Conference.
34 Boserup, op. cit., p. 94.
35 Madhu Kishwar, 'Unpaid, Unrecognized: Women Speak About Housework,' *Manushi, A Journal About Women and Society*, no. 2, March-April 1979, available from Shaheed Prakashan Press, A-794, Nabi Kareem, Paharganj, New Delhi - 55, India, p. 43.
36 Fatima Mernissi, 'Women and Health Service in Morocco,' *ISIS, International Bulletin*, Spring 1978, no. 7, p. 13. Obtainable from Via della Pelliccia 31, 00153, Rome, Italy, or Case Postale 301, 1227 Carouge, Geneva, Switzerland.
37 Gumarekian, op. cit., p. 7.

38   R. Apthorpe, ed., Land Settlement and Rural Development in
      Eastern Africa, Pampala: Nkarga Editions: Transition Books,
      cited in Pala and Seidman, op. cit., p. 13.
39   Boserup, op. cit., p. 55.
40   Paul Bohannan, 'Some Principles of Exchange and Investment
      Among the Tiv,' *American Anthropologist*, vol. 57, February
      1955, p. 69.
41   Lourdes Arizpe, 'Women in the Informal Labor Sector: The Case
      of Mexico City,' *Signs*, vol. 3, no. 1, Autumn 1971.
42   Tomiko Shimado, letter to Alison Raymond Lanier, quoted in
      'Women in the Rural Areas,' *Annals of the American Academy
      of Political and Social Science: Women Around the World*,
      January 1968, Philadelphia, p. 121.
43   Yolanda T. Moses, 'Female Status, the Family, and Male
      Dominance in a West Indian Community,' *Signs*, vol. 3,
      no. 1, Autumn 1977, p. 151.
44   Hanna Papanek, 'Development Planning for Women,' *Signs*,
      vol. 3, no. 1, Autumn 1977, p. 17.
45   Arizpe, op. cit., pp. 28, 30.
46   Ibid., p. 25.
47   Shirley-Ann Hussen, from 'Four Views on Women in the Struggle,'
      Caribbean Women in the Struggle, p. 29.
48   Lois Wasserspring, 'Inequality and Development: Women in Latin
      America,' paper presented at the Wellesley Women and
      Development Conference.
49   Boserup, op. cit., p. 93.
50   Ibid., p. 94.
51   Niara Sudarkasa, 'Women and Migration in Contemporary West
      Africa,' *Signs*, vol. 3, no. 1, Autumn 1977, pp. 178-89.
52   Ann Stoler, 'Class Structure and Female Autonomy in Rural
      Java,' *Signs*, vol. 3, no. 1, Autumn 1977, pp. 74-89.
53   Abu-Lughod, 'Migrant Adjustment to City Life: The Egyptian
      Case,' *American Journal of Sociology*, 67, July 1961, pp. 22-3,
      cited by Deniz Kandiyoti, 'Sex Roles and Social Change:
      A Comparative Appraisal of Turkey's Women,' *Signs*, vol. 3,
      no. 1, Autumn 1977, p. 71.
54   Kandiyoti, op. cit., p. 71.
55   See, for example, Betty Friedan, *The Feminine Mystique*, Dell
      Publishers, New York, 1963.
56   Rhona Baptiste, 'IWY: What it means to us,' reprinted from the
      March 1975 issue of *Der Uberblick*, in *Caribbean Women in
      the Struggle*, pp. 32-3.
57   William Borders, 'Matrimonial Advertising in India's Sunday
      Papers Adapts Itself to Changing Economics and Mores,'
      New York Times, 28 August 1977.
58   Facts on Iran based on article by Mim Kelber, 'Iran: Five Days in
      March,' *Ms. Magazine*, June 1979, pp. 90-96. As this goes to
      press the Khomeini regime is enforcing a strict system of

punishment for persons straying from the rules of Islam, and women's repression is becoming even more severe. In July 1980, 131 women were dismissed from Army headquarters for not wearing covering over their heads. Men charged with adultery receive 100 lashes while women receive the death penalty. Two women accused of operating houses of prostitution were buried up to their chests, covered with hoods and stoned to death. (Doyle McManus, 'The Wages of Sin in Iran are Severe,' *Boston Globe*, 10 July 1980).

59 Achola Pala, 'Definitions of Women and Development: An African Perspective,' *Signs*, vol. 3, no. 1, Autumn 1977, p. 12.
60 Ibid., p. 13.

3 As a woman, I have no country: the diversity of male power

Minimal power societies

1 These societies are called 'manipulative' by Carolyn J. Matthiasson. As she described the category, it 'includes societies in which women feel that they are inferior to men and resort to deceit, withdrawal, artifice or circumvention to attain their own desires.' We feel this term is misleading because to manipulate implies real power to influence actions, reminiscent of the argument that women are responsible for the world because of the way they raise their sons. The behavior she calls manipulative is described in this book as a survival strategy. ed., Carolyn J. Matthiasson, *Many Sisters, Women in Cross-Cultural Perspective*, The Free Press, New York, 1974, p. xviii.
2 Alemnesh Bulti, *Women in the Ethiopian Economy*, unpublished master's thesis, Goddard-Cambridge, 1976-7, pp. 11-12.
3 Ibid., pp. 32, 35.
4 Ibid., pp. 40-41.
5 *Statistical Abstract of Ethiopia*, 1972, cited by Bulti. See also Bulti, p. 24.
6 Susan Bourque and Kay Warren, 'Campesinas and Comuneras: Subordination in the Sierra,' *Journal of Marriage and the Family*, November 1976, pp. 784, 785.
7 Susan Bourque and Kay Warren, talk given at Goddard-Cambridge, 14 April 1977.
8 Bourque and Warren, 'Campesinas and Comuneras', pp. 783-4.
9 Bourque and Warren, talk, op. cit.
10 Bourque and Warren, 'Campesinas and Comuneras', p. 784.
11 Ibid.
12 Bourque and Warren, talk, op. cit.
13 Bourque and Warren, 'Campesinas and Comuneras,' p. 786.
14 Sheila Rowbotham, *Women, Resistance and Revolution*, Vintage

Books, New York, 1972, pp. 236-40.

15   Fatima Mernissi, 'Veiled Sisters,' *New World Outlook*, vol. 31, no. 8, April 1971, p. 39.

16   Rowbotham, op. cit., pp. 241-3.

17   Ibid., p. 243.

18   Ibid., p. 244.

19   Iijuna Aiko, 'Where are we headed? – A Critical Analysis of 30 Years of "Woman's Policy".' Information packet on Women in Japan, distributed by Fabienne Melchior, Goddard-Cambridge, 1976-7, p. 68.

20   Ibid., p. 74.

21   Azuma Hidemi, 'A Child's Death – The Beginning of Struggle for Daycare,' Information packet on Women in Japan, distributed by Fabienne Melchior, Goddard-Cambridge, 1976-7, pp. 24, 77. Committee to Support K-san, 'Give me Back my Child, An Unmarried Working Mother in the Courts,' Information packet on Women in Japan, pp. 47-50.

22   'The "Woman Power" Fraud, C. Itoh and Co.: A Case in Point,' Information packet on Women in Japan, p. 12.

23   Ibid., p. 11.

24   Aiko, op. cit., pp. 71-3.

25   Fabienne Melchior, talk on women in Japan in short course on Women in the Economy, Goddard-Cambridge, 11 November 1976.

Token power societies

26   Carolyn Matthiasson (op. cit. p. xviii) defines societies in this category as 'complementary': 'Composed of cultures in which women are valued for themselves and the contribution they make to society. In these societies women are neither inferior nor superior to men, merely different.' Our descriptions of women's status in societies at the middle of the continuum of women's power shows how we think this 'separate but equal' analysis falls short.

27   Del Martin, *Battered Wives*, Glide Publications, San Francisco, 1976, p. 60. Terry Davidson, *Conjugal Crime*, Hawthorn Books, Inc., New York, 1978, pp. 116-7.

28   'Compliance,' *National Organization for Women News* (Boston), May 1978, p. 4.

29   'Saving the Family,' *Newsweek*, 15 May 1978, p. 68. See also Isabel Sawhill, 'Discrimination and Poverty Among Women Who Head Families,' *Signs*: Journal of Women in Culture and Society vol. 1, no. 3, Autumn 1977, part II.

30   The myth that women control wealth is refuted at greater length in *Women, Money and Power*, Phyllis Chesler and Emily Jane Goodman, William Morrow & Co., New York, 1976.

31   *Equal Times*, Boston, 12 March 1978, p. 4.

32 Marjorie King, 'Cuba's Attack on Women's Second Shift,'
     unpublished paper, Philadelphia, Pa., p. 3.
33 Carrollee Benglesdorf and Alice Hageman, 'Emerging from Under-
     development: Women and Work,' *Cuba Review*, vol. 4, no. 2
     (P.O. Box 206, Cathedral Station, New York, N.Y. 10025), p. 8.
34 Ibid., p. 10.
35 Margaret Randall, 'Introducing the Family Code,' *Cuba Review*,
     vol. 4, no. 2, p. 31.
36 Benglesdorf and Hageman, op. cit., p. 11.
37 *Unesco Statistical Yearbook*, Unesco, Paris, 1978, p. 144.
38 Dr Lajonchere, Ministry of Health. Unpublished interview by
     Anne Kaufman, May 1978, Havana.
39 Dr Valdes Vivó, director, Hospital Rámòn, Gonzalez, Coro.
     Unpublished interview by Anne Kaufman May 1978, Havana.
40 Margaret Randall, unpublished interview by Anne Kaufman,
     May 1978, Havana.
41 King, op. cit., p. 1.
42 Heidi Steffens, 'FMC: Feminine, Not Feminist,' *Cuba Review*,
     vol. 4, no. 2, p. 22.
43 Rowbotham, op. cit., p. 159. For another analysis of women
     under socialism see Hilda Scott, *Does Socialism Liberate
     Women?*, Beacon Press, Boston, 1974.
44 Rochelle Ruthchild, interview by Katherine Parker, June 1980.
45 George St George, *Our Soviet Sister*, Robert B. Luce, Inc.,
     Washington, 1973, p. 68.
46 Ibid., pp. 66-7.
47 William Mandel, *Soviet Women*, Anchor Books, Garden City,
     New York, 1975, p. 239.
48 Magda Cordell and John McHale, *Women in World Terms*, State
     University of New York at Binghamton, 1975, pp. 37, 39.
49 Mandel, op. cit., p. 109.
50 Ibid., pp. 108, 132, 245.
51 St George, op. cit., pp. 60-61.
52 Mandel, op. cit., p. 296.
53 Ibid., p. 219.
54 David Shipler, 'Soviet Women Not Liberated Despite Professional
     Roles,' *New York Times*, 12 August 1976.
55 Mandel, op. cit., p. 232.
56 Most of the information on Sweden is consolidated from the
     following sources: David Jenkins, ed., *Sweden and the Price of
     Progress*, Coward-McCann, New York, 1968; Edmund
     Dahlstrom, *The Changing Roles of Men and Women*, Beacon
     Press, Boston, 1971; Mary Lou Thompson, ed., 'Report to the
     UN, 1968, the Status of Women in Sweden,' *Voices of the New
     Feminism*, Beacon Press, Boston, 1970; and Birgitta Limner,
     'What Does Equality Between the Sexes Imply,' *American
     Journal of Orthopsychiatry*, vol. 41, no. 5, October 1971.
57 Jenkins, op. cit., pp. 195-6.

58   Dahlstrom, op. cit., p. 68.
59   Leonard Downie Jr, 'More Swedes Find Welfare State Too Taxing,' *The Washington Post*, Washington, D.C., 2 September 1979, p. A26.

Negotiating power societies

60   W.J. Goode, *World Revolution and Family Patterns* (New York: Free Press, 1963), p. 373, quoted by Jessie Bernard, 'The Status of Women in Modern Patterns of Culture,' *Annals of the American Academy of Political and Social Science: Women Around the World*, January 1968, Philadelphia.
61   Matthiasson (op. cit., p. xviii) describes these societies as 'ascendant' saying, 'An ascendant society is one in which it may be an advantage at times to be a woman. Being a woman is an advantage at times in other societies; however, the difference is one of frequency. In an ascendant society the basis of the advantage is institutionalized. Ascendancy does not, however, imply matriarchy. There is no evidence that any society has been truly matriarchal in structure.' We appreciated Matthiasson's work since it was the only analysis we found that divided societies from the point of view of women's status, but her feminist analysis is not taken far enough. It assumes that the representation of women in these societies is a privilege for women, rather than mechanisms that limit women's exploitation by men. Feminist anthropologists Kay Warren and Susan Bourque use 'equivalent' power to describe the same power relationship. We chose another word because of the semantic connotation of equal power that 'equivalent' gives, and because we preferred to think of supportive institutions as giving women a base from which to negotiate with men, rather than as giving women equal power with men, which is not possible within a patriarchal framework.
62   Karen Lindsey, 'Murder or Self-Defense? When Battered Women Strike Back,' *Viva*, vol. 5, no. 2, September 1975.
63   Ruth Sidel, *Women and Childcare in China*, Hill and Wang, New York 1972, p. 15.
64   Ibid., p. 51.
65   C.K. Yang, *Chinese Communist Society: The Family and The Village*, MIT Press, Cambridge, Mass., 1959, p. 117.
66   Sidel, op. cit., p. 53.
67   Shirley MacLaine, *You Can Get There From Here*, Bantam Books, New York, 1975, p. 144.
68   Jack Belden, 'Goldflower's Story,' reprinted from *China Shakes The World*, New England Free Press, Somerville, Mass.
69   W. Hinton, *Fanshen*, Vintage Books, New York, 1966, pp. 396-7.
70   J. Hinton, 'Politics and Marriage,' *New China*, June 1976, pp. 32-4.
71   Sidel, op. cit., p. 39

72　Maria Antonietta Macciocchi, *Daily Life in Revolutionary China*, Monthly Review Press, New York, 1972, p. 360.

73　Lisa Rofel, personal communication with Lisa Leghorn, 27 June 1980.

74　From unpublished research conducted by Lisa Leghorn, 1971-3 and 1975, in the south of Togo. See also Liner notes and accompanying essay to *Togo: Music from West Africa*, Rounder Records, 1979.

75　Alison Raymond Lanier, 'Women in the Rural Areas', *Annals of the American Academy of Political and Social Science: Women Around the World*, January 1968, p. 120.

76　John Darnton, 'Ghana Combating Prices, Hoarding,' *New York Times*, 10 July 1976, p. 6.

77　Ibid.

78　Dorothy Vellenga, 'Ghana: Liberation,' *New World Outlook*, vol. 31, no. 8, April 1971, p. 13.

79　*Unesco Statistical Yearbook*, op. cit., p. 144.

80　All information on the Iroquois, unless otherwise noted, is taken from Judith Brown, 'Iroquois Women: An Ethnohistoric Note,' *Toward An Anthropology of Women* ed. Rayna Reiter, Monthly Review Press, New York, 1975; Carolyn Niethammer, *Daughters of the Earth, The Lives and Legends of American Indian Women*, Collier Books, New York, 1977; Eleanor Leacock, 'Women in Egalitarian Societies,' *Becoming Visible: Women in European History*, ed. Bridenthal & Koonz, Houghton-Mifflin, Boston, 1977, pp. 11-35.

81　Diamond Jenness, *The Indians of Canada*, Bulletin no. 65 of the National Museum of Canada (1932) Ottawa, p. 137. B.H. Quain, 'The Iroquois' (1961) in *Cooperation and Competition among Primitive Peoples*, ed. Margaret Mead, Boston; cited in Brown, op. cit., p. 235.

82　Quain, op. cit., cited in Brown, op. cit., pp. 235-6.

83　Reverend Wright, quoted by Lewis H. Morgan, *Houses and House-Life of the American Aborigines*, University of Chicago Press, Chicago, 1965, cited in Brown, op. cit., p. 242.

84　Alexander A. Goldenweiser, 'On Iroquois Work, 1912,' *Summary Report of the Geological Survey of Canada*, Anthropology Division sessional paper 26, Governmental Printing Bureau, Ottawa, p. 469, cited in Brown, op. cit., p. 246.

85　Matthiasson, op. cit., p. xviii.

4　The personal is economic

1　Jessie Bernard, 'The Status of Women in Modern Patterns of Culture,' *Annals of the American Academy of Political and Social Science: Woman Around the World*, January 1968, Philadelphia, p. 6.

2 Nicole M. Friderich, 'Access to Education at All Levels,' *Annals*, pp. 134-43.
3 Ibid.
4 Ibid.
5 Phyllis Ntantala, 'The Women of South Africa,' *New World Outlook*, vol. 31, no. 8, April 1971, p. 20.
6 Bernard, op. cit., p. 8. See also chart, p. 9.
7 Population Council, 'Fertility and Family Planning,' Thailand, 1973.
8 This discussion of birth- and death-rates is based on Jeanne Clare Ridley's article, 'Demographic Change and the Roles and Status of Women' found in *Annals*, January 1968, Philadelphia. This article also contains tables which illustrate the inter-relationship between birth- and death-rates, women's marital status, and women's level of economic activity for a number of different countries. See pp. 17, 19, 20.
9 This concept is derived from Wayne Suttles, 'Affinal Ties, Subsistence and Prestige among the Coast Salish,' *American Anthropologist*, vol. 62, April 1960; Thorstein Veblen, *The Theory of the Leisure Class*, The New American Library, Inc., New York, 1953, pp. 37-40.
10 Robert Cuthbert, 'The Church in Caribbean Development,' *The Role of Women in Caribbean Development*, Report on Ecumenical Consultation, 19-23 July 1971, Caribbean Conference of Churches, Barbados, 1975, p. 10.
11 Carol Stack, *All Our Kin*, Harper & Row, New York, 1974, pp. 29, 63.
12 Nancy Tanner, 'Matrifocality in Indonesia and Africa and Among Black Americans,' *Woman, Culture and Society*, ed. Rosaldo and Lamphere, Stanford University Press, 1974, p. 154.
13 John K. Galbraith, *Economics and the Public Purpose*, Signet, New York, 1973, p. 35.
14 Veblen, op. cit., pp. 56, 68.
15 Fatima Mernissi, 'Veiled Sisters,' *New World Outlook*, vol. 31, no. 8, April 1971, p. 38.
16 Concept partially derived from Phyllis Chester and Emily Jane Goodman, *Women, Money and Power*, William Morrow & Co., New York, 1976, pp. 40-51.
17 Claude Duhamel, 'Le Travail féminin-témoinage,' *Le Travail Féminin*, Congrès de relations industrielles de l'Université Laval, Les Presses de l'Université Laval, Québec, 1967, pp. 130-1.
18 Iijuna Aiko, 'Where are we headed? – A Critical Analysis of 30 years of "Women's Policy".' Information packet on Women in Japan, distributed by Fabienne Melchior, Goddard-Cambridge, 1976-7, p. 69.
19 From Lennox Grant, 'Agony of Our Women to Keep Jobs in Canada,' *Caribbean Contact*, vol. 5, no. 11, March 1978.

20 H.R. Hays, *The Dangerous Sex*, Pocket Books, Simon and Schuster, New York, 1965.

21 William Mandel, *Soviet Women*, Anchor Books, Garden City, New York, 1975, p. 304.

22 As of 1915, up to 50 per cent of women workers in European cities were single parents. Elise Boulding, *Women, Bread and Babies: Directing Aid to Fifth World Farmers*, IWY Bulletin no. 4, United Nations, 1975, pp. 1-2.

23 Adrienne Rich, 'Motherhood in Bondage,' *On Lies, Secrets and Silence*, W.W. Norton, New York, 1979, p. 196.

24 Concept defined by Goodenough (1965) quoted by Stack, op. cit., p. 83.

25 Charlotte Perkins Gilman, *Women and Economics*, Harper & Row, New York, 1966, pp. 40-68.

26 John Hood, 'Can I Talk With a Woman?' *The Role of Women in Caribbean Development*, Report on Ecumenical Consultation, 19-23 July 1971, Caribbean Conference of Churches, Barbados, 1975, p. 53.

27 Rhona Baptiste, 'IWY: What it means to us,' reprinted from the March 1975 issue of *Der Uberblick*, in *Caribbean Women in the Struggle*, sponsored by Caribbean Church Women of the Caribbean Conference of Churches, September 1975, pp. 32-3.

28 John Hood, op. cit., p. 56.

29 Ann Cornelisen, *Women of the Shadows: The Wives and Mothers of Southern Italy*, Vintage Books, New York, p. 157.

30 Jean Kilbourne, quoted by Mary Maynard, 'The Naked Truth,' *Equal Times*, 13 May 1979, pp. 11, 12.

31 Ibid.

32 Catherine A. MacKinnon, *Sexual Harassment of Working Women*, Yale University Press, New Haven and London, 1979, p. 22.

33 Ibid.

34 Gilman, op. cit., pp. 37-8, 54-5.

35 Arlene Eisen Bergman, *Women of Viet Nam*, People's Press, San Francisco, 1974, pp. 87-8.

36 Bernard, op. cit., pp. 12-13.

37 Andrea Dworkin, *Woman Hating*, E.P. Dutton & Co. Inc., New York, 1974, pp. 95-106.

38 Wearing Kimonos has been linked to breast cancer in recent years. Fabienne Melchior, talk on women in Japan in short course on Women in the Economy, Goddard-Cambridge, 11 November 1976.

39 Elizabeth Hood, 'Black Women, White Women: Separate Paths to Liberation,' *The Black Scholar*, April 1978, p. 51.

40 Ibid., p. 47.

41 Kathryn Burkhart, *Women in Prison*, Doubleday & Co., Garden City, New York, 1973, p. 35.

42 Michele Russell, 'Sexism and Racism: The American Reality,' speech given at Conference on Theology in the Americas,

Detroit, August 1975, pp. 12-14.

43 From *History of Woman Suffrage*, vol. 1, reprint of 1881 edition by Hacker Art Books, New York, 1971, pp. 680-1, quoted by Evelyn Hammonds, 'Women and Blacks: Compelled to Compete,' *Sojourner, The New England Women's Journal of News, Opinions and the Arts*, vol. 4, no. 9, May 1979, p. 9.

44 Quoted by Adrienne Rich, 'Disloyal to Civilization,' *On Lies, Secrets and Silence*, W.W. Norton, New York, 1979, p. 285.

45 Hammonds, op. cit. See also statement by Belle Kearney, Mississippi delegate to 1903 NAWSA Convention, quoted by Hammonds.

46 Fannie Lou Hamer, 'The Special Plight and Role of Black Women,' (1971), quoted by Rich, op. cit., p. 278.

47 Barbara Berg, quoted by Rich, Ibid., p. 286.

48 Ella Gross, 'Bridging the Gap,' *Aegis, Magazine on Ending Violence Against Women*, March-April 1979, Box 21033, Washington, D.C. 20009, p. 38.

49 For further examples, see Susan Cavin, quoted by Rich, op. cit., p. 295.

50 See, for example, Tia Cross, Freada Klein, Barbara Smith and Beverley Smith, 'Face-to-Face, Day-to-Day-Racism CR,' *Sojourner, The New England Women's Journal of News, Opinions and the Arts*, vol. 4, no. 9, p. 11.

51 Eliot Liebow, *Tally's Corner, A Study of Negro Streetcorner Men*, Little, Brown & Co., Boston, Mass., 1967, pp. 142, 150.

52 Azuma Hidemi, 'A Child's Death – The Beginning of Struggle for Daycare,' Information packet on women in Japan, distributed by Fabienne Melchior, Goddard-Cambridge 1976-7.

53 Kathleen Barry, *Female Sexual Slavery*, Prentice-Hall, Englewood Cliffs, New Jersey, 1979, p. 155.

54 Marabel Morgan, *The Total Woman*, Pocket Books, N.Y., 1975, p. 96.

55 Alemnesh Bulti, *Women in the Ethiopian Economy*, unpublished master's thesis, Goddard-Cambridge, 1976-7, pp. 19-21.

56 Alemnesh Bulti, interview by Katherine Parker, October 1976.

57 Norma Boujouen, 'Sexual Assault,' *Aegis . . .*, March-April 1979, pp. 9-10.

58 Karen Lindsey, 'Prostitution,' *Sister Courage*, February 1976, p. 44.

59 Andrea Dworkin, 'Safety, Shelter, Rules, Form, Love: The Promise of the Ultra-Right,' *Ms. Magazine*, June 1979, p. 76.

60 *New World Outlook*, vol. 31, no. 8, April 1971, p. 60.

61 Rich, 'Compulsory Heterosexuality . . . ' op. cit.

62 Maxine Hong Kingston, *The Woman Warrior: Memoirs of a Girlhood Among Ghosts*, Vintage Books, Random House, New York, 1977, pp. 72-3.

63 Leah Fritz, *Dreamers and Dealers, An Intimate Appraisal of the Women's Movement*, Beacon Press, Boston, 1979, p. 192.

64 Susan Wadley, 'Women and the Hindu Tradition,' *Signs*, vol. 3, no. 1, Autumn 1977, p. 118.

65 Ester Boserup, *Women's Role in Economic Development*, St Martin's Press, New York, 1970, pp. 45-6.

66 Betsy Warrior, 'The Self-Image of Woman as Shaped by Unpaid Labor,' *Houseworker's Handbook*, Leghorn and Warrior, Cambridge, Mass. 1974, p. 6.

67 John Stuart Mill, *The Subjection of Women*, first published 1869; reprint, Source Book Press, New York, 1970.

68 Marilyn French, *The Women's Room*, Jove/Harcourt Brace Jovanovich, New York, 1978, pp. 109, 111-13.

69 Many thanks to the students in Lisa Leghorn's Women's Studies Class of 1977 at Arlington School in Belmont, Mass., who thought of some of these analogies.

70 Lourdes Arizpe, 'Women in the Informal Labor Sector: The Case of Mexico City,' *Signs*, vol. 3, no. 1, Autumn 1977, p. 35.

71 Fritz, op. cit., pp. 180-81, 187-8.

72 Urmila Bannerjee, 'Parul . . . One of Many,' *Manushi, A Journal About Women and Society*, March-April 1979, available from Shaheed Prakashan Press, A-794, Nabi Kareem, Paharganj, New Delhi – 155, India, p. 4.

73 Janvedna, 'We Bear the Fruit of Their Sins,' reprinted in *Manushi, A Journal About Women and Society*, no. 2, p. 18.

74 Ibid.

75 Barry, op. cit., p. 74.

76 Ibid., p. 76.

77 Ibid., p. 78.

78 Janvedna, op. cit., p. 18.

79 Tanner, op. cit., p. 150.

80 Audre Lorde, 'Scratching the Surface: Some Notes on Barriers to Women and Loving,' *The Black Scholar*, April 1978, p. 34.

81 Ibid., pp. 33-4.

82 Edgar Moyo, *Big Mother and Little Mother in Matabeleland*, History Workshop Pamphlets, Briant Colour Printing, London, 1973, pp. 14-17.

83 Maria Rosa Dalla Costa and Selma James, *The Power of Women and the Subversion of the Community*, The Falling Wall Press, Montpelier, England, 1973, pp. 47-8.

84 Boserup, op. cit., p. 50.

85 Ibid., pp. 37-9.

86 Ibid., p. 48.

87 Ibid., p. 42.

88 Ibid., p. 41.

89 Ibid., p. 39.

90 Claudia Fonseco, 'I didn't choose my husband, my father gave me to him,' *Unesco Courier*, August 1975, Paris, p. 5.

91 Boserup, op. cit., p. 39.

92 Barry, op. cit., p. 163, quoting Remi Clignet, *Many Wives, Many*

Powers, Northwest University Press, Evanston, 1970, p. 17.

93   Père Labat, *The Memoirs of Père Labat, 1693-1705*, translated and abridged by John Eden, Frank Cass & Co. Ltd., London 1970, pp. 76-7.

94   Boserup, op. cit., p. 43.

95   Ibid., p. 47.

96   Dorothy Vellenga, 'Ghana: Liberation,' *New World Outlook*, vol. 31, no. 8, April 1971, p. 30.

97   Ibid., p. 31.

98   Interview of Florence Dolphyne, 'Educating Women to Think Like Equals,' *Unesco Courier*, no. 697, Paris, p. 19.

99   Martha Bulengo, 'No To Polygamy,' *New World Outlook*, vol. 31, no. 8, April 1971, p. 32.

100 Boserup, op. cit., p. 48.

101 Elizabeth Warnock Fernea, *Guests of the Sheik: An Ethnography of An Iraqi Village*, Doubleday and Co., Garden City, New York, 1965, pp. 162-3.

102 Barry, op. cit., p. 157.

103 Mernissi, op. cit., p. 36.

104 Boserup, op. cit., p. 48.

105 Elizabeth Warnock Fernea, *Middle-Eastern Muslim Women Speak*, University of Texas Press, 1977. Quoted by Barry, op. cit., p. 158.

106 Mernissi, op. cit., p. 39.

107 Boserup, op. cit., p. 108.

108 Ibid., pp. 48-50.

109 Ibid., p. 48.

110 Mernissi, op. cit., p. 39.

111 Ibid.

112 Adamson Hoebel, *Anthropology: The Study of Man*, McGraw-Hill Books, New York, 1972, p. 430.

113 Description of the Nayar culture from E. Kathleen Gough, 'Changing Kinship Usages in the Setting of Political and Economic Change among the Nayars of Malabar,' *Journal of the Royal Anthropological Institute*, 82 (1952), pp. 71-88.

114 Interview of Weka-Yawo Aladji by Lisa Leghorn, August 1975, Lomé, Togo.

115 Kingston, op. cit., p. 56.

116 Deniz Kandiyoti, 'Sex Roles and Social Change: A Comparative Appraisal of Turkey's Women,' *Signs*, vol. 3, no. 1, Autumn 1977, pp. 71-2.

117 Cornelisen, op. cit., p. 28.

118 Ibid., p. 219.

119 Ibid., p. 227.

120 Ntozake Shange, *nappy edges*, St Martin's Press, New York, 1978.

121 Neena Vyas and Madhu Jain, 'When Women Protest,' *Manushi, A Journal About Women and Society*, no. 2, p. 31.

122   Susan Brownmiller, *Against Our Will, Men, Women and Rape*,
         Bantam Books, 1975, p. 229.
123   Gabrielle Bernard, statement and elaboration in film, 'We Will
         Not Be Beaten,' distributed by Transition House Films,
         Cambridge.
124   Yolanda and Robert Murphy, *Women of the Forest*, Columbia
         University Press, New York, 1974, pp. 106-8.
125   Alemnesh Bulti, talk given in Women in the Economy short
         course, Goddard-Cambridge, November 1976.
126   Sudesh Vaid, 'Breaking Fear's Silence,' in *Manushi, A Journal
         About Women and Society*, no. 2, pp. 6, 7, 8.
127   Darryl D'Monte, 'Mass Rape – Police the Culprits,' *Manushi,
         A Journal About Women and Society*, no. 2, March-April
         1979, p. 23.
128   Chris Garcia, Connie Destito Guerro, Irene Mendez and Marian
         Mercado, 'La Violación Sexual — the reality of rape,' *Aegis,
         Magazine on Ending Violence Against Women*, March-April
         1979, p. 22.
129   Mercedes Rodríguez-Alvarado, 'Rape and Virginity among Puerto
         Rican women,' *Aegis*, March-April 1979, p. 5.
130   Quotes in article by Margaret Neville, 'Why? A Question of
         Human Rights and Freedom,' *Equal Times*, Boston, 13 May
         1979, p. 8.
131   Ibid.
132   Freada Klein, presentation at Violence Against Women short
         course, Goddard-Cambridge, June 1977.
133   Garcia, *et al.*, op. cit., p. 19.
134   Lisa Leghorn, 'Violence Against Women: A Cross-Cultural
         Feminist Perspective,' included in 'Wife-Battering,' available
         through the American Friends Service Committee – Women's
         Program, 2161 Massachusetts Ave., Cambridge, Mass. 02140;
         Maynard, op. cit., p. 12; Ellen Weber, 'Sexual Abuse Begins at
         Home,' *Ms. Magazine*, April 1977.
135   *Manushi* Editorial Collective, 'How We Look At It,' *Manushi, A
         Journal About Women and Society*, no. 2, March-April 1979,
         p. 3.
136   Boujouen, op. cit., p. 10.
137   Mernissi, op. cit., pp. 36-8.
138   'Fighting Lechery on Campus,' *Time Magazine*, 4 February 1980,
         p. 84.
139   1976 survey in *Redbook Magazine*, quoted in *Sexual Harassment
         at the Workplace*, distributed by the Alliance Against Sexual
         Coercion, P.O. Box 1, Cambridge, Mass. 02139.
140   Catharine MacKinnon, op. cit., pp. 18, 23.
141   Ibid., p. 44.
142   Ibid., pp. 34-5.
143   Ibid., p. 219.
144   Ibid., pp. 220-21.

145   Barry, op. cit., p. 84.
146   Freada Klein, op. cit.
147   'The more things change . . . ' *Boston Globe*, 28 May 1979.
148   R.E.L. Masters and Edward Lea, eds *The Anti-Sex*, The Julian Press, New York, 1964, p. 19.
149   Betsy Hartmann, 'Behind Bamboo Walls,' *Country Women Magazine*, Issue 30: International Women, available from Box 51, Albion, Calif. 95410, pp. 4-5.
150   The following discussion and facts from Barry, op. cit., pp. 33-4, and 73, respectively.
151   Cornelisen, op. cit., p. 164.
152   Karen Lindsey, 'Charges Reduced – And Raised – Little Trial,' *Boston Phoenix*, 12 August 1975, p. 11.
153   Kathryn Burkhart, *Women in Prison*, Doubleday, New York, 1973, p. 231.
154   Marge Piercy, *Woman on the Edge of Time*, Knopf, New York, 1976. Phyllis Chester, *Women and Madness*, Avon, New York, 1972.
155   Coalition Against Institutional Violence Against Women, 'Ward for Violent Women Opens in Worcester,' *Sister Courage*, December 1976. Flora Hass, ' "Violent Women" and Mass. Prisons,' *Boston Phoenix*, 5 October 1976, pp. 29-30.
156   Fran Hosken, *Win News*, 'Female Circumcision: Summary Facts,' and 'Press Release,' available from 187 Grant St, Lexington, Mass. 02173.
157   Lesley Blanch, *The Wilder Shores of Love*, Touchstone Book, Simon and Schuster, New York, 1954, p. 227. Barry (op. cit., pp. 163, 164) also discusses this.
158   Barbara Ehrenreich and Deirdre English, *Witches, Midwives and Nurses*, The Feminist Press, Old Westbury, New York, 1973.
159   Angela Davis, 'Reflections on the Black Woman's Role in the Community of Slaves,' *The Black Scholar*, December 1971, p. 8.
160   Fritz, op. cit., p. 174.
161   Wendy Ifill, 'Creation vs. Procreation,' *Caribbean Women in the Struggle*, p. 46.
162   For a description of population programs as a part of the destruction and containment of Native American people, see Native American Solidarity Committee, 'The Question That You Ask,' reprinted in *Aegis, Magazine on Ending Violence Against Women*, March-April 1979, p. 25.
163   Judy Herman, 'Forced Sterilization,' Urban Planning Aid, Boston, 1976; also Women Against Sterilization Abuse, 5000 Knox St., Philadelphia, PA. 19199, reprinted in *Aegis*, March-April 1979, p. 24.
164   Karen Lindsey, 'To Be Free, Sterilized and a Woman,' *Boston Phoenix*, 12 December 1972.
165   'Population Control,' *Boston CESA Newsletter*, Committee to

End Sterilization Abuse, Boston, 1976.
166   Women Against Sterilization Abuse, op. cit.
167   Herman, op. cit.
168   A 1969 survey in the USSR found that the larger the apartment
space per person, the fewer women want a second child, due
to the correlation of space with education and wider interests.
Mandel, op. cit., p. 235. See also Population Council,
Thailand, op. cit.

5 She who sows does not reap

1   Leah Fritz, *Dreamers and Dealers, An Intimate Appraisal of the
Women's Movement*, Beacon Press, Boston, 1979, p. 166.
2   Hahna Papanek, 'Development Planning for Women,' *Signs*,
vol. 3, no. 1, Autumn 1977, p. 16.
3   Edith Dahlschen, compiler of 'Songs of Zambia,' *New World
Outlook*, vol. 31, no. 8, April 1971, p. 61.
4   Marilyn French, *The Women's Room*, Jove/Harcourt Brace
Jovanorich, New York, 1978, p. 107.
5   Kathleen Barry, *Female Sexual Slavery*, Prentice-Hall, Englewood
Cliffs, New Jersey, 1979, p. 58.
6   Study by Chase Manhattan Bank, cited in Lisa Leghorn and
Betsy Warrior, *Houseworker's Handbook*, Cambridge, Mass.
1974, p. 18. One study of the work week of British
housewives with one child or more found that women worked
an average of 77 hours a week, seven more hours than 15
years ago. Ann Oakley, *The Sociology of Housework*, Martin
Robertson, London, 1974, pp. 93-4.
7   Associated Press, 'Worth of a Mother? $35,000, says article',
Boston Globe, 24 July 1979.
8   Ann Crittendon Scott, 'The Value of Housework', *Ms. Magazine*,
vol. 1, no. 1, July 1972. Also Leghorn and Warrior, op. cit.,
p. 18.
9   Madhu Kishwar, 'Unpaid, Unrecognized: Women Speak About
Housework', *Manushi, A Journal About Women and Society*,
no. 2, March-April 1979, available from Shaheed Prakashan
Press, A-794, Nabi Kareem, Paharganj, New Delhi – 55,
India, pp. 38-9.
10   Maria Rosa Dalla Costa and Selma James, *The Power of Women
and the Subversion of the Community*, The Falling Wall Press,
Montpelier, England, 1973, pp. 11, 33-4. Margaret Benston,
'The Political Economy of Women's Liberation,' New England
Free Press, *Monthly Review*, September 1969, Leghorn and
Warrior, op. cit.
11   Charlotte Perkins Gilman, *Women and Economics*, Harper &
Row, New York, 1966, p. 13.
12   Kishwar, op. cit., p. 43.

13   Ester Boserup, *Woman's Role in Economic Development*,
       St Martin's Press, New York, 1970, pp. 22-4.
14   Zarina Patel, talk given at Goddard-Cambridge, 3 March 1977.
15   Thelma Awori, 'For African Women Equal Rights Are Not
       Enough', *Unesco Courier*, August 1975, Paris, p. 25.
16   Boserup, op. cit., pp. 27-8.
17   Ibid., p. 26.
18   Ibid., p. 68.
19   Ibid., p. 34.
20   Ibid., p. 35.
21   Cliff Conner, 'Hunger, US Agribusiness and a World Famine,'
       Self-Education Packet, 1975, available from Committee for
       Self-Education, 11 Garden Street, Cambridge, Mass. 02138.
22   Michele Russell, 'Sexism and Racism: The American Reality.'
       Speech given at Conference on Theology in the Americas,
       Detroit, August 1975, p. 3.
23   I. Epstein, 'The Jewish Woman in the Responsa,' *Response*, no.
       18, Summer 1973, p. 24.
24   Charlotte Baum, 'What Made Yetta Work? The Economic Role of
       Eastern European Jewish Women in the Family,' *Response*,
       no. 18, Summer 1973, pp. 32-4.
25   Baum, op. cit., p. 36.
26   Ibid., p. 33-7.
27   Betsy Hartmann, 'Behind Bamboo Walls,' *Country Women
       Magazine*, Issue 30: International Women, available from
       Box 51, Albion, Calif. 95410, p. 4.
28   Jane Humphries, 'Women: Scapegoats and Safety Valves in the
       Great Depression', *Review of Radical Political Economy*,
       Spring 1976, pp. 98-100.
29   *The New York Times*, 21 September 1975.
30   Suzanne Stocking, 'Feds Insult Women's Work', *Somerville
       Times*, November 1976.
31   Carolyn Elliot, 'Theories of Development: An Assessment',
       Signs, vol. 3, no. 1, Autumn 1977, p. 7.
32   Lourdes Arizpe, 'Women in the Informal Labor Sector: The Case
       of Mexico City,' *Signs*, vol. 3, no. 1, Autumn 1977, p. 33.
33   Adrienne Rich, *On Lies, Secrets and Silence*, W.W. Norton,
       New York, 1979, p. 302.
34   Paddy Quick, 'Women's Work', *The Review of Radical Political
       Economics*, vol. 14, no. 3, July 1972, p. 17.
35   Vicki Shanamary Gabriner, 'Clerical Workers: Victory at Boston
       University,' *Equal Times, Boston's Newspaper for Women*,
       13 May 1979, p. 6.
36   All statistics in this paragraph come from Gabriner, ibid., p. 6.
37   Janvedna, 'We Bear the Fruit of Their Sins,' reprinted in *Manushi,
       A Journal About Women and Society*, no. 2, p. 18.
38   Kay Longcope, 'Women's Role in Liturgy,' *Boston Globe*,
       14 September 1979, p. 20.

39 Edith Dahlschen, 'Songs of Zambia', op. cit. p. 59.
40 Figures from *McGill Birth Control Handbook*, 1973, available from: P.O. Box 1000 Station G, Montréal 130, Québec, Canada, reprinted in *Our Bodies, Ourselves*, by the Boston Women's Health Book Collective, Simon and Schuster, New York, 1971, p. 114.
41 See, for example, Benston, op. cit.
42 Boserup, op. cit., p. 38.
43 Ibid., p. 50.
44 Susan Wadley, 'Women and the Hindu tradition,' *Signs*, vol. 3, no. 1, Autumn 1977, pp. 124-5.
45 Hartmann, op. cit., p. 5.
46 Ann Cornelisen, *Women of the Shadows: The Wives and Mothers of Southern Italy*, Vintage Books, New York, p. 157.
47 Paul A. Samuelson, *Economics*, McGraw Hill, 1967, p. 118.
48 Papanek, op. cit., p. 18.
49 French, op. cit., pp. 111-12.
50 G. Wilson and M. Wilson, *Analysis of Social Change*, Cambridge University Press, 1945, cited in Achola Pala and Ann Seidman, 'A Model of the Status of Women in Africa.' Paper presented at the Women and Development Conference, Wellesley College, June 1976. For further information contact Pala c/o IDS, University of Nairobi, Kenya, or Seidman, International Development and Social Change Department, Clark University, Worcester, Mass., USA.
51 Boserup, op. cit., pp. 78-9.
52 Anne Hillerman, 'Mothers Face Welfare When Child Support Fails,' *The New Mexican*, 11 May 1980, p. D-1. Leghorn and Warrior, op. cit., p. 35.
53 Staff Report, US Commission on Civil Rights, 'Women and Poverty', June 1974, p. 3.
54 French, op. cit., pp. 234, 278.
55 Boserup, op. cit., p. 41.
56 Ibid., p. 77.
57 National Organization for Women, Displaced Homemakers Bill. For information write to National NOW Office, 425 13th St NW no. 1048, Washington, D.C. 20004.
58 Boserup, op. cit., pp. 79-80.
59 Matilda Joslyn Gage, *Woman, Church and State*, Arno Press, New York, 1972, pp. 436-7.
60 Raka Sharan, 'Factories or Concentration Camps?', *Manushi*, no. 2, pp. 45-6.
61 Kathryn Burkhart, *Women in Prison*, Doubleday & Co., Garden City, New York, 1973, pp. 282, 283, 231, respectively.
62 Ibid., pp. 231, 283.
63 Mona-Josée Gagnon, 'Les Femmes dans le Mouvement Syndical Québécois', *Sociologie et Sociétés*, vol. 6, no. 1, Presses de l'Université de Montréal, May 1974, pp. 21-5. *Québécoise*

Deboutte!, vol. 1, no. 6, Le Centre des Femmes, Montréal, June 1975, p. 51.

64   *ILO: Yearbook of Labor Statistics 1973* in 'Equality of Opportunity, Report VIII', International Labour Office, Geneva, 1975, cited in Magda Cordell and John McHale, *Women in World Terms*, State University of New York at Binghamton, 1975, p. 39; 'Women Workers Today', US Department of Labor, Employment Standards Administration, Women's Bureau, 1976, p. 8. (The US statistic has risen to 59 per cent since that report.)

65   Betsy Warrior, 'The Protection Hoax', *The Female State*, Issue 4, published by Cell 16, Cambridge, Mass., 1970.

66   Barbara Gamarekian, 'World Bank Noting Women's Influence,' *New York Times*, 23 December 1979, p. 7.

67   Alexander Szalai, 'Women's Time,' *Futures*, October 1975, p. 390.

68   Boserup, op. cit., p. 78.

69   Arizpe, op. cit., p. 35.

70   Boserup, op. cit., p. 192.

71   Elise Boulding, *Women, Bread and Babies: Directing Aid to Fifth World Farmers*, IWY Bulletin no 4, United Nations, 1975, p. 7. Data base from: The Changing and Contemporary Role of Women in African Development, UNECA, 1974, Country Reports on Vocational and Technical Training for Girls and Women, UNECA, 1972-4, studies, mission reports, discussions.

72   Ibid., p. 9. *Analyse de la malnutrition au Bushi*, published by *Oeuvre pour la lutte contre le bwaki et la protection de l'enfance*, as quoted by David Mitchnik in *The Role of Women in Rural Development in Zaire*, OXFAM, Oxford, 1972.

73   Claudia Fonseco, 'I didn't choose my husband, my father gave me to him,' *Unesco Courier*, August 1975, Paris, pp. 6, 7.

74   For a description of the Jamaican male's enjoyment of leisure time, see John Hood, 'Can I Talk With a Woman?', *The Role of Women in Caribbean Development*, Report on Ecumenical Consultation, 18-23 July 1971, Caribbean Conference of Churches, Barbados, 1975, p. 53.

75   Beraët Zeki Üngör, 'Women in the Middle East and North Africa and Universal Suffrage,' *Annals of the American Academy of Political and Social Science: Women Around the World*, January 1968, Philadelphia, p. 76.

76   Andrea Dworkin, 'Safety, Shelter, Rules, Form, Love: The Promise of the Ultra-Right,' *Ms. Magazine*, June 1979, pp. 74-6.

77   'Minority Women Workers: A Statistical Overview,' US Dept. of Labor, Women's Bureau, Washington D.C., 1977, pp. 8-9.

78   Boulding, op. cit., p. 8.

79   *Boston Globe*, 6 May 1974.

80   *Area Handbook for India*, US Department of the Army Pamphlet

550-2, cited in Ellen Rosenberg, 'Ecological Effects of Sex Differential Nutrition', presented at the American Anthropological Association Conference, 1 December 1973.

A study of differential growth patterns in men and women due to sexually discriminatory food distribution can be found in Professor Alan Wilson's section of a report to US AID (contract no. AID-DSPE-C-0021) entitled 'Education and Nutrition: Performance and Policy' written by Charles Benson *et al.*, April 1980. Further information on the study and forthcoming publication may be obtained from Judy Balderston or Alan Wilson of the Dept. of Education, University of California at Berkeley. At the World Conference of the UN Decade for Women held in Copenhagen in 1980, the fact that half the world's women live in situations of rural development – often in conditions where food scarcity and hunger are primary problems – was discussed. In a background paper prepared for that conference (no. A-Conf. 92-24), Malak El Chichini, from the office of the UN High Commissioner for Refugees, pointed out that in the world's refugee camps, where hunger is a major issue, two-thirds of the refugees are women.

81　Unicef News Fact Sheet, reprinted in Lisa Leghorn and Mary Roodkowsky, *Who Really Starves? Women and World Hunger*, Friendship Press, New York, 1977.
82　Marie Toure N'Gom, 'The Continuing Effort for Women's Rights,' *Unesco Courier*, no. 697, p. 11.
83　Interview with Alemnesh Bulti, 7 July 1976, Cambridge, Mass.
84　Warrior, 'The Protection Hoax', op. cit.
85　Elizabeth Johnstone, 'Women in Economic Life: Rights and Opportunities,' *Annals of the American Academy of Political and Social Science: Women Around the World*, January 1968, Philadelphia, pp. 107, 109.
86　'Housework Proves Deadly,' *New Women's Times*, vol. 6, no. 10, 9-22 May 1980.
87　Maxine Hong Kingston, *The Woman Warrior: Memoirs of a Girlhood Among Ghosts*, Vintage Books, Random House, New York, 1977, pp. 72-3.
88　Epstein, op. cit., p. 25.
89　Betsy Warrior, 'The Source of Leisure Time' *Houseworker's Handbook*, Cambridge, Mass., pp. 82-5.
90　Tillie Olson, *Silences*, Del Publishing Co., New York, 1978, p. 31.
91　Ibid., p. 37.
92　Ibid., p. 39.
93　Virginia Woolf, *A Room of One's Own*, included in *The Feminist Papers*, ed. Alice S. Rossi, Bantam Books, New York, 1974, p. 641.
94　Karen Lindsey, 'The Women of Heien Japan,' *Women: A Journal of Liberation*, vol. 1, no. 3, Spring 1970, pp. 2-3.

95 Gilman, op. cit., pp. 14-15.
96 Gamarekian, op. cit., p. 7.
97 This is derived from the concept developed by Frédrik Barth in the article, 'Ecological Relationships of Ethnic Groups in Swat, North Pakistan,' *American Anthropologist*, vol. 58, 1956, p. 1086.
98 Elizabeth Warnock Fernea, *Middle-Eastern Muslim Women Speak*, University of Texas Press, 1977, pp. 161-70.
99 See Leghorn and Roodkowsky, op. cit., pp. 22, 29.
100 Excerpts from Thorstein Veblen, *The Theory of the Leisure Class*, in Leghorn and Warrior, op. cit., pp. 89-93.
101 This hypothesis would take a tremendous amount of work to test, since the data is not currently available. However, we feel that the data and graphic presentation of the composite would be well worth the effort to produce it. Some methods for quantifying similar seemingly unquantifiable data in table and graph form have been developed which might prove useful. For example, Sanday's documentation of the relationship of female status in the *public* domain, to female contribution to subsistence (not including domestic labor and child-birth and rearing) in Peggy Sanday, 'Female Status in the Public Domain,' in *Women, Culture and Society*, pp. 189-206.

6 The winds of change

1 Oscar Lewis, *The Children of Sanchez*, Random House, New York, 1961, p. 431.
2 Batya Weinbaum, *The Curious Courtship of Marxism and Feminism*, South End Press, Boston, 1979.
3 Development and the Caribbean Woman,' Summary of Workshops, *The Role of Women in Caribbean Development*, Report on Ecumenical Consultation, 19-23 July 1971, Caribbean Conference of Churches, Barbados, 1975, p. 31.
4 Fatima Mernissi, 'Women, Saints and Sanctuaries,' *Signs*, vol. 3, no. 1, Autumn 1977, p. 106.
5 'Caribbean Women in the Struggle,' reprinted from August 1975 issue of *People* Magazine in *Caribbean Women in the Struggle*, sponsored by Caribbean Church Women of the Caribbean Conference of Churches, September 1975, p. 8.
6 Gemma Ashby and Shirley-Ann Hussen, 'Four Views on Women in the Struggle,' *Caribbean Women in the Struggle*, pp. 23-6.
7 For further elaboration, see Lisa Leghorn, 'Grass-Roots Services for Battered Women: A Model for Long Term Change,' available from the US Commission on Civil Rights' publication of the proceedings of the January 1978 National Consultation on Battered Women.
8 Barbara Smith and Beverly Smith, 'I Am Not Meant to be Alone and Without You Who Understand': Letters from Black

Feminists, 1972-8, *Conditions: Four*, Brooklyn, N.Y., 1979, pp. 62-77.

9 Raka Sharan, 'Factories or Concentration Camps?' *Manushi, A Journal About Women and Society*, no. 2, March-April 1979, available from Shaheed Prakashan Press, A-794, Nabi Kareem, Paharganj, New Delhi – 55, India, pp. 45-6.

10 Janet Jagan, 'Haliman – Sugar Worker of Guyana,' in *Caribbean Women in the Struggle*, pp. 40-2.

11 Norman Lockman, 'Zimbabwe's Strong Economy Poses Its Own Problems,' *Boston Globe*, 17 June 1980, pp. 1, 8.

12 Interview of Mrs Issam Abdul Hadi, 'Flowers of Fatah,' in *New World Outlook*, vol. 31, no. 8, April 1971, pp. 40-1.

13 Ina M. Beasley, 'Education is the Key for Women,' in *Annals of the American Academy of Political and Social Science: Women Around the World*, January 1968, Philadelphia, p. 156.

14 Ibid.

15 Joyce Holder, 'Tea Parties and Old Lace,' in *Caribbean Women in the Struggle*, pp. 53-4.

16 Josephine Trinidad, 'The Emancipation of the Antillean Woman,' in *Caribbean Women in the Struggle*, pp. 40-42.

17 Jennifer Arthur, 'Spanish Women,' *Women: A Journal of Liberation*, vol. 3, no. 4, pp. 7-8.

18 Deborah Lee Davis, 'A Feminist Movement in Argentina,' unpublished thesis, Mt Holyoke Dept. of Latin American Studies, 1979, pp. 21-2, 39, 56, 64. Available in Mt Holyoke College Library.

19 *News Highlights* (UN, Governments and NGO's), United Nations Decade for Women, Equality, Development and Peace, bulletin no. 2, second quarter 1978, Branch for the Advancement of Women, Room, DC-1033, United Nations, N.Y. 10017.

20 I. Epstein, 'The Jewish Woman in the Responsa,' *Response*, no. 18, Summer 1973, p. 25.

21 Ibid., pp. 26, 27.

22 Ibid., pp. 27, 28.

23 Fatima Mernissi, 'Veiled Sisters,' *New World Outlook*, vol. 31, no. 8, April 1971, pp. 38-9.

24 John Hood, 'Can I Talk With a Woman?' *The Role of Women in Caribbean Development*, p. 54.

25 Margery Wolf, 'Chinese Women: Old Skills in a New Context,' *Woman, Culture and Society*, ed. Rosaldo and Lamphere, Stanford University Press, 1974, p. 159.

26 Susan Bourque and Kay Warren, talk given at Goddard-Cambridge, 14 April 1977 *Power of Women Journal*, no. 3, Henley on Thames, January 1975, p. 3.

27 Zarina Patel, presentation at Goddard-Cambridge International Speakers Series, 3 March 1977.

28 Beasley, op. cit., p. 156.

29 Alison Raymond Lanier, 'Women in the Rural Areas', *The Annals of the American Academy of Political and Social Science:*

Women Around the World, January 1968, p. 123.
30   Le Théâtre des Cuisines, 'Môman Travaille Pas, A Trop
      D'ouvrage!', Les Éditions du Remue-Menage, 1976.
31   Carrolee Benglesdorf and Alice Hageman, 'Emerging from Under-
      development: Women and Work,' *Cuba Review*, vol. 4, no. 2
      (P.O. Box 206, Cathedral Station, N.Y. 10025), p. 8.
32   Japan Ministry of Labor, Women's and Minor's Bureau, 'Report
      on the Status of Women in Japan,' (Tokyo, 1962), pp. 21-5,
      quoted by Alison Raymond Lanier, op. cit.
33   Ashby, op. cit., p. 24.
34   Nojiri Yoriko, 'Women's Occupational Diseases,' Information
      Packet on Women in Japan, pp. 14-16.
35   'Caribbean Women in the Struggle', op. cit., p. 9.
36   *Off Our Backs: A Feminist News Journal*, May 1979.
37   Mary Crowe, 'Human Rights and Freedom,' *Equal Times*, 13 May
      1979, p. 10.
38   Monica Sjoo, 'Sweden, Now We are "Equal",' *Power of Women*,
      vol. 1, no. 4, London, Summer 1975, pp. 12-13.
39   Kathleen Barry, *Female Sexual Slavery*, Prentice-Hall, Englewood
      Cliffs, New Jersey, 1979, p. 62.

7   The economy of the world of women

1   Oscar Lewis, *The Children of Sanchez*, Random House, New
      York, 1961, pp. 38, 57.
2   Ibid., p. 440.
3   Michelle Zimbalist Rosaldo, 'Woman, Culture and Society: A
      Theoretical Overview,' in *Woman, Culture and Society*,
      pp. 29-30.
4   See, for example, Sarah Wright, *This Child's Gonna Live*, Dell
      Publishers, New York, 1971. Adrienne Rich pointed this
      example out to us.
5   Kris Rosenthal, Professor of Sociology, Brandeis University,
      Waltham, Mass. Interview by Lisa Leghorn, 9 November 1979.
6   Lillian Smith, 'Autobiography as a Dialogue between King and
      Corpse,' quoted in Rich, *Lies, Secrets and Silence*, pp. 277-8.
7   Eliot Liebow, *Tally's Corner, A Study of Negro Streetcorner
      Men*, Little Brown & Co., Boston, Mass., 1967, p. 213.
8   Hylan Lewis, 'Culture, Class and the Behavior of Low Income
      Families,' paper prepared for Conference on Views of Lower
      Class Culture, New York, 27-29 June 1963 (mimeographed),
      p. 43, cited by Liebow, op. cit., pp. 208-9, 221.
9   See Rosenthal interview, op. cit.
10   Ibid.
11   See, for example, Emily Culpepper, 'Female History/Myth
      Making,' *The Second Wave*, vol. 4, no. 1, Cambridge, 1975;
      Elizabeth Gould Davis, *The First Sex*, Penguin Books,

Baltimore, 1972; Elizabeth Fisher, *Woman's Creation, Sexual Evolution and the Shaping of Society*, Anchor Press/Doubleday, Garden City, New York, 1979.

12 Paula Webster, 'Matriarchy: A Vision of Power,' *Towards an Anthropology of Women*, ed. Rayna Reiter, Monthly Review Press, New York, 1975, pp. 152-3, synopsis of Davis's position.

13 See Eleanor Leacock, 'Women in Egalitarian Societies,' *Becoming Visible: Women in European History*, ed. Bridenthal & Koonz, Houghton-Mifflin, Boston, 1977, pp. 11-35; Ruby Rohrlich-Leavitt, 'Women in Transition: Crete and Sumer,' in *Becoming Visible*, pp. 36-59; Elisa Buenaventura-Posso and Susan Brown, 'Forced Transition from Egalitarianism to Male Dominance: The Bari of Columbia,' *Women and Colonization*, Mona Etienne and Eleanor Leacock, eds, Praeger, 1980, pp. 109-33.

14 Earl Grant, Ancient Egypt Lecture Series, October 1975-April 1976, Tufts University, African American Cultural Center, Medford, Mass.

15 See Melville Herskovitz, *Dahomey*, vol. 1 and 2, J.J. Augustiy, New York, 1934. Also Audre Lorde, 'Scratching the Surface: Some Notes on Barriers to Women and Loving,' *The Black Scholar*, April 1978, p. 33.

16 Reuter, *New York Times*, 20 July 1976, 'Graves 2,000 Years Old Show German Women Were Soldiers.'

17 Webster, op. cit., p. 155.

18 Charlotte Perkins Gilman, *Herland*, Pantheon Books, New York, 1979.

19 Marge Piercy, *Woman on the Edge of Time*, Alfred A. Knopf, New York, 1976; Joanna Russ, *The Female Man*, Bantam Books, New York, 1975; Suzi McKee Charnas, *Motherlines*, Berkley Publishing, New York, 1979; Sally Miller Gearhart, *The Wanderground, Stories of the Hill Women*, Persephone Press, Watertown, Mass., 1978.

20 Rosenthal, op. cit.

21 For example, Donna Allen, 'The Women's Revolution: The Political Significance of the Genetic Differences Between Men and Women' *No More Fun and Games*, no. 5, Cambridge, Mass.

22 See, for example, Betsy Warrior, 'Man as an Obsolete Life Form', *No More Fun and Games*, no. 2, Cambridge. Valerie Solanis, *SCUM Manifesto*, Olympia Press, 1967.

23 Shulamith Firestone, *The Dialectic of Sex: The Case for Feminist Revolution*, William Morrow, New York, 1970, p. 270.

24 Interview with Gisele Halimi, 'Feminine Values: A Capital to be Developed,' *Unesco Courier*, no. 697, pp. 14-15.

25 Lewis Morgan, *League of the Iroquois*, Corinth Books, New York, 1962, p. 323, quoted in Judith Brown, 'Iroquois Women, An Ethnohistoric Note,' *Toward An Anthropology of Women*, ed. Rayna Reiter, Monthly Review Press, New York, 1975, p. 245.

26 John Davies, *History of the Caribby Islands*, London, 1666,
      pp. 1-35, quoted by Jesse Walter Fewkes in *The Aborigines of
      Porto Rico and Neighboring Islands*, US Government Printing
      Office, 1907.

27 Père Labat, *The Memoirs of Père Labat, 1693-1705*, translated
      and abridged by John Eden, Frank Cass & Co. Ltd., London,
      1970, pp. 107-9.

28 Ibid., pp. 104-5.

29 J. Antoine Jarvis, *Brief History of the Virgin Islands*, The Art
      Shop, St Thomas, Virgin Islands, 1938, p. 22.

30 William Curtis Farabee, *The Central Caribs*, Anthropological
      Publications, The Netherlands, 1967, p. 41.

31 Labat, op. cit., pp. 103, 104, 105.

32 Ibid., p. 103.

33 Ibid., pp. 104-5.

34 'Women and Disarmament' statement from *News Highlights*
      (UN, Governments and NGO's), United Nations Decade for
      Women, Equality, Development and Peace, bulletin no. 2,
      second quarter 1978, Branch for the Advancement of Women,
      Room DC-1033, United Nations, N.Y. 10017.

35 Liebow, op. cit., p. 213.

36 Michele Russell, 'Sexism and Racism: The American Reality.'
      Speech given at Conference on Theology in the Americas,
      Detroit, August 1975, p. 4.

37 Carroll Oliver, 'On Black Feminism and Culture', from
      unpublished letter distributed by Audre Lorde to women in
      the Northeast Black Feminist Network.

38 Diane Bell, 'Desert Politics: Choices in the "Marriage Market",'
      in *Women and Colonization*, p. 244.

39 James Seaver, *Life of Mary Jemison*, Matthews Brothers and
      Bryant, Buffalo, 1880, pp. 69-71, quoted by Brown, op. cit.,
      p. 244.

40 Liebow, op. cit., pp. 131-2, 135-6.

41 Robert Staples, 'The Myth of Black Macho: A Response to Angry
      Black Feminists,' *The Black Scholar*, March-April 1979,
      pp. 26, 28.

42 See Charles Nordhoff and James Norman Hall, *Pitcairn's Island*,
      Pocket Books, New York, 1962. This example was pointed out
      to us by Betsy Warrior.

43 G.T. Basden, *Among the Ibos of Nigeria*, Barnes & Noble, New
      York, 1966, p. 95; C.K. Meek, *Law and Authority in a
      Nigerian Tribe*, Oxford University Press, London, 1937; Lisa
      Leghorn and Mary Roodkowsky, *Who Really Starves? Women
      and World Hunger*, Friendship Press, New York, 1977, p. 114.

44 Rosaldo, op. cit., p. 39.

45 Janvedna, *We Bear the Fruit of Their Sins*, reprinted in *Manushi,
      A Journal About Women and Society*, no. 2, March-April
      1979, available from Shaheed Prakashan Press, A-794, Nabi

Kareem, Paharganj, New Delhi – 55, India, p. 18.

46 Alemnesh Bulti, interview by Katherine Parker, October 1976.

47 Lillian Anderson, *Up and Down the Virgin Islands*, Equity Publishing Corp., Orford, N.H., 1963, pp. 31-2.

48 Fatima Mernissi, 'Women, Saints and Sanctuaries,' *Signs: Journal of Women in Culture and Society*, vol. 3, no. 1, Autumn 1977, pp. 101-12.

49 Ibid., pp. 101-2.

50 Ibid., pp. 103, 104, 105.

51 Oscar Lewis, op. cit., pp. 455-6.

52 Rosenthal, interview, op. cit.

53 Margery Wolf, 'Chinese Women: Old Skills in a New Context,' *Woman, Culture and Society*, ed. Rosaldo and Lamphere, Stanford University Press, 1974, p. 159.

54 Urmila Bannerjee, 'Parul . . . . One of Many,' *Manushi*, no. 2, pp. 4-5.

55 Deniz Kandiyoti, 'Sex Roles and Social Change: A Comparative Appraisal of Turkey's Women,' *Signs*, vol. 3, no. 1, Autumn 1977, p. 72.

56 See Leghorn, 'Social Responses to Battered Women,' available from Know, Inc., P.O. Box 86031, Pittsburgh, Pa. 15221.

57 Karen Lindsey, 'Murder or Self-Defense? When Battered Women Fight Back,' *Viva*, vol. 5, no. 12, New York, September 1978.

58 Rhona Baptiste, 'IWY: What it means to us,' reprinted from the March 1975 issue of *Der Uberblick*, in *Caribbean Women in the Struggle*, sponsored by Caribbean Church Women of the Caribbean Conference of Churches, September 1975, p. 33.

59 Annie Jiagge, 'Politics: A Woman's Job,' *New World Outlook*, vol. 31, no. 8, April 1971, p. 13.

60 Adrienne Rich, 'On Privilege, Power and Tokenism,' excerpt from commencement speech given at Smith College, 7 May 1979, printed in *Ms. Magazine*, September 1979, pp. 42-3.

61 Toni Morrison, 'Cinderella's Stepsisters,' excerpt from Barnard College commencement address, May 1979, printed in *Ms. Magazine*, September 1979, pp. 41-2.

62 Kathleen Barry, *Female Sexual Slavery*, Prentice-Hall, Englewood Cliffs, New Jersey, 1979, p. 102.

63 Andrea Dworkin, 'Safety, Shelter, Rules, Form, Love: The Promise of the Ultra-Right,' *Ms. Magazine*, June 1979, pp. 62-76.

64 Kathryn Burkhart, *Women in Prison*, Doubleday & Co., Garden City, New York, 1973, pp. 54-5.

65 Excerpt from Adrienne Rich, 'The Phenomenology of Anger,' *The Second Wave*, vol. 2, no. 2, Cambridge, Mass., 1972; See also Charlotte Perkins Gilman, *The Yellow Wallpaper*, The Feminist Press, Old Westbury, New York, 1973.

66 Fatima Mernissi, as quoted by Judy Foreman in 'Unveiling of the Arab Dilemma,' *Boston Globe*, 25 May 1980, p. C1.

67 Mildred Daley Pagelow, (Univ. of Calif. – Riverside), 'Sex Roles,

Power and Woman Battering,' paper presented to the Ninth World Congress of Sociology, August 1978, Uppsala, Sweden, p. 12, available from Pagelow, 1111 Liberty Lane, Anaheim, Calif. 92805.

68 Kris Rosenthal, from lecture to Fall 1979 Brandeis Sociology class.
69 Karen Horney, *Feminine Psychology*, W.W. Norton, New York, 1967.
70 Pagelow, op. cit., p. 12.
71 Ashley Montagu, *The Natural Superiority of Women*, Macmillan, New York, 1968, p. 42, quoted by Pagelow, op. cit., p. 12; See also Jane Alpert, 'Mother-Right; A New Feminist Theory,' *Ms. Magazine*, August 1973.
72 Phyllis Chesler, 'A psychologist takes on male mythology,' *Ms. Magazine* 6 (1): 50, 79, 1978, quoted by Pagelow, op. cit., p. 13.
73 From discussion in Rosenthal interview, op. cit.
74 Andrea Dworkin, *Woman Hating*, E.P. Dutton, New York, 1974, pp. 134, 136, quoted by Pagelow, op. cit. p. 13.
75 Pagelow, op. cit., p. 24.
76 Adrienne Rich, 'Compulsory Heterosexuality and Lesbian Existence,' *Signs*, vol. 5, no. 4, *Journal of Women in Culture and Society*, University of Chicago Press, Summer 1980.
77 Karen Horney, 'Distrust Between the Sexes,' *Masculine/Feminine*, ed. Betty and Theodore Roszak, Harper & Row, New York, 1969, p. 112.
78 Rosaldo, op. cit., pp. 25-6, summarizing Chodorow, 'Family Structure and Feminine Personality,' in the same work.
79 Ibid., pp. 27-8.
80 Felicia Ifeoma Ekejiuba, 'Introduction: Women and Symbolic Systems,' *Signs*, vol. 3, no. 1, Autumn 1977, p. 91.
81 Rosaldo, op. cit., pp. 36, 39.
82 Ibid., pp. 40-41.
83 Ibid., p. 40.
84 Dorothy Vellenga, 'Ghana: Liberation,' *New World Outlook*, vol. 31, no. 8, April 1971, p. 26.
85 Gilman, *Women and Economics*, Harper & Row, New York, 1966, p. 338.
86 Lisa Rofel, personal communication with Lisa Leghorn, November 1979.
87 Marilyn French, *The Women's Room*, Jove/Harcourt Brace Jovanovich, New York, 1978, pp. 80-81.
88 Rosenthal, interview, op. cit.
89 See, for example, Ester Boserup, *Woman's Role in Economic Development*, St Martin's Press, New York, 1970, pp. 56-7.
90 Judith Moore, personal communication with Lisa Leghorn, 15 April 1979.
91 Anna Gyorgy and friends, *No Nukes: Everyone's Guide to*

Nuclear Power, South End Press, Boston, Mass., 1979.

92 Marian Leighton, 'Anarcho-Feminism and Louise Michel,' *Black Rose: Journal of Contemporary Anarchism*, no. 1, Box 474, Somerville, Mass. 02144, pp. 30-35.

93 Wolf, op. cit., p. 159.

94 Rich, 'Compulsory Heterosexuality', op. cit.

95 Betsy Hartmann, 'Behind Bamboo Walls,' *Country Women Magazine*, issue 30: International Women, available from Box 51, Albion, Calif. 95410, p. 6.

96 Boserup, op. cit., p. 64.

97 Monica Sjoo, 'Sweden, Now We Are Equal,' *Power of Woman*, vol. 1, no. 4, London, Summer 1975, pp. 12-13.

98 'When Women Stop Everything Stops,' *Power of Women Journal*, vol. 1, no. 5, London, 1976, pp. 18-19.

99 Ann M. Patterson Ligon, 'Are these the Peacemakers? An International Relations Study,' unpublished thesis, available from Ann Patterson Ligon, Goddard College, Plainfield, Ut 05662, USA.

100 'A Feminist Call to Action,' c/o Feminist Women for Peace/ S.O.S., 6 Durham Street, Boston, Mass. 02115.

101 See interview with Dr Helen Caldicott in *New Roots*, March-April 1980. Information also available from Wo-men for Survival, 96 School Street, Cambridge, Mass. 02139.

102 See Karen Lindsey, 'Murder or Self-Defense?' op. cit.

103 Boserup, op. cit., p. 64.

104 See, for example, Norman Lockman, 'Zimbabwe's Strong Economy Poses Its Own Problems,' *Boston Globe*, 17 June 1980.

105 Boserup, op. cit., pp. 80-81.

106 Interview of Devaki Jain, *Unesco Courier*, no. 697, Paris, pp. 4-5.

107 Ibid., pp. 3-4.

108 Some liberal capitalist economists have devised some mechanisms for partially redistributing the ownership of capital in the United States. Although without feminist focus, it provides food for thought for possible mechanisms for transforming some patriarchal economic institutions. See 'Making New Capitalists – A Creative Response to Income Inequities,' Proceedings of the Executive Seminar in National and International Affairs, Department of State publication, April 1978. For further information on Consumer, Employee and General Stock Option Plans, contact Kelso & Co., 111 Pine St, San Francisco, Calif. 94111.

109 Rosenthal, interview, op. cit.

110 See, for example, Merlin Stone, *When God Was a Woman*, The Dial Press, New York, 1976; Elaine Pagels, *The Gnostic Gospels*, Random House, New York, 1979; Diane Mariechild, *Womancraft: The Conscious Development of Psychic Skills We All Possess*, Boston, 1976, obtainable from the author at

105 Elmwood Ave., Quincy, Mass. 02170.

111   Kay Longcope, 'Women's Role in Liturgy,' *Boston Globe*,
14 September 1979, p. 20.

112   Rosenthal, interview, op. cit.

113   See, for example, Audre Lorde, 'Scratching the Surface . . .',
op. cit., p. 32.

114   Nawal El Sadawi, Fatima Mernissi, Mallica Vajarathon, 'A Critical
Look at the Wellesley Conference,' *Quest, A Feminist
Quarterly* vol 4, no. 2, pp. 102, 106.

115   Maria Isabel Barreno, Maria Teresa Horta, Maria Velho da Costa,
The Three Marias, New Portuguese Letters, Doubleday & Co.,
New York, 1975.

116   Diana Russell, *Crimes Against Women: The Proceedings of the
International Tribunal*, Les Femmes, Milbrae, Calif., 1976.

117   *ISIS, International Bulletin*. Obtainable from Via della Pellicia 31,
00153, Rome, Italy, or Case Postale 301, 1227 Carouge,
Geneva, Switzerland.

118   Fran Hosken, *Win News*, 'Female Circumcision: Summary Facts,'
and 'Press Release,' available from 187 Grant St, Lexington,
Mass. 02173.

119   *Manushi* no. 2, pp. 22, 24.

120   Deborah Lee Davis, 'A Feminist Movement in Argentina,'
unpublished thesis, Mt Holyoke Dept. of Latin American
Studies, 1979, pp. 11, 16, 20, 42.

121   *Sojourner*, The New England Women's Journal of News, Opinions
and the Arts, vol. 4, no. 8, April 1979, p. 3, and Kate Millett,
speech given at (and videotaped) Harvard University, 8 March
1980.

122   'Towards a Canadian Feminist Party,' Feminist Party of Canada,
Maple, Ontario, April 1979, available from Box 322, Maple,
Ontario.

123   This concept was well articulated by Gabrielle Bernard, a Boston-
area feminist, in the Transition House film, 'We Will Not Be
Beaten,' available from: Transition House Films, 120 Boylston
St, no. 707, Boston, Mass. 02116.

Index